Language Curriculum Innovation in a Chinese
Secondary School

Yan Zhu

Language Curriculum Innovation in a Chinese Secondary School

A Study of Teacher Cognition and Classroom Practices

 Springer

Yan Zhu
College of Foreign Languages and Literature
Fudan University
Shanghai
China

ISBN 978-981-10-7238-3   ISBN 978-981-10-7239-0   (eBook)
https://doi.org/10.1007/978-981-10-7239-0

Library of Congress Control Number: 2017958838

Printed on acid-free paper

This Springer imprint is published by Springer Nature
The registered company is Springer Nature Singapore Pte Ltd.
The registered company address is: 152 Beach Road, #21-01/04 Gateway East, Singapore 189721, Singapore

Acknowledgements

Despite all the hardships encountered along the way, the Danyang Project has been a productive and rewarding learning experience. I would like to take this chance to express my gratitude to all those people who so generously supported my Ph.D. research project, on which this book is based.

First and foremost, my deepest gratitude goes to Prof. Dingfang Shu, for all his warm encouragement, valuable advice, and unconditional support, which made the completion of this book possible. Particularly, I would like to extend my sincere thanks to Prof. Shu for initiating the Danyang Project and pushing it forward despite all the unexpected difficulties. Without this project, I could have never had the chance to go beyond the university–school boundary and witness the numerous deeply entrenched problems in Chinese secondary classrooms. It is these problems, I believe, that will continue to motivate my research as my career unfolds.

I am also deeply grateful to Prof. Rod Ellis, for his enlightening and insightful advice on this project, for his always prompt and helpful feedback on my manuscripts, and for his continuous encouragement, which helped me through hard times during this arduous journey.

Moreover, my sincere gratitude goes to the people who were involved in this project at Huanan Experimental School: Mr. Suorong Zhang, Mr. Wenzhong Wang, Mr. Xuping Wang, Ms. Yufang Yin, and many others. My special gratitude goes to Ms. Mingdi Li, Mr. Huijun Chen, Ms. Wenjun Zhou, Mr. Yingchun Zhang, and Ms. Yaqin Jing, for letting me step into their lives, for showing me such great trust, and for giving me the chance to observe the changes that took place over these years. I am especially grateful to the students and parents who enthusiastically participated in the Danyang Project.

Contents

Abbreviations

CCP Central Committee	The Central Committee of the Communist Party of China
CLT	Communicative Language Teaching
DP	The Danyang Project
EP	Exploratory Practice
FLT	Foreign Language Teaching
HES	Huanan Experimental School
LAP	Language Achievement Performance
MOE	Ministry of Education
PT	Project Teacher
SEC	The State Education Commission
SHMEC	Shanghai Municipal Education Committee
SISU	Shanghai International Studies University
TBLT	Task-based Language Teaching
TRG	Teaching Research Group
YS	Yanling School (the rural school where Marian volunteered to teach)

List of Figures

List of Tables

Abstract

Dealing with educational changes is an essential component of a foreign language teacher's professional life. However, although a focal question in almost all curriculum innovation projects is whether and how a newly implemented educational intervention brings about changes in teachers' cognition and classroom practices, there is hardly a study detailing the trajectory of teachers' changes within curriculum innovation, from an in-depth and longitudinal perspective. The present study aims to fill this research gap.

This book reports on a 4-year ethnographic study of a foreign language curriculum innovation project at a Chinese secondary school. The present study is part of the Danyang Project, a large-scale university–school collaborative project sponsored by the Shanghai Municipal Education Committee, and jointly run by Shanghai International Studies University, located in Shanghai, and Hunan Experimental School, a secondary school in Danyang, Jiangsu Province. The Danyang Project attempted to tap into deeply entrenched problems in Chinese secondary foreign language classrooms through implementing an innovative curriculum, highlighting learner autonomy and communicative language teaching. A total of 10 teachers, who taught 12 project classes to an estimated 697 students, participated in the Danyang Project. To educate and support the project teachers, a school-based in-service teacher education program was implemented at the outset of the innovation project.

This study was motivated by four research questions: (1) What changes took place in the Danyang teacher's cognition? (2) What changes took place in her classroom practices? (3) What was the relationship between the changes in teacher's cognition and the changes in her classroom practices? (4) What factors influenced the teacher's implementation of the Danyang Project?

This study depicts the idiosyncratic attributes of teacher cognition and classroom teaching practices at different phases of the Danyang Project, to delineate the trajectory of teachers' change over its span. Five stages of the Danyang Project are addressed in this book, including the pre-project stage (May 2009–August 2009); the top-down stage (September 2009–December 2011); the bottom-up stage (January 2012–March 2013); the exam preparation stage (April 2013–June 2013);

and the post-project stage (July 2013–January 2014). This study draws on field notes, ethnographic and formal in-depth interviews, teaching journals, and classroom observations to collect research data, yielding a huge preliminary data bank.

One focal informant, Marian (pseudonym), was selected from a group of project teachers, due to the typicality and richness of research data concerning her cognition and classroom practices, yielding a selected data bank consisting of field notes (121,533 Chinese words), interview transcripts (71,516 words), teaching journals (142,189 Chinese words), and over 202 minutes' video-recorded lessons. A dyad of lessons taught by one non-project teacher and one project teacher was also comparatively analyzed, and individual post-observation interviews conducted with both to triangulate the data.

This study addresses the following aspects of teacher cognition: (1) meaning versus form in foreign language teaching; (2) learner participation and learner autonomy; (3) providing corrective feedback; (4) using textbooks; and (5) attitudes toward the innovation project. Teachers' classroom practices were examined against a framework of effective language teaching formulated to inform the Danyang Project, which included seven aspects of classroom instruction: (1) time allotment to different activities of a lesson; (2) choice of instructional materials; (3) teacher talk—quantity/types of questions asked; (4) learner talk—amount/average length per move; (5) participatory organization; (6) focus on meaning versus form; and (7) discourse structures, including IRF and student-initiated exchanges.

Qualitative data were analyzed inductively and cyclically, following a procedure of open coding and axial coding, generating 137 open codes and 11 coded themes, which in turn yielded nine patterns. Video-recorded lessons taught by Marian were annotated with ELAN (v.4.6.1) and their transcripts coded per the effective classroom instruction framework. Data analysis produced the following answers to the research questions:

(1) The project teacher's cognition changed in accordance with the goal of the innovative project, but the trajectory of change was much more tangled and complicated than what was initially expected.

(2) Changes in the project teacher's teaching practices roughly took on an "N" shape. That is to say, the newness of the teacher's and her students' behaviors reached a dramatically high level when the innovation project was at its height; as the innovation project faded, classroom instruction returned to a more traditional format, albeit with some new teaching behaviors.

(3) Consistency between teacher cognition and classroom practices was found at the pre-project, bottom-up, and post-project stages. At the top-down and exam stages of the Danyang Project, the changes in the teacher's cognition did not conform to the changes in her classroom practices. Thus, it was found that the stress that caused the tension between the teacher's mental world and outside realities was likely a salient factor in the variations in her cognition and classroom practices, at different stages.

(4) The teacher's implementation of curriculum innovation was influenced by intra- and inter-personal factors. The former included the cognitive and affective

processes that influenced her responses to the educational intervention, when learning and trying out a new pedagogy, and when reflecting on its impact on language learning. The latter encompassed the external variables mediating teacher learning.

Drawing on the research findings, an exploratory model of foreign language teacher cognition and practices is proposed. The model hypothesizes two types of teacher cognition: explicit cognition and implicit cognition. Explicit cognition is likely to relate to teachers' planned practices, while implicit cognition is likely to relate to teachers' incidental practices. There is a bidirectional interface between these two types of teacher cognition, and teacher cognition is accessed based on contextual realities that impact the teacher's pedagogical decisions.

Implications for foreign language curriculum innovations in the Chinese context and suggestions for future studies are presented, given the present study's limitations.

Keywords Curriculum innovation · Teacher cognition · Classroom practices
In-service teacher education program · University–school collaboration project

Chapter 1
Introduction

The present study reports on a longitudinal EFL curriculum innovation project situated at a junior secondary school in the city of Danyang, Jiangsu Province, China, known as the Danyang Project (hereafter shortened to DP). This chapter first contextualizes this university-school collaborative project in historical and socio-political terms, by providing brief overviews of English language curriculum innovation, English language education at secondary schools, and the foreign language teacher education system in China. It then moves on to summarize several accessible and representative university-school collaborative projects in EFL settings. The last section gives an introductory overview of the Danyang Project, and its teacher education program.

1.1 English Curriculum Innovation of Secondary Education in China: History and Status Quo (1977–2012)

The history of English teaching in China dates from 1903, when the nationwide Handpicked Charter Schools were mandated to provide an English course as part of the national education system (Hu, 1999). From a historical perspective, the history of English education in China has been intricately intertwined with social, political, and economic factors (Adamson & Morris, 1997; Hu, 2002, 2005). Adamson & Morris (1997) provided a historical review of English curriculum evolvement in China, and documented the idiosyncratic features of China's national English curriculum at five stages, from the founding of the People's Republic of China (PRC) to the end of 20th century, as is shown in Table 1.1.

Examining the ongoing evolvement of Chinese education, Yi (2010) conducted a similar, 30-year study spanning the period from the inception of the Reform and Opening-up Policy in 1978, to 2008, proposing a four-phase division to examine

© Springer Nature Singapore Pte Ltd. 2018
Y. Zhu, *Language Curriculum Innovation in a Chinese Secondary School*,
https://doi.org/10.1007/978-981-10-7239-0_1

Table 1.1 A historical review of the features of the English curriculum in China (Adapted from Adam & Morris, 1997, p.7)

Period	Timeline	Macro national priorities	Role of English
The end of soviet influence	1956–1960	National socialist construction	Access to scientific and technical information
Toward quality in education	1960–1966	Quality in education to support development	Developing cultural and scientific knowledge
The cultural revolution	1966–1976	Social revolution	Vehicle for propaganda
Modernization under Deng Xiaoping	1977–1993	Economic modernization	Developing trade; cultural and scientific knowledge
Toward nine years' compulsory education	1993–1997	Economic modernization and compulsory schooling	Developing trade; cultural and scientific knowledge

specific features at different historical stages: (1) restoration (1978–1984), in which a preliminary but fundamental system was constructed shortly after the termination of the Cultural Revolution; (2) development (1985–1991), in which essential advancements, in terms of teaching goals and approaches, were incorporated into the national English syllabus; (3) adjustment (1992–2000), in which the notion of quality-oriented education was emphasized, and greater autonomy and flexibility granted in the implementation of national syllabi in regional educational settings; and, (4) a new round of curriculum reform (1999–2008), which was characterized by on-going implementation of quality-oriented education (Yi, 2010, p. IV).

As can be seen from Yi's study, the period following the enactment of the Reform and Opening-up policy witnessed an imperative expansion of English education provision in China, due to the country's rapid social and economic development. An observable consequence of this trend is that a good command of English has become widely acknowledged as a privileged prerequisite for individual citizens' educational and professional development. In recent years, with China's entry into WTO and its hosting of such influential international events as the 2008 Beijing Olympics and the 2010 Shanghai Expo, learning English is of paramount importance in both social and educational settings.

The importance of secondary education in the national English curriculum is largely self-evident, as will be addressed in Sect. 1.2 of this chapter. In the present study, I regard the release of influential official documents and national curricula as critical points of division, and therefore propose five phases of national curricular innovation, as follows.

(1) The first phase: 1977–1985

A trial English syllabus for secondary schools was issued by the Ministry of Education (MOE) in 1978, and later revised in 1980. These two syllabi advocated employing grammar-translation and audio-lingualism in English language teaching. Two years later, a third version of the English teaching syllabus was released that

Table 1.2 A summary of the major features of national English teaching curricula of secondary education in China (1977–1985)

Time	Title	Teaching goals	Recommended teaching approach	Overall allocated time (teaching hours)	Textbooks
1978/ 1980	A trial/ formal English syllabus for secondary schools	(1) Provision of carefully selected basic linguistic knowledge; (2) Laying two foundations, i.e., basic knowledge and basic skills; (3) Developing intellectual abilities.	A mixture of the grammar-translation and audiolingualism	656	A package of mandated textbooks for secondary courses including: (1) 6 books for junior secondary schools; (2) 2 books for senior secondary schools
1982	A revised version of the prior documents	Remained unchanged	Remained unchanged	960 (in curriculum for humanity studies) 932 (in curriculum for science studies)	A largely revised version of the package of mandated textbooks

maintained the basic approaches to language teaching found in the previous documents, but significantly raised the requirements for learners at key secondary schools. Table 1.2 (based on Curriculum and Textbook Research Institute, 1999; Hu, 2002; MOE, 1978, 1982) below, summarizes the syllabi in this phase.

As can be seen from the table, the syllabi enacted in this phase were centralized in nature, because of nation-wide requirements for using a uniform set of mandated textbooks and a set of fixed teaching goals, regardless of regional and institutional variations. Nonetheless, the issuing and implementation of these curricula laid the foundation for secondary English education in China, after the decade of turmoil resulting from the Cultural Revolution.

(2) The second phase: 1986–1992

China embarked on a round of national education reform with the enactment of the *Decision on Reforming China's Educational System* (CCP Central Committee, 1985) and the *Compulsory Education Law of the People's Republic of China* (CPC, 1985). In this period, three English syllabi were released, included the *English syllabus for full-time secondary schools* (SEC, 1986), the *English Syllabus for*

Table 1.3 A summary of the major features of secondary English curricula (1986–1992) (Based on Curriculum and Textbook Research Institute, 1999; Yi, 2010)

Time	Title	Suggested teaching approaches	Overall allocated time (teaching hours)
1986	*English Syllabus for Full-Time Secondary Schools*	Explicit instruction plus language practice	Starters from junior secondary schools: 500 (junior) +432 (senior)
			Starters from senior secondary schools: 552
1988	*English Syllabus for Nine-year Compulsory Education Full-time Junior Secondary Schools*	Explicit instruction plus communicative activities	Three-year junior secondary school learners: 300
			Four-year junior secondary school learners: 536
1990	*English Syllabus for Full-time Secondary Schools*	Explicit instruction plus language practice	Starters from junior secondary schools: 500 (junior) +426 (senior)
			Starters from senior secondary schools: 552

Nine-year Compulsory Education Full-time Junior Secondary Schools (SEC, 1988), and the *English Syllabus for Full-time Secondary Schools* (SEC, 1990). In a significant step forward, all three curricula established enhancing learners' communicative competence as one of the major goals of English teaching. The recommended teaching approaches and mandated textbooks, however, contained very limited indications of the communicative principles to be taught, and teaching approaches underpinned by behaviorism still played a dominant role, despite some functional-notional conceptions scattered in the syllabi. The other indicator of progress in the design of these curricular standards was their recognition of the variations that existed among different institutions. The third development of this round of syllabus design was that the policy was based on rich empirical data from a nation-wide survey conducted by the MOE (SEC at that time). The survey involved 105 key and 35 general secondary schools, totaling 58,070,000 students and 1614 teachers, and was the first and largest nation-wide investigation of education since the foundation of the PRC (Liu, 2008). Table 1.3 summarizes important specifications in secondary English curricula at this stage.

(3) The third phase: 1993–2000

The third phase of curriculum innovation in English education commenced when CCP Central Committee & State Council released the *Program for China's Educational Reform and Development* (CCP Central Committee, 1993), an influential document emphasizing the prioritized and fundamental status of education in society, and proposing a movement towards quality-oriented education. This was followed by the enactment of the *English Syllabus for Nine-year*

Table 1.4 A summary of the major features of secondary English curricula (1993–2000) (Based on Curriculum and Textbook Research Institute, 1999)

Time	Title	Suggested teaching approaches	Allocated time (teaching hours)
2000	*English Syllabus for Nine-year Compulsory Education Full-time Junior Secondary Schools*	an integrated approach stressing language use	4/week
2000	*English syllabus for full-time senior secondary schools*	an integrated approach stressing language use	12/week 384 in total

Compulsory Education Full-time Junior Secondary Schools (MOE, 2000a) and the *English Syllabus for Full-time Senior Secondary Schools* (MOE, 2000b), which came on the heels of the implementation and amendment of three consecutive trial syllabi. Two significant contributions to English education syllabus design in this phase were: (1) explicit statements regarding language and culture; and, (2) the adoption of the "one syllabus with multiple textbooks" principle, which shattered the monopoly of a uniform set of mandated textbooks (Table 1.4).

(4) The fourth phase: 2001–2010

The next round of curriculum innovation in basic education in China began with the advent of the new millennium. It was, in fact, the eighth round of curriculum innovation in the history of the PRC, the previous seven rounds having taken place in 1949–1952, 1953–1957, 1958–1965, 1966–1976, 1977–1985, 1986–1992, and 1993–2000, respectively (Yi, 2008, p. 177). What characterized this phase of change was its guiding principle of pushing forward the implementation of quality education to develop all-around learners, as advocated by two guiding government documents at that time: the *Decision on Deepening Educational Reform and Promoting Quality Education* (CCP Central Committee & State Council, 1999), and the *Decision on Reform and Development of Basic Education* (State Council, 2001). In line with the principles advocated in these documents, the MOE released *the Outline of Basic Education Curriculum Reform (Trial)* (MOE, 2001a), a package of course standards informing and regulating the teaching of all courses, ranging from pre-schools to senior secondary schools. At the same time, the *English Course Standard for Full-time General Senior Secondary Schools of Compulsory Education (Experimental)* (MOE, 2001b) was issued. A recognizable change in this round of curriculum innovation was the use of the term *curriculum* to replace *syllabus*, indicating an effort to 'guide' teaching, rather than 'prescribe' it. Furthermore, the new course standard formulated a set of language proficiency scales to ensure a coherent transition between different educational stages, and to achieve conformity with international practice.

(5) The fifth phase: a new national curriculum (MOE 2012-present)

Sinc 2011, this above-mentioned trend in national curriculum innovation has been intensified and expanded, with the enactment of the *English Curriculum for Compulsory Education* (2011) (MOE, 2012), the latest national English curriculum for basic education in China. The curriculum explicitly states the rationale for English learning, and its importance for the development of both individual learners, and the whole country. It also maintains both an instrumental and humanistic orientation for English courses at all levels, in addition to an eclectic teaching approach that stresses a balanced integration of explicit and implicit language instruction, and the adjustment of teaching goals to cater more to learners' needs (Wang, 2013), as indicated in the following explanation of the curriculum's rationales.

> First, the new curriculum emphasizes quality education, promoting learner development through language learning. Second, it caters to all students, taking into consideration the Chinese language learners' individual differences. Third, it sets integrated objectives, taking into account the progressive and consistent attributes of language learning. Fourth, it stresses the learning process, valuing using the target language in real situations. Fifth, it reforms assessment methods, focusing on assessing comprehensive skills in using English. Sixth, it enriches learning resources, exploring, and expanding various sources and platforms to facilitate language leaning.

> (MOE, 2012, pp. 3–4)

The overall goal of the new English curriculum is "to develop preliminary and comprehensive skills in using English, to promote cognitive and intellectual development, and to enhance integrated humanistic quality through language learning" (MOE, 2012, p. 8). More specifically, its goals are elucidated in five discrete, but interrelated aspects, including "language skills, linguistic knowledge, affective factors, learning strategies, and cultural awareness" (*ibid*). Regarding each aspect, there is a continuum of target requirements, ranging from Level 1 to Level 5, in which Level 1 prescribes the specific requirements to be achieved by the end of primary schooling, and Level 5, by the end of junior secondary schooling.

Corresponding to the rationales and goals, eight general principles of English teaching are also recommended in the new curriculum, to inform and facilitate teachers.

> (1) English teaching should cater to all students, and lay the foundations for English language development for every student.
> (2) English teaching should emphasize language use, and aim to develop learners' skills in using English.
> (3) English teaching should stress learning strategies, and foster learner autonomy.
> (4) English teaching should raise learners' consciousness of cross-cultural differences, and develop learners' cross-cultural communication competence.
> (5) English teaching should be adaptive to contextual realities, and teachers should use textbooks innovatively.
> (6) English teachers should draw on a wide range of instructional resources, and improve the efficiency of learning.
> (7) English teachers should organize extracurricular activities, and expand the platform for learners to learn.
> (8) English teachers should develop the professional capacity to meet the requirements of the new curriculum.

> (MOE, 2012, pp. 25–33)

Furthermore, the appendices of the new curriculum include sample lesson plans for teaching learners of different proficiency levels, to demonstrate how to implement these principles in classroom instruction.

1.2   A Brief Overview of English Secondary Education in China

Normally, English education in China consists of English courses offered for three to six years at primary schools, five to six years at secondary schools, two to four years in undergraduate study, and one to four years in postgraduate study. The proportion of time reveals how important secondary education is in individual learners' formal schooling experience. Secondary education plays a crucial role in English education in China, serving an estimated population of 80 million English learners, compared to the approximately 40 million learners at primary schools and specialized/vocational schools (Hu, 2005, p. 17). Demographic statistics released by the MOE indicate student enrollment at secondary schools has steadily increased in recent years, climbing from 60 million in 1997, to 85 million in 2005, before gradually declining to 75 million in 2011 (MOE, 2013[1]). According to the latest MOE statistics, there are now approximately 80 million students enrolled in general secondary schools in China, the majority of whom learn English as a foreign language (Hu, 2009; Liu, 2008).

Given the large population of learners and the pivotal position of secondary education in China's formal schooling system, it could be argued that the significance of English teaching at secondary schools is self-evident; as Shu et al. (2012a) remarked, "among [the] many problems ingrained in foreign language teaching in China, those entrenched in secondary education are of critical significance" (2012a, p. I).

1.3   A Brief Overview of Foreign Language Teacher Education System in China

1.3.1   The Foreign Language Teacher Education System in China

After decades of development, China has built up a complete and systematic teacher education system. In his study, Hu (2005b) gave a comprehensive description of the pre-service and in-service foreign language teacher education programs in China, as summarized in Table 1.5.

---

[1]http://www.moe.gov.cn/publicfiles/business/htmlfiles/moe/s7382/index.html.

Table 1.5 A summary of pre-service and in-service foreign language teacher education programs in China (Based on Hu 2005b)

Pre-service foreign language teacher education programs	
Settings	Teacher education courses
Normal schools	• Language courses (language as linguistic forms)
(*zhongdeng shifan xuexiao*)	• Language proficiency courses (little regard to communicative effectiveness)
	• Pedagogical content knowledge
Teachers colleges	(lack in fundamental areas of knowledge)
(*gaodeng shifan zhuanke xuexiao*)	• Other courses: political theory, physical education, etc.
Normal universities	
(*shifan daxue*)	

In-service foreign language teacher education programs		
Settings		Teacher education courses
Informal settings	Teaching research group (*jiaoyanzu*)	• Collaborative syllabus design/lesson planning
		• Classroom observation
		• End-of-semester work report
Formal settings	Education college (*jiaoyu xueyuan*)	• Seminars, workshops, short-term courses with the award of professional/training certificates
	(in-house or at selected schools)	
	Tertiary teacher education institutions	• Long-term (1–2 years) off-the-job courses that lead to degree or diploma
		• Short-term intensive programs during school holidays
	Self-study higher education system	• Courses and exams that lead to higher-education diplomas
	Distance learning agencies	• Programs that lead to higher education certificates or diplomas
	Overseas institutions and organizations	• Teacher education programs jointly managed with Chinese universities
		• Overseas-based in-service training programs

Pre-service foreign language teacher education programs	
Settings	Teacher education courses
Normal schools (*zhongdeng shifan xuexiao*)	• Language courses (language as linguistic forms) • Language proficiency courses (little regard to communicative effectiveness)
Teachers colleges (*gaodeng shifan zhuanke xuexiao*)	• Pedagogical content knowledge (lack in fundamental areas of knowledge)
Normal universities (*shifan daxue*)	• Other courses: political theory, physical education, etc.

(continued)

Table 1.5 (continued)

In-service foreign language teacher education programs

Settings		Teacher education courses
Informal settings	Teaching research group (*jiaoyanzu*)	• Collaborative syllabus design/lesson planning • Classroom observation • End-of-semester work report
Formal settings	Education college (*jiaoyu xueyuan*) (in-house or at selected schools)	• Seminars, workshops, short-term courses with the award of professional/training certificates
	Tertiary teacher education institutions	• Long-term (1–2 years) off-the-job courses that lead to degree or diploma • Short-term intensive programs during school holidays
	Self-study higher education system	• Courses and exams that lead to higher-education diplomas
	Distance learning agencies	• Programs that lead to higher education certificates or diplomas
	Overseas institutions and organizations	• Teacher education programs jointly managed with Chinese universities • Overseas-based in-service training programs

1.3.2   The National Teacher Training Program in China

The incessant curricular changes in China have caused increasing concern about the qualifications and professional development of foreign language teachers. Recognizing the need for qualified English teachers to ensure the implementation of national educational changes, the National Teacher Training Program (*Guopei Jihua*; hereafter NTTP) was initiated by the MOE and the Ministry of Finance, in 2010 (MOE, 2010). Jointly operated by the two ministries, the program is the largest national level teacher training project aimed at enhancing the professional capacity of teachers, ranging from kindergartens to primary and secondary schools, with teachers from rural areas being granted priority admission. Though three years' implementation is not sufficiently long to realize substantive changes in teachers' perceptions and practices, the need for on-going evaluation on the NTTP's effectiveness is clear (Yu, 2010; Zhu, 2010). Several studies (Duan, 2013; Zhu, 2010) have reported emerging problems with the NTTP, including its adoption of a top-down approach, and neglect of trainees' needs; therefore, it is suggested that institutional and individual factors be addressed when implementing the program.

In the NTTP, the teacher trainees are normally so-called "backbone" teachers, who are privileged to be selected and are expected to promote curriculum innovation after they finish the program and return to their schools. This de-contextualized elite training model has also adopted by other top-down in-service teacher training programs at various administrative levels in China.

1.3.3   The Effectiveness of Teacher Education System in China

Despite the enormity of the teacher education infrastructure in China, a relatively small amount of research has evaluated its effectiveness. Studies (Hu, 2005; Yuan, 2001) report that most in-service teacher education programs in China focus more on granting certificates, than on developing participants' professional capacity. Although the population and professional qualifications of foreign language teachers have greatly increased in recent decades, there has long been a gloomy gap between the quality of language teachers available, and the demands of curriculum reforms (Hu, 2005; Nunan, 2003; Yu, 2001).

Analyzing the situation of pre-service EFL teacher education in China, Hu (2005) claimed "continuing professional development is the most important way to strengthen professional education" (Hu, 2005, p. 679). Other studies (see for example Carless, 1997; Kırkgöz, 2008; Li, 1998) have added our understandings of how on-going in-service teacher education plays a pivotal role in changing teachers' perceptions of and capacity in their professional life. Based on this recognition, the Danyang Project strives for an appropriately situated and more efficient approach to language teachers' professional development.

1.4   Research on University-School Collaboration Project

It is a long-standing and widely-practiced endeavor to implement curriculum innovation through university-school partnerships or collaborations (see, for example, Bullough & Kauchak, 1997; Lee, 2013; Peters, 2002; Thomas et al., 2012). In different parts of the world, university-school collaborations are a major mechanism to support and facilitate education changes and promote teachers' professional development, to increase learner achievement outcomes (see, for example, Cornelissen et al., 2011; Gardner, 2011; Littleton, 1998; Serrano, 2012). In the field of second/foreign language teaching, there is a relatively long history of university-school collaboration; Table 1.6, lists a few representative and influential cases in ESL/EFL settings.

The three Chinese university-school collaboration projects had some features in common with the Bangalore projects. First, the projects were not based on a one-to-one cooperative model; rather, the partnership was built up between one university and several primary or secondary schools. Second, the initiators might not necessarily be experts specializing in foreign language teaching; Feng, for example, is a renowned scholar whose research interest is modern education theory and comparative education.

The Chinese university-school innovative projects listed in Table 1.6 are not as influential as their international counterparts, perhaps partially due to readership factors, as most project reports and studies were published in Chinese.

Table 1.6 A list of university-school collaborative innovation projects in EFL/ESL contexts

Projects	Directors	Rationales	Time line	Institutions	Models
Bangalore/Madras Communicational Teaching Project (CTP) (Beretta, 1990; Beretta & Davie, 1985; Brumfit, 1984)	N. S. Prabhu	Unconscious grammar construction; Focus on meaning; Task-based language teaching	1979–1984	8 classes in primary and secondary schools in Bangalore and Madras, South India	School-based, with outside researchers
Promoting English teachers' educational innovation for the development of students' English language competence —a university-school collaborative AR (Wang et al., 2010; Wang & Mu, 2013)	Qiang Wang (Centre for Foreign Language Education and Teacher Education) (CFLETE)	Professional development of secondary foreign language teachers through collaborative action research with university researchers	July, 2007–May, 2009	12 teacher educators/ researchers from Beijing Normal University, 3 education superintendents and 38 backbone English teachers from 13 senior secondary schools in Beijing	School-based, with outside researchers and support from local administration
Transcendence Basic Education Experiment (He, 2005a, 2005b)	Kekang He (Beijing Normal University)	Language consciousness hypothesis; (He, 2005)	Phase 1: Sep. 2000-	2 primary school classes in Grade 1, a total of 80 students, Nanshan Experimental School, Shenzhen, China	School-based, with outside researchers and support from local administrators
			Phase 2: Jun. 2002-	2 primary school classes in Grade 2, totaling 90 students, Nanhai Experimental School, Foshan, Guangzhou, Guangdong, China	
			Sep. 2002-	2 primary school classes in Grade 1, East Dongfeng Road Primary School, Dongshan District, Guangdong, China	

(continued)

Table 1.6 (continued)

Projects	Directors	Rationales	Time line	Institutions	Models
			Phase 3: Mar. 2003-	15 multi-leveled primary schools in Nanshan District, Shenzhen, China; Up to 19 participant primary schools in Nanshan District by Mar. 2004;	
			Phase 4: Commencement time untold	More than 110 primary schools in Guangzhou, Shenzhen, Zhongshan, Beijing, Dalian, Xiamen, Baoding, Foshan.	
			Jun.,2004	Fengning county, Hebei Province (under-developed rural area)	
Bilingual Education and Integrated English Program (Feng, 2002, 2012)	Zengjun Feng (South China Normal University, Guangdong)	Localization of Bilingual Education in Chinese context	Commencement time unavailable, up to 12 years by Dec., 2011	A total of approximately 20 primary schools and kindergartens in Guangdong and Anhui Provinces, China	School-based, with outside researchers and support from local administrators

Nevertheless, one cannot ignore that there is still a gap to be filled with respect to theoretical and methodological issues concerning university-school collaborative projects in China. A close look at the projects listed in Table 1.6 reveals several inherent limitations.

First, the innovation projects lack sufficient justifications for their rationales, and there is an apparent lack of low-inference accounts of how the projects have been implemented. Though accessible publications relating to the projects unanimously report their ultimate success, hardly any validated schemes have been adopted to evaluate program effectiveness, in terms of learners' learning outcomes. Therefore, it is hard to say whether these projects, among the numerous innovative projects in different parts of China, have been as overwhelmingly successful as reported, within a relatively short period.

Moreover, the reported outcomes are too optimistic to fit into the S-shaped diffusion curve widely used to describe how changes take place in educational innovation, indicating "it always takes longer to implement than expected" (Rogers, 1983; Markee, 1997, p. 58). Therefore, the author has reservations about the projects' reported 'successful' outcomes, and the ensuing expeditious dissemination of innovative principles.

Last, though the word 'experiment' is quite frequently used in the Chinese context to refer to beneficial educational innovations, one needs to be cautious about selecting 'experiment' as a research method in empirical studies involving these innovative projects. Obviously, the complexity of the research context, combined with the lengthy timespan of the project, makes it virtually impossible to conduct an experimental or quasi-experimental study in which dependent and independent variables are strictly manipulated. Moreover, the long duration of some projects is likely to jeopardize ethical norms of scientific research, as participants might be continuously exposed to treatment with pedagogies that are potentially harmful (Wen, 2011).

Reflecting on the limitations of innovation projects in the Chinese EFL context, it is necessary to conduct a study with a grounded rationale and rigorous research design, to investigate how EFL curriculum innovation is initiated and implemented in a specific Chinese educational setting. The present study strives to fill in the research gap by presenting a trustworthy account of the Danyang Project, documenting its both achievements and the situations that could constrain its implementation.

1.5   An Overview of the Danyang Project and Its Teacher Education Program

1.5.1   History

The Danyang Project was initiated in the spring of 2009. It was jointly conducted by Shanghai International Studies University (SISU), a leading Chinese university with prestigious foreign language and applied linguistics programs, and Huanan

Experimental School (HES), Danyang, Jiangsu Province, a nine-year school consisting of a six-year primary sector and a three-year junior secondary sector. Since its establishment in 2004, HES has grown rapidly and gained much popularity among local parents, because of students' outstanding academic performance.

Prof. Dingfang Shu from SISU, the initiator of the DP, once said, "it has long been my dream to conduct a longitudinal study on English teaching reform at a secondary school" (Shu et al., 2012a: p. I); the opportunity to do so arose when Mr. Zhang, the principal of HES, met with Prof. Shu, in early 2009. During that meeting, Mr. Zhang expressed concerns about the current situation and entrenched problems in basic education in China. Prof. Shu sympathized with him, and they decided to embark on the Danyang Project.

Mr. Zhang is a special-grade math teacher[2] with more than 30 years' teaching and school management experiences. As the principal of HES, Mr. Zhang is a powerful and determined leader, with tremendous charisma and energy. Though not an English teacher, he is quite interested in and concerned about issues relating to English learning and teaching. Since the outset of the DP, Mr. Zhang had been enthusiastically supportive of it, firmly believing experts and researchers from SISU would bring greater academic success to HES, and further enhance its reputation. Mr. Zhang's cordiality is evident, as HES offered SISU researchers accommodation and in-city transportation, in addition to a spacious office where researchers could work and hold small-scale sessions of the teacher education program. In addition, when working at HES, researchers had free access to such resources as the library, the lecture hall, conference rooms, and IT labs.

Having the principal's support is an essential prerequisite for launching a university-school collaborative innovation. Shortly after several informal meetings between the principal and Prof. Shu, university researchers began their pre-project investigation, in April 2009. In August of that year, both parties signed an official contract of collaboration, signaling the formal commencement of the project (Shu 2012a, b). Also in 2009, Prof. Shu started to supervise three new PhD students at SISU—An, Wang, and Geng. The three PhD students were interested in curriculum innovation, and their research proposals were incorporated into the DP agenda; thus, they automatically became the project's first group of co-investigators. Meanwhile, at HES, Mr. Wang (a deputy principal and special-grade math teacher) was given responsibility over the project, and two head teachers of English teaching research groups (TRGs), Ms. Yin and Ms. Huang, were called upon to facilitate managing the DP.

As the above description shows, it is quite clear that the DP had a top-down character from the very beginning. At the outset of the DP, the innovative curriculum was implemented radically through intensive teacher training sessions, in which researchers demonstrated lesson plans and instructional materials the teachers were then required to follow and use. Despite its initial difficulties, the

---

[2]Special-grade teacher (*Teji Jiaoshi*) is the title of the highest professional level for teachers in basic education in China.

project had some achievements towards the end of the top-down stage, as learners and teachers won prestigious awards in numerous province- and nation-wide contests.

Despite the initial beneficial effects of the top-down approach, DP was in a dilemma two years later, as there was strong resistance against its innovative principles and, even worse, the distortions of those innovative practices carried out by project teachers. The issue of teacher resistance will be discussed in detail in Chaps. 4 and 5. Nevertheless, from the end of 2011, the DP gradually shifted to a bottom-up approach, which was more lenient in planning and practice, taking into consideration the situations that restricted the implementation of new teaching practices. At this stage, more teachers' voices were attended to, and a supportive model was adopted in its teacher education program, one in which teachers' needs and enquiries were regarded as major issues that informed teacher learning activities.

In December 2010, the project team won a national education award issued by MOE. In September 2011,[3] after running for over two years without external funding, the Danyang Project was approved as an Innovative Project, and sponsored by the Shanghai Municipal Education Committee (hereafter SHMEC), with funding totaling RMB 60,000. In April 2014, the project team won a municipal-level education award issued by SHMEC.

At the time of writing, DP has been underway for nearly five years. In the beginning of 2014, the project was temporarily halted because it was short of hands. It is not surprising, in retrospect, that a friendly and constructive partnership was formed between SISU and HES through years of cooperation. Despite all the hardships both parties experienced during the collaboration, they both agree the benefits of the project outweighed the drawbacks.

Acknowledging the transformative effects of the DP on the development of PhD students, Shu (2013) proposed an integrative model of educating PhD students using the off-campus base of the innovative research project. He argued that participating in the innovative project was beneficial for PhD students in terms of bridging the gap between theory and practice, as it allowed them to get out of the library and apply what they had learned in real language classrooms. By doing so, Shu claimed, PhD students would be more likely to relate their doctoral research with practical needs in the field. On HES' side, after several years' of continual contact, the people there were quite friendly to university researchers, treating them as external colleagues. HES staff espoused the idea that the secondary school and the university mutually benefit from the collaborative research project.

The present study covers the timeline from May 2009 to January 2014.

---

[3]Project code: 12ZS061, retrieved from http://kyc.shisu.edu.cn/s/22/t/2/1a/c4/info6852.htm.

1.5.2   Aims

At the outset of the DP, its overarching aim (as stated both by SISU and HES) was to improve the effectiveness of foreign language learning, which was also the goal for educational innovation projects in general. Pertaining to this common core goal were a series of peripheral objectives, including fostering learner autonomy, facilitating the project teachers' professional development, enhancing the academic prestige of HES, etc.

Despite their congruous recognition of DP's core and peripheral objectives, SISU and HES adopted different perspectives in pursuit thereof. SISU, as a research-oriented university, maintained a researcher's stance, regarding the DP as a research project seeking effective and feasible remedies for deeply-rooted problems with FLT in China (An, 2012a, 2012b; Geng, 2012a, 2012b; Shu, 2012a, 2012b; Wang, 2012a, 2012b; Yuan, 2012, 2013). On the other hand, HES took a practitioner's perspective, expecting that researchers, or 'experts' in their words, were academically and professionally competent to equip them with expertise to foster effective teaching, which in turn would result in students' success in English learning.

1.5.3   Principles of the Innovative Curriculum

Two main principles, literally expressed as "intensive teaching and autonomous learning" (*jizhong jiaoxue, zizhu xuexi*), were explicitly stated as the DP's guide-lines—given the reality of the venue, concisely-phrased rhetoric was deemed more conducive to the acceptance of innovative ideas than academic terminologies. However, this short phrase could scarcely contain the full principles underlying curriculum in the DP, which included:

(1) A balanced curriculum can be built to develop learners' explicit linguistic knowledge and communicative competence. Learning can be achieved through exposing learners to sufficient and suitable language input and using the target language.
(2) The effectiveness of an innovation project is evaluated by learners' learning outcomes, including their linguistic competence and socio-affective factors that mediate their language learning.
(3) Learner autonomy can be fostered in and outside classrooms at secondary schools.
(4) Curriculum innovation provides language teachers with an optimal space for professional development. School-based teacher education programs are a beneficial and effective complement to traditional off-site teacher training courses.
(5) The experimental school, as well as the project teachers, plays a seminal role in assimilating and disseminating innovative ideology and practices.

1.5.4 Components

DP was comprised of relatively independent but interrelating sub-projects, with individual researchers taking primary responsibility for their own sub-projects, which were also the focus of their doctoral theses. Meanwhile, there were regular team meetings in which researchers consulted with each other to formulate research proposals, construct teacher education plans, and sort out emerging problems. Table 1.7, summarizes the sub-projects encompassed in the DP.

As shown in Table 1.7, the Danyang Project's components covered the key elements of learner needs analysis, course design, material development, classroom instruction, assessment, and teacher development in a foreign language curriculum (Richards, 2001). One could argue there was not much newness revealed in this innovative curriculum; however, as Ellis (1997) reminded us, innovation can be conceived of in two different ways—i.e., as "absolute innovation" or as "perceived innovation"—with the DP falling into the latter category, because "the change is perceived as innovatory by the practitioners who adopt it" (Ellis, 1997, p. 27).

Overall, DP intended to implement theoretically sound innovative principles, and did not exclude the possibility that absolute innovation could be generated in the process. A typical example was needs analysis, which was by no means innovative, in terms of its theoretical background and development in the field, but was almost completely new to the teachers and students at HES. Other innovative artifacts, as shown in Table 1.7, included Language Achievement Performance (LAP hereafter) classes, school-based textbooks, ELP-based assessment (assessment based on English learning portfolio), and a multi-interactive teacher education model.

As discussed earlier in this chapter, stakeholders involved in the DP unanimously aimed to carry it forward in a sustainable way, by keeping it a system open

Table 1.7 Researchers and their sub-projects in the DP

Researchers	Timeline	Sub-projects (Titles of Doctoral Theses)
An, L.	April 2009–December 2011	*The Role of Textbooks in Modifying Teacher Beliefs and Practices: A Project-based Study in Middle Schools in China* (An, 2012)
Geng, F.	April 2009–December 2011	*Developing Learner Autonomy and Language Speaking Proficiency through LAP Class—A Project-based Research at a Secondary School in China* (Geng, 2012)
Wang, B.	April 2009–January 2013	*Fostering Learner Autonomy via ELP-Based Assessment in the Chinese Context* (Wang, 2012)
Yuan, Y.	April 2010–January 2013	*Multi-interactive Model of School-based English Teacher Education: Theory and Practice* (written in Chinese) (Yuan, 2013)
Zhu, Y.	April 2011–January 2014	*An Ethnographic Study on Foreign Language Teacher Cognition and Classroom Practice within Curriculum Innovation in a Chinese Secondary School* (Zhu, 2014)

to new sub-projects. To ensure the ethical appropriateness and technical feasibility of newly-developed sub-projects, all research proposals underwent rigorous group review before being introduced to HES.

1.5.5   Project Participants

So far, a total of 10 university researchers have participated in the DP, five of whom have based their doctoral studies (An, 2012; Geng, 2012; Wang, 2012; Yuan, 2013; Zhu, 2014) on it. Researcher participants involved in the project comprised of PhD students and post-doctoral fellows under the supervision of Prof. Shu, the initiator of the DP. The length of involvement of researcher participants in the project varied individually, mainly depending on how closely their PhD studies were associated with the DP. Most researchers went into the field after gaining background knowledge about the DP through reading and scrutinizing project documents, and would be oriented to the environment by the experienced researchers. When a sub-project for which one researcher was responsible came to an end, she would withdraw to focus on writing her doctoral thesis; however, most such withdrawn researchers remained in contact with project teachers and researchers in the field, through on-line communication.

A predominant criterion for selecting project teachers (hereafter PTs), as Shu has stated, was whether they "acknowledge the rationale of the DP and show willingness to spend extra time participating in its teacher education program. Above all, they ought to be interested in innovating their teaching and research" (2012b, p. 3). Due to its "top-down approach" (Wang, 2012b, p. 70), participation in the first stage of the DP was effectively an obligatory work list item for project teachers. However, the situation began to change in August 2012, with the graduation of the first group of students from project classes; teachers who had finished three years' teaching in project classes could now decide whether to stay or leave, and more new teachers were nominated to participate in the DP. Taking the first duo of PTs as an example, one (Alex) decided to withdraw, whereas the other (Judy) chose to stay in the DP; at the same time, three new participants joined in. Table 1.8 shows the demographic background of the project teachers; all the names in the table are pseudonyms.

1.5.6   The Teacher Education Program of the DP

At the very beginning of the DP, a school-based teacher education program was launched to help project teacher implement innovation principles and deal with emerging problems. At the top-down stage of the DP, the teacher education program was situated in a positivistic paradigm, in which learning was defined as an internal cognitive process, isolated from the social context in which it was situated (Lenneberg, 1967). In the positivistic perspective, teachers could learn about the

Table 1.8 The demographic information of teacher participants in the DP (September 2014)

Timeline	Teacher	Gender	Age	Number of students
August 2009–June 2012	Judy	Female	31	50
	Alex	Male	40	52
August 2010–June 2013	Frank	Male	32	54
	Marian	Female	40	55
August 2011–June 2014	Julia	Female	33	105
	Grace	Female	33	57
August 2012–present	Judy	Female	31	106
	Rosa	Female	30	57
	Helen	Female	31	57
	Flora	Female	31	104

Table 1.9 The teacher education program at the top-down stage

Strategy	Procedure
Seminar	(1) Teacher educators prepared theoretical principles, demonstrative lesson planning and recommended instructional materials to be presented in seminars (2) Teacher educators and PTs met for seminars in which PTs listened attentively and took notes (3) PTs raised questions for discussion
Unfocussed classroom observation	(1) Teacher educators developed a global observation scheme (see Appendix 1) in consultation with project teachers (2) Teacher educators observed project teachers' classrooms using the scheme. They also took notes on prominent issues relating to the class they had observed (3) After observation, teacher educators provided feedback for improving teaching

content and teaching practices transmitted to them, and develop pedagogical expertise during their early years of teaching (Johnson, 2009). Thus, the major components encompassed in the teacher education program were seminars and unfocussed classroom observation. Before organizing the seminars, teacher educators normally spent a large amount of time preparing documents to inform PTs on such issues as what to teach and how to teach. Usually, the seminars were educator-dominated, with PTs taking notes while the researcher presented prepared contents (Table 1.9).

At the top-down stage, classroom observation was unfocussed; that is, a global observation scheme was used, and no specific aspects of teaching were attended to. Observation was conducted to evaluate whether PTs' practices reflected what they had learned in teacher training seminars. Apart from seminars and classroom observation, the PTs were required to construct teaching profiles enclosing documents such as professional background form, teaching journals, teaching evaluation form, teaching videos, certificates of merit, etc. In this phase, PTs were required to write daily teaching journals, which were sent to teacher educators via email, generating weekly replies containing very detailed comments on salient issues revealed therein the journals. Each teacher's journals were separately reviewed by at least two teacher educators.

On entering its bottom-up stage, the teacher education program gradually shifted to an interpretative epistemological perspective, informed by the recognition of teacher learning as socially-negotiated process (Stenhouse, 1975). With an adoption of a socio-cultural paradigm, the teacher education program began to perceive PTs as "users and creators of legitimate forms of knowledge who make decisions about how best to teach their L2 students within complex socially, culturally, and historically situated contexts" (Johnson, 2006, p. 239). Through the lens of interpretative epistemology, teacher education was perceived as the exploration of the complexities of teachers' mental lives (Freeman, 2002), and of the context in which they make sense of their work. That is to say, PTs were regarded as active agents who could construct personalized teaching theories, rather than passive recipients of the knowledge and ideas to which they were exposed (Zhuang & Huang, 2014).

In this phase, the teacher education program adopted a teacher-centered approach that valued PTs' prior experience as language learners and teachers, acknowledged the complexity of the context in which teachers' work was situated, and perceived teacher development as the individualized theorization of teaching praxis through interpersonal and intrapersonal interaction. The major strategies employed in teacher education programs were exploratory action research and focused classroom observation, which were designed in response to PTs' enquiries, and implemented to facilitate and scaffold teacher learning. Major procedures of exploratory action research and focused classroom observation are documented in Table 1.10.

Along with these two major strategies employed in teacher education program was a supportive framework offering on-going and timely assistance to project teachers. At the bottom-up stage, it was no longer the PTs' obligation to write teacher journals and develop teacher profiles; instead, they were encouraged to write reflectively on teaching scenarios of critical meaning, rather than keep an account of mundane matters in their daily routine. Consequently, there was an apparent decrease in the number of teaching journals submitted at this stage; nevertheless, each journal was still reviewed by at least two teacher educators, and timely and meticulous feedback supplied. In addition, the PTs' inquiries were promptly responded to with constructive advice or accessible resources.

On average, teacher educators visited HES once every two weeks, staying for roughly three days each time. Apart from regular work in teacher education programs, they also took advantage of their time in the field to communicate with principals, head teachers of TRGs, and non-project teachers, as well as to participate in such school-based teacher-development activities as teaching contests and public lesson observations. They frequently contacted students in project classes, through both informal exchanges and formal interviews. As time passed, teacher educators gradually built rapport with people at HES. In her studies, Yuan (2012, 2013) documented in detail how this took place, despite the myriad hardships

Table 1.10 The teacher education program at the bottom-up stage

Strategy	Procedure
Exploratory action research	(1) PTs raised questions relating to teaching and learners (2) Teacher educators helped PTs to formulate operationalized research questions and assisted the teachers to prepare exploratory action research proposals by referring to relevant literature, sharing personal research experiences, providing feedback to research proposals, etc. (3) PTs negotiated with teacher educators on issues emerging in the process of action research (4) PTs completed the action research and submitted the action research reports, on which teacher educators gave constructive feedback
Focused classroom observation	(1) PTs raised questions relating to specific aspects in his or her classroom instruction (2) Teacher educators constructed tailored observation schemes focusing on aspects that a teacher expected to be attended to (see for example in Appendix 2 an observation scheme devised to observe participatory structure of classroom interaction). And PTs were informed of the rationales behind the scheme and were trained to use it to observe specific aspects in classroom instruction (3) Information was collected through focused classroom instruction to provide feedback on specific aspects of the teachers' teaching for teacher reflection (4) Around one month later, the aspects of instruction that had been observed and reflected upon were observed again following the same procedure

teacher educators had to overcome at the beginning of the project. Only through intensive contact with local people can an ethnographic study gather sufficient information about socio-political realities in the field. Such regular but detached contacts in the field enabled researchers to observe the school and teachers, while mitigating the observer's paradox (Labov, 1972).

1.6 Summary

This chapter has situated the study in a historical and socio-political background, by outlining secondary English curriculum innovation and the foreign language teacher education system in China. Based on an introductory discussion of university-school collaborative projects, the rationale on which the Danyang Project was initiated was elucidated. Then, the chapter briefly introduced the Danyang Project and its teacher education program, including its history, aims, curriculum principles, components, and project participants, as well as the distinct teacher education approaches adopted at two major stages of the project.

Chapter 2
Theoretical Framework of the Study

This chapter is composed of three sections. The first presents the theoretical underpinnings that have informed teacher educators and practitioners of the Danyang Project in pursuit of effective FLT classroom instruction. This is followed by the second section, reviewing the literature to date on curriculum innovations. The final section provides a synthesis of the mainstream theories concerning language teacher cognition and practices.

2.1 Effective Teaching in FLT Classrooms: Theory and Research

2.1.1 Effective Teaching in FLT Classrooms

The early history of research in second language acquisition and foreign language teaching is infused with studies exploring, verifying, and comparing pedagogies in pursuit of effective teaching methods and techniques (Hedge 2000; Richards & Rodgers 1986, 2001; Ur, 1996). Method-oriented studies made strides in pursuing effective teaching methods in specific aspects of language teaching, including reading, listening, writing, and grammar, or in adopting a broader view by considering the ecological teaching context in which learner, teacher, material, and syllabus factors play mediating roles. One prominent commonality of these studies lies in their research purpose of prescriptively offering effective teaching methods for language teachers to follow.

Though it may sound plausible to give teacher education program teachers or trainees hand-on toolkits, it might be potentially haphazard for them to follow a prescribed teaching agenda without understanding or believing in the underlying theoretical principles. Thus, the construct of 'method' should be addressed, before

© Springer Nature Singapore Pte Ltd. 2018
Y. Zhu, *Language Curriculum Innovation in a Chinese Secondary School*,
https://doi.org/10.1007/978-981-10-7239-0_2

what it means to be 'effective' is examined. Richards, Platt, and Platt (1992) defined 'method' as:

> A way of teaching language which is based on systematic principles and procedures, i.e., which is an application of view of how a language is beset taught and learned (Platt & Platt, 1992, p. 228).

Ellis (2012) defined 'method' as:

> A pedagogic construct enshrined in a set of principles and techniques that specify how specific acts of teaching are to be performed (Ellis, 2012, p. 52).

The above definitions, though systematic and specific, are not flawless, as they are built on a relatively isolated domain of teaching beliefs and conceptions. In his seminal work, *Language Teaching Analysis*, Mackey (1965) speculated that method "means so little and so much" (Mackey, 1965, p. 139). Along with the endeavor to seek definite and operational tips for guiding teachers' practice, there have always been voices reacting against the confinement of methods in language teaching. Two major approaches are eclecticism and principled teaching.

Eclecticism suggests that teachers develop their own 'method' in teaching. For example, Harmer (2001, 2007) recognized the difficulty of choosing the optimal approach for a specific teaching situation, and proposed "pragmatic eclecticism" (Harmer, 2001, p. 97) by suggesting alternative models to PPP as coherent frameworks for its operation. He further observed that such learner factors as age and character, combined with a teacher's own beliefs and preferences, were likely to influence his or her pedagogical decisions. Eclecticism, irrespective of its avoidance of dogmatic adherence to any one enclosed method, is of limited use; as Stern criticized, "eclecticism is still based on the notion of a conceptual distinctiveness of the different methods" (1983, p. 428). Widdowson (1990) also observed that, "if by eclecticism is meant the random and expedient use of whatever technique comes mostly readily to hand, then it has no merit whatever" (1990, p. 50). Thus, despite its important ability to shift teachers from being passive recipients in transmission-based teacher development models, to constructive actors forming their own methods through intuitive, contextualized decisions, eclecticism has been criticized for being too vague to follow, mainly due to its underlying conception of clear boundaries between methods.

Other approaches opposed to the notion of 'method' that could be included in this broad category include the post-method approach and principled teaching, which share a common discontent with the construct of 'method.'

2.1.2   Post-method Approach

This subsection does not exclusively examine "post-method pedagogy" (Kumaravadivelu, 1994, 2001, 2003, 2006); instead, it attempts to depict broadly the era characterized by the notion of informed, enlightened, and dynamic teaching, including such widely-recognized and -accepted concepts as communicative language teaching (CLT) (Breen & Candlin, 1980; Littlewood, 1981; Savignon, 2002; Yalden, 1981; among others) and task-based language teaching (TBLT), which shows strong characteristics of CLT (Ellis, 2003, 2009, 2012).

Kumaravadivelu (2001, 2003, 2006) conceptualized post-method pedagogy as a three-dimensional system, consisting of three fundamental parameters—particularity, practicality, and possibility. In addition, a macrostrategic framework is formulated with macro and micro strategies. The macrostrategies are listed here:

(1)   Maximize learning opportunities;
(2)   Facilitate negotiated interaction;
(3)   Minimize perceptual mismatches;
(4)   Activate intuitive heuristics;
(5)   Foster language awareness;
(6)   Contextualize linguistic input;
(7)   Integrate language skills;
(8)   Promote learner autonomy;
(9)   Ensure social relevance; and
(10) Raise cultural consciousness.

(Kumaravadivelu, 2006, p. 201)

The framework formulates a general guideline for teachers to implement in their own specific teaching contexts. Neither communicative language teaching (CLT) nor task-based language teaching (TBLT) are considered methods, only approaches derived from theoretical, empirical, and experiential knowledge from L2 teaching and learning. CLT and TBLT both formulate broad principles for language teachers and acknowledge various meaning-oriented classroom practices, which are departures from traditional methods of language teaching. Brown noted seven inter-related characteristics of CLT:

(1)   Overall goals. CLT suggests a focus of all the components of communicative competence.
(2)   Relationship of form and function. Language techniques are designed to engage learners in the pragmatic, authentic, functional use of language for meaningful purposes.
(3)   Fluency and accuracy. A focus on students' "flow" if comprehension and production and a focus on the formal accuracy of production are complementary principles underlying communicative techniques.
(4)   Focus on real-world contexts. Students in a communicative class ultimately must use the language, productively and receptively, in unrehearsed contexts outside the classroom.
(5)   Autonomy and strategic involvement. Students are given opportunities to focus on their own learning process through raising their awareness of their own styles of learning and through the development of appropriate strategies for production and comprehension.
(6)   Teacher roles. The role of the teacher is that of facilitator and guide, not an all-knowing font of knowledge.
(7)   Student roles. Students in a CLT class are active participants in their own learning process.

(Brown, 2007, p. 46–47)

Ellis (2009) summarized five characteristics of the main approaches of TBLT, as follows:

(1) the provision of opportunities for natural language use;
(2) learner-centeredness;
(3) focus-on-form;
(4) the kind of task; and
(5) the rejection of traditional approaches to language teaching.

(Ellis, 2009, pp. 224–225)

2.1.3 Teaching by Principles

Brown (2001, 2007) noted language teachers' choices should be based on grounded principles—that is, what we know for certain about second language acquisition and teaching, despite the unknown mysteries in the field. He maintained that teachers are more likely to undertake "enlightened" teaching when associating teaching decisions and practice with principles derived from research. In this way, teaching is a more confident process, as teachers are aware of the rationales for employing a classroom technique, and know how to evaluate its utility after using it (2001, p. 15; 2007, p. 63). In the 3rd edition of his book, *Teaching by Principles*, Brown (2007) enumerated 12 principles for learner autonomy and willingness to communicate, including two items changed from his previous set of principles (Brown, 2001), as synthesized in Table 2.1.

2.1.4 Principles of Effective Teaching

Based on research findings to date, Ellis (2005) formulated the following 10 widely-quoted principles for language instruction on second language acquisition and language teaching:

Principle 1. Instruction needs to ensure that learners develop both a rich repertoire of formulaic expressions and a rule-based competence.
Principle 2. Instruction needs to ensure that learner focus predominantly on meaning.
Principle 3. Instruction needs to ensure that learners also focus on form.
Principle 4. Instruction needs to be predominantly directed at developing implicit knowledge of the L2 while not neglecting explicit knowledge.
Principle 5. Instruction needs to consider the learner's 'built-in syllabus.'
Principle 6. Successful instructed language learning requires extensive L2 input.
Principle 7. Successful instructed language learning also requires opportunities for output.
Principle 8. The opportunity to interact in the L2 is central to developing L2 proficiency.
Principle 9. Instruction needs to take account of individual differences in learners.
Principle 10. In assessing learners' L2 proficiency it is important to examine free as well as controlled production.

(Ellis, 2005, pp. 210–221)

Table 2.1 Principles of language learning and teaching (Based on Brown, 2007, pp. 62–81)

Category	Principles	Statements of the principles
Cognitive principles	1. Automaticity	Efficient second language learning involves a timely movement of the control of a few language forms into the automatic, fluent processing of a relatively unlimited number of language forms. Overanalyzing language, thinking too much about its forms, and consciously lingering on rules of language all tend to impede this graduation to automaticity
	2. Meaningful learning	The process of making meaningful associations between existing knowledge/experience and new material will lead toward better long-term retention than rote learning of material in isolated pieces
	3. The anticipation of reward	Human beings are universally driven to act, or "behave," by the anticipation of some sort of reward—tangible or intangible, short-term or long-term—that will ensue as a result of the behavior
	4. Intrinsic motivation	The most powerful rewards are those that are intrinsically motivated within the learner. Because the behavior stems from needs, wants, or desires within oneself, the behavior itself is self-rewarding; therefore, not externally administered reward is necessary
	5. Strategic investment	Successful mastery of the second language will be due to a large extent to a learner's own personal "investment" of time, effort, and attention to the second language in the form of an individualized battery of strategies for comprehending and producing the language
	6. Autonomy	Successful mastery of a foreign language will depend to a great extent on learners' autonomous ability both to take initiative in the classroom and to continue their journey to success beyond the classroom and the teacher.
Socioaffective principles	7. Language ego	As human beings learn to use a second language, they also develop a new mode of thinking, feeling, and acting—a second identity. The new "language ego," intertwined with the second language, can easily create within the learner a sense of fragility, a defensiveness, and a raising of inhibitions
	8. Willingness to communicate	Successful language learners generally believe in themselves and in their capacity to accomplish communicative tasks, and are therefore willing risk takers in their attempts to produce and interpret language that is a bit beyond their absolute certainty. Their willingness to communicate results in the generation of both output (from the learner) and input (to the learner)

(continued)

Table 2.1 (continued)

Category	Principles	Statements of the principles
	9. The language-culture connection	Whenever you teach a language, you also teach a complex system of cultural customs, values, and ways of thinking, feeling, and acting. Especially in *second* (as opposed to *foreign*) language-learning contexts, the success with which learners adapt to a new cultural milieu will affect their language acquisition success, and vice versa, in some possibly significant ways
Linguistic principles	10. The native language effect	The native language of learners exerts a strong influence on the acquisition of the target language system. While that native system will exercise both facilitating and interfering effects on the production and comprehension of the new language, the interfering effects are likely to be the most salient
	11. Interlanguage	Second language learners tend to go through a systematic or quasi-systematic developmental process as they progress to full competence in the target language. Successful interlanguage development is partially a result of utilizing feedback from others
	12. Communicative competence	Given that communicative competence is the goal of a language classroom, instruction needs to point toward all its components: organizational, strategic, and psychomotor. Communicative goals are best achieved by giving due attention to language use and not just usage, to fluency and not just accuracy, to authentic language and context, and to students' eventual need to apply classroom learning to previously unrehearsed contexts in the real world.

Later, McIntyre et al. (2009) proposed a six-principle model of effective language teaching for diversified language learners. Grounded in the Vygotskian teaching-learning framework, the principles include: Joint productive activity; Language learning across the curriculum; Contextualization; Rigorous curriculum; Instructional conversation; and Family involvement. The last principle is "a way to help students connect their prior experience and knowledge with academic content" (McIntyre et al., 2009, p. x).

More recently, Richards and Bohlke (2011) proposed the following eight principles for effective language classroom instruction:

(1) Your lesson reflects high professional standards.
(2) Your lesson reflects sound principles of language teaching.
(3) Your lesson addresses meaningful learning outcomes.
(4) Your lesson provides opportunities for your learners to take part in extended practice with using language in a meaningful way.
(5) Your lesson is effectively managed.

(6) Your lesson is a coherent sequence of learning activities that link together to form a whole.
(7) Your lesson creates a motivation to learn and provides opportunities for success.
(8) The lesson reflects your personal philosophy of teaching.

(Richards & Bohlke, 2011, pp. 1–14)

To summarize, these above sets of principles draw on research findings in education, second language acquisition, and language teaching to extract factors that could be manipulated to improve the effectiveness of language classroom instruction, including curriculum issues, classroom climate, teachers' pedagogical expertise, learners' individual attributes, etc. Informative as these principles are, they arguably have limited implications for improving FLT instruction effectiveness in Chinese classrooms, given the idiosyncratic attributes of Chinese learners and teachers, and the realities of Chinese educational settings. Hence, it is necessary to associate general principals with context-specific factors in Chinese classrooms.

2.1.5 Studies on Effective Language Teaching in China

Recognizing the contributions made by mainstream studies on effective language teaching worldwide, studies in Chinese contexts attend more to the peculiarities of FLT classrooms in China. In pursuit of systematic principles for effective foreign language classroom teaching in Chinese contexts, as well as their implications for informing teacher development, SFLEP[1] has been hosting the National College English Teaching Contests since 2010, and has made continual efforts addressing this essential issue (Shu, 2010, 2011, 2012c, 2013b; Yang, 2011; Wang & An, 2012; Zhu, 2013). Commenting on a selected contestant's teaching scenario in the 1st SFLEP Cup National College English Teaching Contest, Yang noted:

> [This teacher] has a quite good command of English, with satisfactory accuracy, native-like pronunciation, and intonation. He has well maintained the balance between input and output in lesson planning. In addition, he has acquired a solid foundation of linguistics and applied linguistics, and has capacity of classroom organizations as well. Apparently, this teaching scenario is an illustrative example of effective foreign language teaching.

(Yang, 2011, p. 15)

Also, reflecting on some problems in the national teaching contest mentioned above, Shu pointed out that "organization, content and effect" were three essential indicators for evaluating foreign language classroom instruction (Shu, 2010, p. 30), emphasizing that "the key issue is effect, more specifically, to what extent have the pedagogical objectives been fulfilled" (*ibid*).

---

[1]SFLEP, Shanghai Foreign Language Education Press, is one of the leading publishing houses specializing in foreign language education in China.

Zhu's (2013) study, in pursuit of a theoretical framework against which to evaluate an outstanding classroom teaching episode in the 3rd SFLEP National Foreign Language Teaching Contest, proposes a framework containing seven essential factors contributing to the effectiveness of foreign language classroom teaching:

(1) appropriate teaching objectives;
(2) feasible lesson planning;
(3) various teaching materials;
(4) adaptive teaching skills;
(5) harmonious classroom climate;
(6) effective classroom assessment;
(7) in-depth reflection on teaching

(Zhu, 2013, p. 50)

The studies to date have formed a large bulk of research exploring the principles contributing to the effectiveness of FLT classroom instruction in China, and have been recognized as a substantive move towards "developing a set of FLT theories with Chinese characteristics" (Shu, 2005, p. 2). Nevertheless, most of these studies are notably general in nature, drawing primarily on arguments rather than empirical research findings, thus generating disappointingly few implications for classroom practitioners. Therefore, formulating a micro-framework for effective classroom instruction in Chinese FLT contexts would fill an existing research gap, and was a substantial goal of the author in the Danyang Project.

2.2 The Rationale for the Framework of Effective Teaching that Informs the DP

Overall, the construct of teaching effectiveness could be formulated using either a theory-laden or data-driven approach. As the latter normally draws on longitudinal process-product research, which is beyond the scope of this study, the present study adopted a theory-laden approach, by examining and synthesizing extant research on aspects of L2 classroom instruction. As noted by Ellis (2012), "at one level, 'teaching' is discourse" (p. 75), to unfold the complexity of classroom instruction, this study takes a discourse perspective to view classroom instruction.

Classroom discourse is "the type of language used in classroom situations" (Richards et al., 2000, pp. 64–65). It has idiosyncratic forms and functions, in comparison with languages used in interactions in other situations. To some extent, the quality of classroom discourse is a decisive indicator of teaching effectiveness; however, it has been universally recognized that classroom interaction per se is a highly complex process (Walsh, 2011), as evidenced by the proliferation of classroom-based research in the field, and the on-going controversies over certain critical issues. Despite existing ambiguities that motivate classroom-based research, this study draws on what has been found so far based on empirical evidence to guide, calibrate, and evaluate PTs' classroom behaviors, to construct a theoretical framework to bolster the DP teacher training program. The purpose of this effective teaching framework is two-fold—to provide a set of objectives for teacher training programs, and to establish criteria for observing and evaluating concrete changes in PTs' teaching behaviors. As student's contributions are an indispensable part of classroom discourse, this framework also encompasses aspects pertaining to learner behaviors.

2.2.1   Socio-Cultural Theory of Language Learning

In the realm of second language acquisition research, there have long existed two mainstream theoretical perspectives (interactionist-cognitive and socio-cultural) on the fundamental questions of what is language learning, and how learning takes place. According to socio-cultural theory, language learning is both an interpsychological and intrapsychological process (Vygotsky, 1981) taking place through the mediation of social interaction. From a socio-cultural perspective, language learning is perceived as a process rather than a product, and, more specifically, a process of development rather than acquisition; "development does not proceed as the unfolding of inborn capacities, but as the transformation of innate capacities once they intertwine with socio-culturally constructed mediation means" (Lantolf & Pavlenko, 1995, p. 109). Hence successful language learning involves a developmental process of shifting from 'other-regulated' activity to 'self-regulated' activity (see Table 2.2). In this sense, socio-cultural theory has blurred the distinction between "language learning and language using" (Lantolf & Pavlenko, 1995, p. 116). As Sfard (1998) put it, there is not a clear boundary between 'acquisition' and 'participation'.

An important construct in socio-cultural theory of language learning is the zone of proximal development (ZPD), which is defined by Vygotsky as:

Table 2.2 Types of 'development' in sociocultural theory (Ellis, 2012, p. 239)

1	The learner is unable to produce a specific target form even with assistance.
2	The learner demonstrates that with substantial assistance he/she can use a specific linguistic feature (x), which previously he/she could not use
3	The learner demonstrates that subsequently he/she can use x in the same or similar context but now requires less assistance than on the previous occasion
4	The learner subsequently demonstrates that he/she can now use x in the same or very similar context in which he/she had used it previously without any assistance
5	The learner is now able to employ x on different occasions in new contexts and with different interlocutors without any assistance (i.e., 'transfer of learning' has taken place)

...the distance between the actual development level as determined by independent problem solving and the level of potential development as determined through problem-solving
under adult guidance or in collaboration with more capable peers.

(Vygotsky, 1978, p. 86)

This definition was later fine-tuned by Ohta (2001, p. 9) to better suit FLT contexts:

For the L2 learner, the ZPD is the distance between the actual developmental level as
determined by individual linguistic production, and the level of potential development as
determined through language produced collaboratively with a peer or teacher.

(Ohta, 2001, p. 9)

It is evident from both definitions above that learning involving ZPD entails
learners' participation in collaborative activities with others (teacher, peers, tutor,
etc.). An essential question herein is how a socio-cultural viewpoint on language
learning informs FLT classroom instruction; accordingly, the present study examines operational aspects of classroom instruction that have been informed by
socio-cultural theory.

2.3   Defining Terms of Discourse Units

The present framework is largely informed by the findings of a series of seminal
studies on classroom discourse (for example, Sinclair and Coulthard, 1975; Spada
& Fröhlich, 1995; Nassaji & Wells, 2000; Wells, 1996). Before elaborating on the
framework, it is necessary to define a hierarchy of discourse units. In this study, the
smallest component of discourse is *move*, which is "the minimal contribution a
speaker can make to an exchange" (Ellis 2012, p. 87). *Exchanges*, which combine
"reciprocally-related moves" (Wells, 1996, p. 78), in turn comprise a *sequence*. An
exchange consists of obligatory *initiation* move and *response* move, and probably a
follow-up move, constituting the IR(F) pattern (Sinclair & Coulthard, 1975) or
'triadic dialogue' (Lemke, 1990).

According to Wells (1996), there are two types of exchanges: *nuclear exchanges*
and *bound exchanges*. Nuclear exchanges independently contribute "new content to
the discourse" (*ibid*, p. 78), while bound exchanges, as the name suggests, are affil-
iated with nuclear exchanges in some way. Bound exchanges in turn are classified into
three categories. The first is *preparatory exchange*, which signals the beginning of a
new sequence, such as the bid-nomination exchanges in classroom discourse. The
second category is *dependent exchange,* which deals with certain aspect of nuclear
changes by means of exemplification, expansion, and justification. The third is *embedded exchange*, which deals with problems in the on-going exchange.

The unit at the next higher level to exchange is *sequence*, which comprises at
least one obligatory nuclear exchange and optional bound exchanges. The largest
unit for analyzing classroom discourse is *episode*, which "consists of all the talk

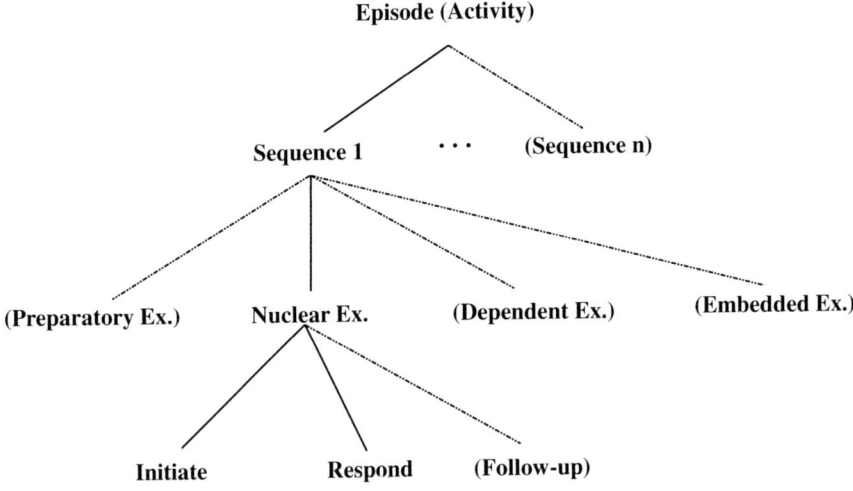

Fig. 2.1 The organization of spoken discourse (Wells, 1996, p. 79)

produced in carrying out a single activity, or one of its constituent tasks" (Wells, 2000, p. 383). The constituent structure of moves, exchanges, sequences, and episode is illustrated in Fig. 2.1.

2.3.1 The Framework

(1) Instructional Objectives and Activities

In his pioneering schemata of activity theory (see Fig. 2.2), Engeströme (1999, 2001) noted the "object" predicts the orientation of a certain activity, and springs from the motive for a consequence (Lantolf & Thorne, 2013). In this model, the object means the "raw material" or "problem space" at which the activity is targeted, and which is transformed into "outcomes" through mediating tools (Engeströme, 1993, p. 67). In his later publication, Engeströme maintained that, "the object gains motivating force that gives shape and direction to activity… determines the horizon of possible action" (Engeströme, 1999). To apply this model into FLT classroom instruction, we could say the object is the "problem space," or instructional objectives that cater to the needs of learners and gains motivating force to give shape and direction to classroom activities.

Three criteria are proposed to address issue relating to instructional objectives and activities, given the significance thereof. First, there should be clear goals set to develop learners' linguistic, affective, and social competence in classroom instruction, no matter implicitly or explicitly stated. Second, the time allotment for different teaching and learning activities should align with instructional objectives.

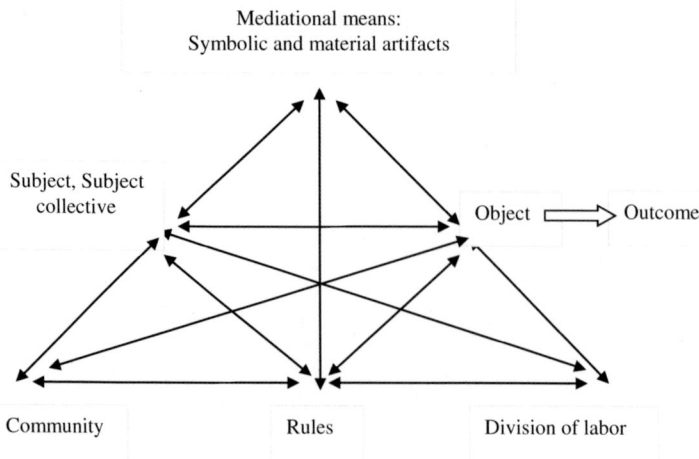

Fig. 2.2 The activity system (based on Engeströme, 1999, 2001)

Third, the sequence of the transition between activities should basically follow a protocol progressing from other-regulated learning towards self-regulated learning.

(2) **The Choice of instructional materials**

The term "instructional materials" in this study does not exclusively refer to mandated textbooks for Chinese basic education, which are normally prescribed by central or local educational administrations, but to "anything which is used to help language learners to learn" (Tomlinson, 2011, p. viii), including mandated materials and materials adapted from available resources. In the specific constitutional setting of this study, mandated instructional materials contain a set of textbooks and supplementary materials (*jiaofu ziliao*), including PPTs, worksheets, exercise worksheets, etc., collaboratively developed by teachers working in the same TRG.

Per socio-cultural theory, there is an indirect relationship between humans and the world, such that "human thinking is mediated by culturally organized and transmitted symbolic meaning" (Lantolf, 2012, p. 57). Physical and symbolic tools mediate human learning (Vygotsky, 1978), and instructional materials play an important mediating role in FLT classrooms, to regulate learners' language development. In other words, instructional materials are cultural tools facilitating learning in transforming and reconstructing the resources and practices to which learners are exposed, rather than merely vehicles or conduits for linguistic knowledge.

This redefined role of instructional materials challenges language teachers to rectify their traditional recognition of textbooks as authoritative teaching guides that prescribe what and how to teach. As claimed by Tomlinson (2008), many current ELT materials tend to have divergent influence on language acquisition and development. Thus, in most pedagogical settings, it is up to language teachers to choose, evaluate, and adapt instructional materials. Overall, the objective of material adaptation is to "maximize the appropriacy of teaching materials in context" (McDonough et al., 2013, p. 67). It takes considerable expertise and capability to accommodate instructional materials to the realities in FLT classrooms; for example, teachers undertake "predictive and retrospective evaluation" (Ellis, 1997, p. 36) of textbooks to make pedagogical decisions, and must test the "suitability and effectiveness" of teaching materials in their teaching practices (Ellis, 2010, p. 52).

Grounded on the rationale elaborated so far, how FLT teachers use instructional materials is considered a prominent indicator of teachers' professional development. An array of teacher training sessions was incorporated in the DP to facilitate PTs' learning to effectively choose, adapt, and use instructional materials.

(3) **Teacher talk**

Teacher talk is defined as "that variety of language sometimes used by teachers when they are in the process of teaching" (Richards et al., 2000, p. 471). As Ellis (2012) has put it, "teacher talk is the defining feature of many classrooms" (p. 119). Early studies (for example, Thornbury, 1996; Walsh, 2002) sought general features of teacher talk likely to effect language learning, and applied their findings to teacher training. However, in the socio-cultural perspective, there are hardly any general characteristics of teacher talk that are universally effective, regardless of contextual factors. How much and what a teacher speaks does has no implications for teaching effectiveness, without considering the micro-contextual realities in language classrooms, such as instructional objectives and learner factors.

In this part teacher talk is addressed in a focused sense; how it combines reciprocally with learner talk will be discussed later, within the discussion of discourse structure. This study addresses the quantity and quality, respectively, of teacher talk by examining the duration and length of teacher talk, teacher's speaking speed, and two types of teacher questions. This study investigates to what extent quantity of teacher talk contributes to classroom discourse at different stages of curriculum innovation.

A widely-adopted taxonomy to describe teacher questions is the distinction between display questions and referential questions (Long & Sato, 1983). A display question is about "whether the addressee has knowledge of a particular fact or can use a particular linguistic item correctly" (Ellis, 1994, p. 700), while a referential question is "genuinely information seeking" (ibid, p. 721). It is a theoretical presupposition in this study that, while teachers' open-ended referential questions provide more space for communication in language classrooms, close-ended display questions to which the teacher knows the answers are a necessary component of classroom talk. Brock (1986) found learner responses to referential questions were significantly longer and more syntactically complex than were their responses to display questions. The application of this widely accepted notion has been implemented in teacher training programs as well (Cullen, 1997; Thornbury, 1995). However, Wu (1993), in a study of ESL students in Hong Kong, found learners' responses were restrictive rather than elaborate, regardless of question type, while Long and Crookes (1992) found display questions elicited more student turns; thus, caution should be exercised not to overemphasize the superiority of referential questions over display questions. The display question also plays an indispensable role in classroom discourse; as Lee (2006) suggested, they "are central resources whereby language teachers and students organize their lessons and produce language pedagogy" (p. 691).

A synthesis of the research to date on referential and display questions equips this study with an integrative stance on the use of different question types, justified by the "goals and agenda of the educational institution" (Ho, 2005, p. 297).

(4) Learner talk

In the present study, learner talk is defined as the utterances contributed by learners to classroom discourse. The language a learner uses in classrooms is reciprocally interrelated to teacher talk, and this sub-section mainly addresses how the quantity and quality of learner talk shapes the overall landscape of classroom discourse. Learners' contributions were examined in terms of time and length to reveal learner participation in classroom discourse. However, quantity of learner talk alone provides only an elaborate description, thus the average length per move was also examined to describe its general feature.

Another aspect of learner talk addressed here is its restrictiveness—i.e., how much of what students is partially or fully repeating what they are exposed to in classroom instruction. As with the different types of teacher questions, the taxonomy of learner talk here does not indicate a rigid bisection between restricted and unrestricted learner talk, but an ecologically sound distribution of two types of learner talk to conduce effective language learning. Restricted learner talk, which is omnipresent in traditional classrooms featuring drill practice, has a facilitative impact on language learning (for example, Roebuck & Wagner, 2004; Shrestha,2013; Skehan, 1998). However, in her study, Duff (2000) illustrated drill practice activities can also become burdensome to learners. From a socio-cultural perspective, "repetition is seen as a valuable tool for achieving self-regulation" (Ellis, 2012, p. 177).

Unrestricted learner talk, which is more likely to involve learners' free production, is more likely to resemble authentic interaction, and is conductive to language learning according to the basic tenets of communicative language learning. It is through free production that learners participate in classroom interaction in which language development is achieved from other-regulated to self-regulated learning.

(5) Participatory organization

Participatory organization refers to "the way in which students are organized" (Spada & Fröhlich, 1995, p. 15). In this study, participatory organization is operationalized as different combinations of interlocutors in classroom interaction. So far, an abundance of research has informed the present study with empirical evidence of the mediating role played by student-centered interaction in language learning. From a socio-cultural perspective, Donato's (1994) study supported that "learners can provide guided support to their peers during collaborative L2 inter-actions in ways analogous to expert scaffolding" (Donato, 1994, p. 51). Studies also found learner-centered classroom discourse provides more opportunities for nego-tiation, in comparison with teacher-centered discourse (Antón, 1999). Also, peer-peer collaborative dialogue mediates second language learning; it is essential to inform learners of the justification of peer mediated learning (Swain et al., 2002), and learners are involved in peer assistance through co-construction and prompting (Foster & Ohta, 2005).

This study examines participatory organization in language classrooms by broadly classifying it into two types—teacher-student interaction and student-student interaction. The former is further divided into sub-categories according to how learners participate in interaction with the teacher; specifically, whether a learner speaks in a monologue, spontaneously responds to the teacher with other peers, or speaks in chorus with other students.

(6) Focus on meaning versus forms

Traditional language teaching based on structural syllabi has targeted building linguistic competence by emphasizing grammatical rules, or "focus on forms" (Long, 1991). In focus-on-forms instruction, the target language is treated as an object to be learned, rather than a tool for communication, and language learning as habit formation (Skinner, 1957). When teaching is directed at linguistic forms, activities involving drill repetition and memorization are abundant in language classrooms. Though the linguistic resources learners develop through focus-on-forms instruction play a role in learner's interlanguage development, linguistic competence cannot be fully developed without providing learners opportunities to focus on meaning (Ellis, 2005). However, activities targeted at meaningful communication should not exclude attention to linguistic forms. According to Schmidt's Noticing Hypothesis (1990, 1993), second language learning involves learners' conscious mental processes. Focus-on-form instruction targeting mapping meaning and form is also supported by Long's (1985, 1996) interaction hypothesis, which argues that negotiated interaction facilitates language development. Thus, focus-on-form pedagogy informs the basic tenet of curriculum innovation in the DP—that is, the primary focus of classroom instruction is on meaning and attention should also be given to linguistic forms (Ellis, 2005).

When dealing with micro-analyses of classroom interaction in this study, 'meaning-focused' exchanges refer to the reciprocal moves in which information transaction occurs, while 'form-focused' exchanges mainly deal with linguistic features of the target language, including grammatical, phonological, or lexical forms. 'Meaning and form' exchanges comprise those speech acts combining information transaction and elaboration of a linguistic aspect.

(7) Discourse structures

IRF exchange, or the 'triadic dialogue' as referred by Lemke (1990), is a three-part exchange structure that is ubiquitous and dominant in all classrooms (Ellis, 2012). As its name suggests, the IRF exchange pattern consists of a teacher-initiation move, a student-response move, and a follow-up move by the teacher. van Lier (1994) listed eight main characteristics of the IRF exchange:

(1) It is three turn long.
(2) The first and the third turn are produced by the teacher, and the second one by the student.
(3) The exchange is started and ended by the teacher.
(4) The student's turn is sandwiched between two teacher's turns, and is often brief and elliptical in nature.
(5) The first teacher's turn is designed to elicit some kind of verbal response from a student. The teacher often already knows the answer (is 'primary knower').
(6) The second teacher's turn (the third turn in the exchange) is some kind of comment on the second turn, or on the 'fit' between the second and the first.
(7) It is often clear from the third turn whether or not the teacher was interested in the massage contained in the response, or merely in the form of the answer, or in seeing if the student knew the answer or not.
(8) If the exchange is part of a series, as is often the case, there is behind the series a plan and a direction determined by the teacher. The teacher 'leads' the students.

(van Lier 1994: 73)

While the ubiquity of triadic dialogues or IRF patterns in classroom discourse is widely acknowledged (Lemke, 1990; Waring, 2009; Wells, 1993), how IRF exchanges induce opportunities for language learning remains controversial. Studies (Kasper 2001; Lerner 1995) have reported the IRF pattern has limited effects on learning, given the limited space it provides for learner participation and negotiation. However, other researchers (for example, Gourlay, 2005; Nassaji & Wells, 2000; Seedhouse, 1996; Waring, 2009) hold different views, in support of the facilitative contribution of IRF exchanges. Ellis (2012) maintained that "IRF is not a monolithic structure, but, in fact, highly varied" (p. 91). His view is in line with what van Lier's (2000) proposed 'IRF continuum' (p. 94), in which he argued that it is the depth of processing involved that determines its contribution to learning. According to van Lier, the continuum ranges from 'recitation' at the bottom, to 'display' and 'recognition' in the middle, and 'precision' at the top.

Motivated by a communicative approach for language learning, the DP adopted an integrative perspective to examine IRF patterns as an indicator of communicativeness in FLT classes. In addition, the initiation and response moves were regarded as operational domains teacher education programs could target to enhance PTs' professional expertise. Traditional classrooms are infused with an enclosed form of IRF, in which the response moves are restricted in form and normally induce classroom interaction that is not oriented towards the exchange of meaning. In this study, teachers' making interactive decisions to deploy initiation and follow-up moves to accommodate learners' level of cognitive processing and provide opportunities for free production with exemplification, expansion, and verification, is perceived a sign of development (Cullen, 2002). As the constituent structure illustrated in Fig. 2.1 reveals, the IRF pattern's contribution to language learning depends largely on whether and how the teacher manipulates the initiation move and follow-up move in the nuclear exchange to create one or more subsequent dependent exchanges in which extended learner production is elicited, as illustrated in the following two episodes, selected from two classroom discourses the research observed:

Episode 2.1

(1)	T: (Pointing to a picture on PPT a slide) What does this man do?	I	Nuclear exchange
(2)	S: He is a singer.	R	
(3)	T: Right. Sit down, please.	F	

Episode 2.2

(1)	T: (Pointing to a picture on a PPT slide) What does this man do?	I	Nuclear exchange
(2)	S: He is a singer.	R	
(3)	T: Right.	F	
(4)	T: Why do you think he is a singer?	I	Dependent exchange
(5)	S: Because he performs on the stage with fancy costume.	R	
(6)	T: Yes, you're very clever.	F	

In the two episodes shown above, the same question asked by the teacher constituted the initiation move in the nuclear exchange. Obviously, the teacher was the primary knower when asking this question. What distinguishes these two excerpts is the third move. As Episode 2.1 shows, the teacher put an end to communication by giving an evaluative comment on the student's response, whereas in the same move of Episode 2.2, the teacher added another question, to which she was the secondary knower and let the student justify his answer to the first question; this question generated a subsequent dependent exchange in which space was created for language learning to take place.

Another prominent aspect of IRF research focuses on the initiator to examine teacher-led or student-initiated IRF exchanges. Ernst (1994) put forward the talking circle as a communicative activity to generate opportunities for student-led talk. In Johnson's study (1995), she provided examples of student-initiated talk that assimilates adult-child interaction in authentic out-of-class interactions, and is conducive to L1 learning. Ellis (2012) also pointed out "task-based teaching affords opportunities for student-initiated discourse" (p. 92). It can be found from relevant studies that student-initiated talk is more likely to take place when traditional teacher-fronted classrooms are converted into student-centered ones, or in activities featuring communicativeness. In the present study, providing opportunities for student-initiated exchanges was perceived as an indicator of teachers' departure from traditional pedagogy.

To sum up, the framework for effective language teaching that informs the DP highlights building a vibrant classroom community where the teacher makes numerous interactive decisions and maneuvers, to co-construct interaction with learners that contributes to the achievement of instructional goals. As can be shown in the principles above, the notion of effective teaching in the Danyang Project indicates a strong inclination to depart from traditional teacher-fronted teaching pedagogy, which is based on structural syllabus, focuses predominantly on language forms, and draws largely on grammar-translation or PPP methods. Nevertheless, formulation of these principles and framework alone does not guarantee successful implementation, and involves changing teachers' cognitions and practices to implement innovative pedagogy (see for example, Carless, 2003; Fullan, 2001; Kırkgöz, 2008).

2.4 Curriculum Innovation: Theory and Research

2.4.1 Defining Curriculum Innovation

Curriculum innovation is defined in various ways, several of which are summarized in Table 2.3, that reveal some general characteristics of curriculum innovations. First, curriculum innovation is targeted at enhancing students' learning and development, and is often managed in a planned manner. Second, curriculum innovation is enacted through the development and implementation of educational products (i.e., instructional materials, methodological skills, etc.) that reflect new values and ideology. Third, curriculum involves possible changes in stakeholders' beliefs and behaviors. Fourth,

Table 2.3 A summary of definitions of curriculum innovation

Researcher	Definition
Rogers (1983, p. 11)	"…the documented infusion of new content or methodology to a course of study to improve or enhance student learning. Curriculum innovation is defined as broad initiatives, and not the nuances or idiosyncratic shifts that occur from teacher to teacher or classroom to classroom."
Markee (1997, p. 46)	"Curriculum innovation is a managed process of development whose principal products are teaching (and/or testing) materials, methodological skills, and pedagogical values that are perceived as new by potential adopters."
Fullan (2001, p. 25)	(1) the possible use of new or revised materials (instructional resources such as curriculum materials or technologies), (2) the possible use of new teaching approaches (i.e., new teaching strategies or activities), and (3) the possible alteration of beliefs (e.g., pedagogical assumptions and theories underlying particular new policies or programs)."
Marsh (2009, p. 114)	"A working definition of innovation is the planned application of ends or means, new or different from those which exist currently in classroom, school or system, and intended to improve effectiveness for the stakeholders."

curriculum innovation is enacted within a multi-dimensional socio-cultural system encompassing learners, teachers, school administrators, parents, etc.

To a certain extent, it can be argued that the history of foreign language teaching has been spurred by curriculum innovations. From audiolingualism, which stresses habit formation, to the Natural Approach, which features communication in classrooms and meaning-focused teaching, to the communicative approach and task-based language teaching, which emphasize meaning-oriented communication, while still attending to linguistic forms.

Markee (1997) distinguished between "primary innovation," which consists of the core dimensions of educational change, and "secondary innovations," which are the organization developments underpinning the primary innovation. He maintained that "the function of secondary innovations is restricted to enabling primary innovations" (1997, p. 53).

According to Ellis (1997), there are two types of innovation—"absolute innovation" and "perceived innovation." The former contains completely new proposals yet to be testified in practice, while the latter refers to ideas or practices that are new to the specific practitioners (pp. 26–27). Drawing on the scarcity of innovatory pedagogical proposals generated in SLA, Ellis suggested most innovations in this field fall into the second category.

Applying what has been discussed so far to the Danyang Project, it could be found that its underlying notions and implementation process conform to the characteristics of curriculum innovation in general. Apart from those common features, the DP is a perceived innovation implemented in a longitudinal and intensive manner.

2.4.2 Influencing Factors of Implementing Curriculum Innovation

Disappointing or even frustrating as it may sound, numerous studies worldwide have reported that large scale curriculum innovations are seldom implemented in teaching practice in the manner their developers or policy makers expected (for example, Zheng, 2005; Zheng & Davison, 2008; China; Carless, 2001, 2003, 2004; Hong Kong; Li, 1998; South Korea; Curdt-Christiansen & Silver, 2012, 2013; Singapore; Orafi & Borg, 2009; Libya; Tomlinson, 1990; Indonesia). What factors influence the implementation and effectiveness of curriculum innovation? Table 2.4 synthesizes empirical findings addressing this question.

Apart from the influencing factors listed in Table 2.3, Ellis (1997) synthesized four components that could contribute to the implementing effect of curriculum innovation: (1) socio-cultural context; (2) practitioners' personal traits and expertise; (3) how the method is implemented; and, (4) the attributes of innovation.

In a similar but more elaborated way, Markee (1997) suggested the following general principles to implement a curriculum innovation:

Table 2.4 A synthesis of factors influencing innovation from empirical studies

Studies	Settings	Factors influencing innovation
Carless (2003)	Primary schools in Hong Kong	Teacher beliefs, teacher understandings, the syllabus time available, the textbook and the topic; preparation and the available resources; the language proficiency of the students (2003, p. 485)
Li (1998)	Secondary schools in South Korea	Difficulties caused by the teacher, the students, and the educational system
Curdt-Christiansen and Silver (2012, 2013)	Primary schools in Singapore	Centralized educational structures, examination-oriented systems, and societal cultural frameworks (2013, p. 246)
Orafi and Borg (2009)	Secondary schools in Libya	Teacher training, established practices, assessment, teachers' perceptions of students' abilities
Tomlinson 1990	Indonesian junior and senior high schools	The attitudes and personality of the teacher; rapport between students and teacher; locally appropriate version of the communicative approach (Tomlinson, 1990, p. 36)
Zheng (2005), Zheng and Davison (2008)	A Chinese secondary school	External factors, internal factors and situated forces

Principle 1. Curricular innovation is a complex phenomenon.

Principle 2. The principal job of change agents is to effect desired changes.

Principle 3. Good communication among project participants is a key to successful curricular innovation.

Principle 4. The successful implementation of educational innovations is based on a strategic approach to managing change.

Principle 5. Innovation is an inherently messy, unpredictable business.

Principle 6. It always takes longer to effect change than originally anticipated.

Principle 7. There is a high likelihood that change agents' proposals will be misunderstood.

Principle 8. It is important for implementers to have a stake in the innovations they are expected to implement.

Principle 9. It is important for change agents to work through opinion leaders, who can influence their peers.

(Markee, 1997, pp. 172–179)

Drawing on research findings from a large number of empirical studies, Underwood (2012) reviewed factors reported to have hindering effects on mandated curriculum innovation, including "difficult classroom conditions, the absence of training, an unsupportive school environment, insufficient resources, and mismatched, high-stakes assessment" (pp. 911–912). Fullan (2001) listed nine factors, divided into three categories—characteristics of change, local characteristics, and external factors—that influence the implementation of an innovation project (see Fig. 2.3).

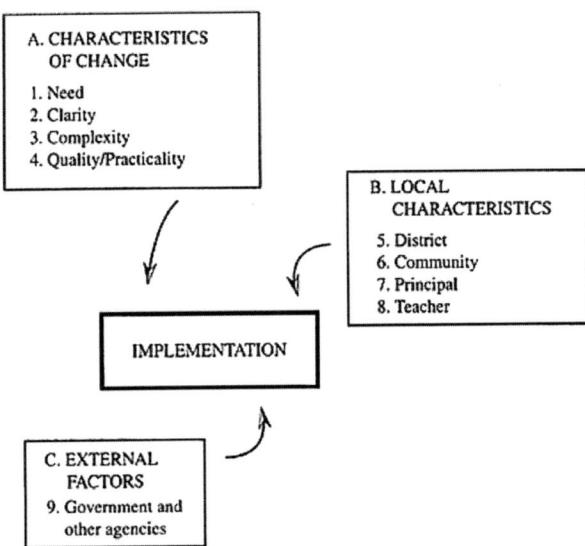

Fig. 2.3 Interactive factors affecting implementation (Fullan, 2001, p. 47)

Both theoretical and empirical studies add our understandings of the components influencing the implementation of curriculum innovation, which roughly fall into three categories. The first is perception—that is, how stakeholders perceive or believe about the change and its potential effects. The second is contextual condition—specifically, the policy that guarantees financial and intellectual resources are provided to support the innovation. The last is implemental realities –in other words, how the process of enactment is organized and coordinated, how stakeholders involved interact with each other, and how opinion leaders in the community influence the trajectory of change. These components have also been referred to as "the subjective reality of curriculum implementation" (Underwood, 2012, p. 911).

These components are interrelated, and work dynamically to influence what is happening in educational settings. As Markee (1997) noted, "curricular innovation is a complex and multidimensional phenomenon" (p. 39). Other researchers have offered congruent views (for example, Carless, 2003; Kırkgöz, 2008; Orafi & Borg, 2009) stating that, among all change agents involved in educational change, teacher factors (e.g., teacher belief, perception, attitude, thinking, decision-making, knowledge, and practices) play a pivotal role. As stated by Orafi & Borg (2009), "the uptake of an educational innovation can be limited when it is not congruent with and does not take into consideration the cognitive and contextual realities of teacher's work" (p. 243).

2.5 Teacher Cognition: Theory and Research

2.5.1 Defining Teacher Cognition

The last three decades have witnessed the development of research on teacher cognition. While signaling the robustness of the domain of enquiry, the proliferation of terminologies in these studies has also admittedly led to "definitional confusion" (Clandinin and Connelly, 1987; Eisenhart et al., 1988; Woods, 2011). For the sake of simplicity and conformity, the present study adopts the umbrella term 'teacher cognition,' defined by Borg (2006) as "the complex, practically-oriented, personalized, and context-sensitive networks of knowledge, thoughts and beliefs that language teachers draw on in their work" (2006, p. 272). In his later publication, Borg (2012) proposed three core constructs of language teacher cognition—how teachers "think, know, and believe" (2012, p. 11). This definition of teacher cognition aligns with Ellis's (2004) definition of teacher beliefs as "statements teachers made about their ideas, thoughts, and knowledge that are expressed as evaluations of what 'should be done', 'should be the case', and 'is preferable'" (2004, p. 244).

2.5.2 Teacher Cognition and Teaching Practices: Consistency or Inconsistency

In recent years, teacher cognition has attracted considerable research interest. In the field of language teacher education, the bulk of research has explored the correspondence between teacher cognition and teaching practices, addressing the recurrent question of whether these two conceptual areas exist in consistent juxtaposition in language teachers' career life (Basturkmen, 2012).

There is a consensus that a teacher's belief system plays an essential role in a his or her teaching practice, by informing, motivating, guiding, or shaping his or her decision-making process and pedagogical behaviors (Borg, 2003, 2011; Burns, 1992; Fang 1996; Johnson, 1992). A proliferation of research since the beginning of the 1990s has yielded findings that have range from being very inconsistent, to being highly consistent. For instance, Johnson (1992) investigated how three ESL teachers' theoretical beliefs corresponded with their pedagogical practice, and found there was consistency between literacy instruction and those teachers' theoretical orientation. Similar results were found in other studies (see, for example, Allen, 2002; Kern, 1995; Richardson et al., 1991). However, not surprisingly, inconsistency between language teachers' beliefs and teaching practices was reported by researchers (Kumaravadivelu, 1993; Phipps & Borg, 2009; Roehler & Duff, 1991). Despite the controversy over whether and how language teachers' belief systems affects their pedagogical practice, it is nearly certain the two are interactively and dialogically related, rather than mutually exclusive (Borg, 2003; Fang, 1996).

2.5.3 Factors Contributing to the Interplay between Teacher Cognition and Teaching Practices

A vital point here, however, is what accounts for the consistency or inconsistency between teachers' practices and their stated cognition. A synthesis of relevant literature sheds light on how personal, educational, and contextual factors influence how teachers' cognition and practices intertwine and interact.

In respect to the personal dimension, mainstream studies support the claim that individual teachers' prior learning experience, or "apprenticeship of observation" as lexicalized by Lortie (1975), largely influences their cognition (Freeman, 1993; Holt Reynolds, 1992; Nespor, 1987). In his oft-cited review article, Borg (2003) found teachers' preliminary ideas about language teaching were largely governed by their own experiences as language learners, and changes in trainee teachers' behaviors did not necessarily result in changes in their cognition. Other studies (see, for example, Johnson, 1994; Numrich, 1996; Woods, 1996) also reported how teachers' prior experience shaped their cognition and pedagogical decisions. In sum, the formation and transformation of teachers' cognition or practice is influenced by their prior learning experience, i.e., how they were taught by their teachers and how they learned as language learners. However, the bulk of research so far has provided little evidence to justify how teachers' prior working experience informs, influences, or interacts with their cognition and teaching practices.

Another central issue is whether, or to what extent, teacher education affects the relationship of between teacher cognition and teaching practice. Research, however, offers conflicting perspectives on the effectiveness of teacher education programs, both pre- and in-service, in changing teachers' cognitions. For instance, Kagan's (1992) widely-referenced review suggests no significant relationship between teacher education and teacher cognition; however, this claim could be regarded as premature, as subsequent studies found evidence of cognitive and behavior change in trainees (see, for example, Freeman, 1993; Peacock, 2001; Richards et al., 1996). The lack of consensus on such core issues as what counts as evidence of cognition, and how to measure its change highlights the themes to be investigated: the uniqueness of individual development, as opposed to a monolithic developmental pathway; the distinction and interaction between teachers' cognitive change and behavioral change; and, the mechanisms underpinning the process of change (Borg, 2003).

In addition to the personal and educational dimensions discussed above, the role of context in the agreement or conflict between teachers' cognition and practice has also been documented by a large body of literature. Contextual factors include the complexity and dynamics inside classrooms (Johnson, 1992a; Nunan, 1992), the students (Bailey 1996; Graden 1996), the school (Crookes & Arakaki, 1999; Richards & Pennington, 1998; Spada & Massey, 1992), and the social realities in the community and society (Burns, 1996). Dominant research has drawn on

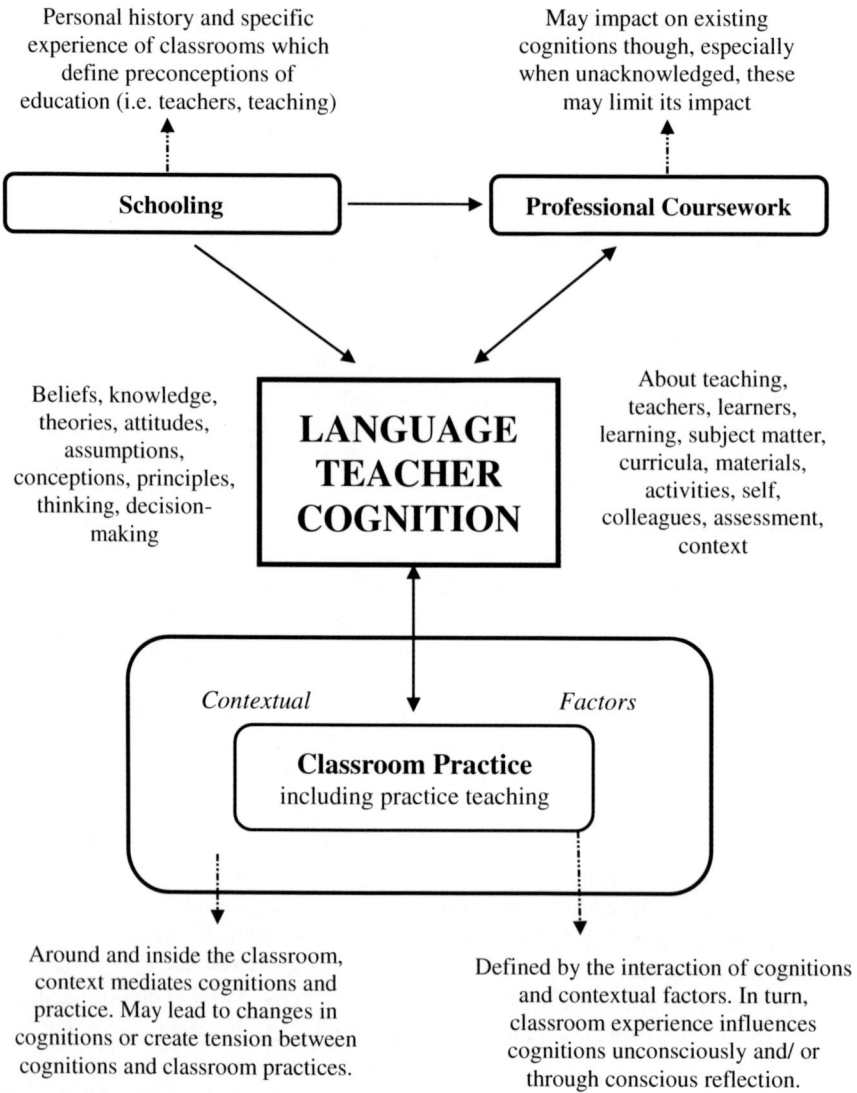

Personal history and specific experience of classrooms which define preconceptions of education (i.e. teachers, teaching)

May impact on existing cognitions though, especially when unacknowledged, these may limit its impact

Schooling ——→ **Professional Coursework**

Beliefs, knowledge, theories, attitudes, assumptions, conceptions, principles, thinking, decision-making

LANGUAGE TEACHER COGNITION

About teaching, teachers, learners, learning, subject matter, curricula, materials, activities, self, colleagues, assessment, context

Contextual   *Factors*

Classroom Practice including practice teaching

Around and inside the classroom, context mediates cognitions and practice. May lead to changes in cognitions or create tension between cognitions and classroom practices.

Defined by the interaction of cognitions and contextual factors. In turn, classroom experience influences cognitions unconsciously and/ or through conscious reflection.

Fig. 2.4 Elements and processes in language teacher cognition (Borg, 2006, p. 283)

contextual factors as constraints explaining teachers' compromised or deviant practices, in relation to their stated beliefs. Nevertheless, the literature expresses reservations about this supposed causal relationship, and a longitudinal study is needed to investigate whether and how changes in context lead to teachers' cognitive and behavioral changes.

Borg's breakthrough work on language teacher recognition formulates a framework (illustrated in Fig. 2.4) for teacher cognition in which personal, context-specific, and social dimensions of language teachers are addressed. This largely overcomes the drawbacks of such earlier models as Belief, Assumptions, and Knowledge (BAK) (Woods, 1996) and Teacher Perspectives Inventory (TPI) (Pratt et al., 1998), both of which drew on teachers' individual and personal cognition.Figure 2.3 indicates the factors influencing language teacher cognition are schooling, professional coursework, and classroom practice, among which schooling is the only factor that has unidirectional effects; schooling also influences professional coursework in a unidirectional way. The figure shows mutual interaction between professional work and classroom practices, and language teacher cognition. This suggests that, although professional training does shape language teacher cognition, programs that do not consider trainees' prior learning experience, or that ignore their formed beliefs are likely to be unsuccessful. Borg's framework suggests classroom practices' relationship with language teachers' cognition is bidirectional and nonlinear, and that both are mediated by contextual factors outside and inside the classroom.

To summarize, most research supports the claim that language teachers' classroom practices are underpinned by their cognition; however, there is a paucity of studies documenting how changes in teachers' cognition and classroom practices take place and interact within curriculum innovation, and how they interact and interrelate with each other. These issues are of pivotal importance to language teachers and teacher educators, as it is a routine professional practice to deal with changes in language teachers' career life. These issues and the research gap they manifest have motivated the present study.

2.6 Summary

This chapter has reviewed extant studies of effective language classroom instruction, and formulated an operational framework by which to observe and examine whether and how changes took place in teachers' teaching behaviors in the DP. Given that the DP was a school-based curriculum innovation project, designed in alignment with the national foreign language curriculum innovation in Chinese basic education, curriculum innovation and the factors influencing its implementation are also reviewed. The third part of this chapter examined the relationships between two fundamental constructs in this study—teacher cognition and teaching practices—and justified the need to address these issues through longitudinal study.

Chapter 3
Research Design

This chapter elucidates the research design of this study. It begins by formulating the research questions and locating the study in an appropriate research paradigm. The research informants and settings are then introduced, before focusing on the five stages of the study. The subsequent subsections address the methods utilized for data collection, and describe how different types of data were analyzed.

3.1 Research Questions

The present study is motivated by the following research questions:

(1) What changes took place in the Danyang teacher's cognition?
(2) What changes took place in his/her classroom practices?
(3) What relationship is there between the changes in the teacher's cognition and changes in his/her classroom practices?
(4) What factors influenced the teacher's implementation of the Danyang Project?

3.2 Research Paradigm

3.2.1 Why an Ethnography?

As stated by Larsen-Freeman and Long (1991),

> …what is important for researchers is not the choice of a priori paradigms or even methodologies, but rather to be clear on what the purpose of the study is and to match that purpose with the attributes most likely to accomplish it.
>
> (Larsen-Freeman & Long, 1991, p. 14)

© Springer Nature Singapore Pte Ltd. 2018
Y. Zhu, *Language Curriculum Innovation in a Chinese Secondary School*,
https://doi.org/10.1007/978-981-10-7239-0_3

The present study documents the emergent process through which changes, if there are any, took place over time in language teachers' cognition and, in turn, their teaching practices. It also addresses the dialectic and complex relationship between teachers' cognition and practices, and the intermediating factors that contribute to or inhibit the implementation of curriculum innovation. Due to the complex and non-linear nature of classroom research, psychometric research was deemed inadequate to "produce the definitive answers that some researchers expect" (Ellis, 1990a, p. 67). Given the broad, longitudinal, and dynamic attributes of this study, there was no more appropriate way to seek answers to the research questions than stepping into the venue under study and becoming part of it.

The present study is "descriptive" (Ellis, 2012, p. 41) in nature. It adopted an ethnographic approach, as its intent was to collect data as a detailed account of "people's behavior in naturally occurring, ongoing settings, with a focus on the cultural interpretation of behavior" (Watson-Gegeo, 1988, p. 576). This study spanned more than four years, depicting the trajectory of change over a long period, and is thus a longitudinal study in its design. It shares the three major characteristics of a typical ethnographic study identified by Nunan and Bailey (2010): involving longitudinal enquiry; being comprehensive; and viewing people's behavior in cultural terms.

Being descriptive, and ethnographic in particular, does not indicate this study exclusively collected and analyzed qualitative data. The author does not regard qualitative and quantitative data as two dichotomous entities, with a clear-cut boundary between text and numbers; rather, she accepts the conviction that ethnographic data are the textual or numerical forms into which first-hand experiences of the social world are converted (Dörnyei, 2007; Ellis and Barkhuizen, 2005; Richards, 2003). Overall, this study adopted a naturalistic epistemology, with the basic ideology that reality is socially constructed; it also embraced some defining characteristics pertaining to the descriptive research tradition, as summarized by Ellis (2012):

(1) It provides a detailed account of a specific instructional setting with an *emic* perspective.
(2) It investigates one or two cases in depth and does not seek to generalize beyond them.
(3) The researcher "enters into the community and become immersed in its culture" (Dörnyei, 2007, p. 130), and the study is carried out without any intervening.
(4) The observed phenomenon is understood in specific cultural and social contexts.
(5) It adopts the principles of the grounded theory (Glaser & Strauss, 2008), that is to say, a research-then-theory approach. Data are analyzed inductively to build a theory.
(6) The quality of this study relies on its trustworthiness, which demonstrates the research findings conforms to the data collected and reveal the stances of different participants.

(Ellis, 2012, p. 42)

3.2.2 *From* Emic *Investigation to* Etic *Analysis*

The distinction between *emic* and *etic* perspectives stems from Pike's (1964) division between phonemic and phonetic attributes of speech sounds. *Emic*, as stated by Watson-Gegeo, "refers to culturally based perspectives, interpretations, and categories used by members of the group under study to conceptualize and encode knowledge and to guide their own behavior" (1988, p. 580). Conversely, *etic* is not culturally specific, and is "based on the use of frameworks, concepts, and categories from the analytic language of the social sciences" (Watson-Gegeo, *ibid*).

This study adopted an *emic* perspective to collect firsthand field data, and thus built a data bank with rich and authentic accounts of the ethnographer's experience. In doing so, context-specific language—i.e., the terms used by people in the setting—were used in its data collection process. For example, in the setting under investigation, teachers tended to use the phrase "phonological appearance" (*yuyin mianmao*) to refer to learners' pronunciation and intonation. When the researcher came to the field, she had to map academic terminologies with their corresponding institutional semantics, acquire the context-specific language, and use it in communication with people in the setting. Similarly, all the data were noted down or transcribed verbatim to faithfully record people's behaviors and their articulated beliefs.

When analyzing data and reporting research findings, however, the *etic* perspective was adopted, primarily out of the consideration for the study's comparability and dissemination in the academic community. Taking an outsider's stance is conducive to terminological consistency. Thus, in this study, both *emic* and *etic* perspectives are parallel and serve distinct purposes.

3.2.3 *Status of the Researcher and Research Ethics*

As the ethnographer was an insider in the research venue, the study's trustworthiness and objectivity are likely to be questioned. However, there is no denying that one of the unique strengths of ethnography is its ability to "illuminate locally relevant understandings and ways of operation" (Murchison, 2010, p. 13) about the complexity of human lives. "Being there" (Bradburd, 1998; Watson, 1999) was the only way to achieve the study's purposes.

As is the convention when conducting an ethnographic study, the researcher's role and intention were disclosed to the informants, and the tangible benefits and possible risks they might experience by participating were explained. To protect human informants from unnecessary negative outcomes, only teachers who had volunteered and given their informed consent were associated with this project; moreover, they could withdraw at any stage. In return for the help they got from the project school and those teacher participants, researchers did volunteer work to contribute to the development of both the school and individual teachers (Shu, 2013), such as providing the entire package of teacher education program embedded in the DP, free of charge. Also, the initiator enlisted his personal resource to help the project school start an exchange program with a renowned secondary school in Heidelberg, Germany. This kind of mutually beneficial collaboration was a prerequisite for the sustainable implementation of this longitudinal project.

3.2.4 Quality Control of This Study

Ethnography, like other qualitative research methods, has been criticized as not being adequately rigorous or scientific. This is understandable, as most researchers are accustomed to experimental studies, and do not feel safe or comfortable unless research findings can be supported by statistical analysis. This uncertainty is characterized by Nunan and Bailey (2010) as "persistent tension":

> However, a tension between ethnography and the experimental method persists. This tension reflects the fact that the two traditions are underpinned by different beliefs about what counts as evidence, how that evidence should be interpreted, and what the role of the researcher is within the research process. In short, these two research cultures reflect two different ways of looking at the world.
>
> (Nunan & Bailey, 2010, p. 188)

To counterbalance the possible criticism the ethnography might be subject to, this study ensured its transparency and trustworthiness by adhering to three principles—working in a team; using both an internal supervisor and external guidance; and employing data triangulation.

(1) Work in a team

As introduced in Chap. 1, this study is part of the Danyang Project, which involved a group of researchers doing substituent studies therein. All researchers involved shared the responsibility for and made contributions to building a data bank for the whole project. It was a regular working procedure to send preliminary drafts of project documents (e.g., field notes, reviewed teaching journal, project agenda, periodic project report, etc.) for group review. Normally, fellow researchers offered meticulous and helpful comments in response to any enquiry (see Appendix 6 for a selected excerpt of a project agenda under group review). The comments were often centered on such aspects as rationales, theoretical soundness, empirical feasibility, appropriateness of materials, etc.

(2) Internal supervisor and external consultants

Throughout the years of implementing the Danyang Project, there were regular meetings between the researcher and her supervisor and co-researchers to discuss its

Table 3.1 Types of triangulation in the study

Types of triangulation	How data were collected
Data triangulation	• Project teacher participants • Non-project teacher participants • Peripheral teachers in the setting • Principals of the school
Methods triangulation	• Field notes: detailed and thick account of what's been observed during every visit to the school • Classroom observation (with observation schemes, video- and audio-recorder) • Interviews (formal and informal) • Teaching journals, action research reports, etc
Theory triangulation	• Second language acquisition • Effective language teaching • Theory of educational change • Teacher cognition and practices
Researcher triangulation	• A total of six researchers contributed to the project in collaboration

updates and emerging problems. The meetings were generally based on information collected through field work by research team members. As the supervisor was the initiator and leading researcher of the DP, he visited the school under study on a regular basis, which helped to raise the trustworthiness of the data collection procedure in the present study. Apart from the internal supervision, the DP also involved a group of external consultants, who made occasional visits to the research venue and offered the researcher helpful advice on its design and implementation.

(3) Triangulation

The present study incorporated triangulation as a quality control strategy to ensure its validity. By so doing, the researcher could check data from one source against those from another; reaching the same conclusion increased confidence (Hammersley & Atkinson, 1983; Nunan & Bailey, 2010; van Lier, 1988), while inconsistencies revealed deeper meanings of the data (Patton, 2002). Four types of triangulation are generally used in qualitative research—data triangulation, theory triangulation, researcher triangulation, and methods triangulation (Denzin, 1978). The triangulation resources used in this study are documented in Table 3.1.

3.3   The Study

3.3.1   Research Informants

As mentioned in Chap. 1, a total of 10 project teachers (PTs) at HES have participated in the Danyang Project, with new PTs joining in at the beginning of each new academic year, from 2009 to 2012. In September 2012, one project teacher withdrew from the project due to her resignation. The demographic information for the participating PTs is documented in Table 1.8, in Chap. 1. This study is embedded in the DP, and covers its timeline from May 2009 to January 2014.

Among the 10 teachers under investigation, two (given the pseudonyms Frank and Marian) completed a complete round of teaching from Level 7 to Level 9 during this study. A close look at the two teachers' CVs and professional documents shows Marian's demographic background (i.e., age, gender, educational background, work experience) was quite representative of the teachers at HES, while her professional capacity (based on her CV) placed her near the middle of the teaching staff of HES. Due to Marian's typicality, she was selected as the focal informant for the present study.

Selecting Marian as the focal informant was "purposive rather than random" (Ellis & Barkhuizen, 2005, p. 260), and was partly due to her having participated in the project for the entire duration (from Level 7 to Level 9) of junior secondary schooling. The other major reason was that Marian's professional profile showed she was at a fairly average professional level before joining in the project, which made it possible to ensure her typicality among the group of 10 project teachers.

Born in 1974, Marian was 35 years old when she joined the DP. She started her teaching career in 1996, after finishing a three-year pre-service teacher education diploma program. By the time she participated in the DP, she had been teaching English for fourteen years, including three years at HES (Huanan Experimental School) and eleven years at a county-level secondary school. She received her Bachelor of English Education from 2001 to 2004, through a correspondence program offered by a provincial teacher college. For Marian, the Danyang Project was the first and longest formal school-based in-service teacher education program in which she had participated.

In this study, selecting Marian as a core informant and other PTs as peripheral informants was not a preemptive decision. Rather, as the researcher's role in the research venue was two-fold (i.e., as researcher and teacher educator), it was neither ecologically possible nor ethically appropriate to focus exclusively on one teacher for four years' visits. The behaviors, emotions, voices, and interactions of other PTs were observed and accounted in detail, to form a data pool providing rich information and insights about the cultural and socio-political background of the research venue.

Apart from project teachers, people who were directly and indirectly associated with the project were also included in this study. For instance, Marian's students and the principals who took charge of the project were formally and informally interviewed, in addition to constant formal and informal exchanges with the director of English teaching division and the class adviser (*ban zhuren*) of the class taught by Marian. In addition, other university researchers were indispensable informants who interacted with local people, and collaboratively constructed the overall picture of this study.

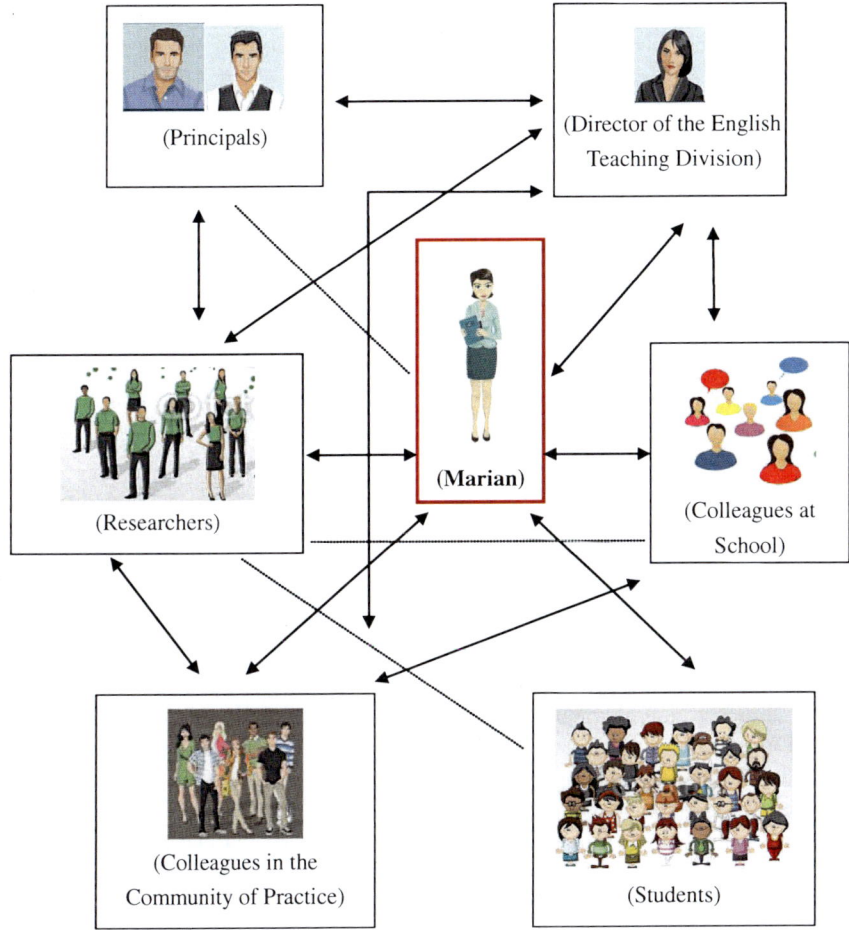

Fig. 3.1 The network of focal and peripheral participants

The interrelated network containing focal and peripheral informants is illustrated in Fig. 3.1, below. The solid lines with bi-directional arrows indicate direct and dialogic connections between people; the dotted lines indicate indirect connections. For example, the solid line with bi-directional arrows connecting Marian and researchers is a signal of their close collaboration, while the dotted line linking Marian and the principals signifies she did not contact principals regularly in the setting. As Murchison (2010) stated, "[i]n interpersonal relationships and the interactions that they influence or give rise to, ethnographers have the opportunity to study culture and society in action" (p. 145). This diagram is informative in that it displays the complexity of interpersonal relationships in which a project teacher was involved in the curriculum innovation project, and also sheds light on the complexity of the research venue.

3.3.2 Research Setting

The venue under investigation, as documented in Chap. 1, was an ordinary public school (containing a six-year primary sector and a three-year junior secondary sector) in Danyang, a city of approximately 960,400 covering an area of 1059 square kilometers[1] in Jiangsu Province. The school, the Hunan Experimental School (HES), was founded in 2004, and is quite popular in the area due to its good academic reputation. At the end of 2013, there were a total of 48 English teachers at HES—36 teaching junior secondary classes and 12 teaching primary classes.

The junior secondary sector of HES contained three levels of students (Level 7–9), with 18 classes in each level. The number of students in each class ranged from 55 to 60. Most English teachers taught two classes, with the overall teaching hours per week being seven for Level 7, six for Level 8, and six for Level 9 (each teaching 'hour' lasted 40 min). Apart from regular classroom teaching, English teachers also served as administrators, class advisors, deputy class advisors, youth league committee members, etc. Usually, teachers who taught the same group of students were assigned into the same office, which was often close to their students' classrooms.

English teachers who taught the same level of students were all under the academic guidance of the same teaching research group (TRG) (literally, a grade lesson-planning group (*nianji beike zu*) consisting of a group leader, two or three core group members, and several ordinary group members. The group leader and core group members were called backbone teachers (*gugan jiaoshi*), and were paid for their work in the TRG. The director of the English Teaching Division oversaw three grade-level TRGs. The organizational structure of TRGs is illustrated in Fig. 3.2.

At HES, English teachers received promotions based on their professional merits in teaching and research, in addition to completing a compulsory amount of teaching hours. How teachers performed in teaching public lessons or teaching contests was documented as proof of good teaching, and participation in research projects and publications was taken as a research achievement. In general, a secondary school teacher began his or her teaching career as secondary Grade 2 teacher (*erji jiaoshi*), and then moved up to become a Grade 1 teacher (*yiji jiaoshi*), a superior grade teacher (*gaoji jiaoshi*), and, eventually, a special grade teacher (*teji jiaoshi*).

---

[1]http://baike.baidu.com/subview/56498/10828180.htm?fr=aladdin.

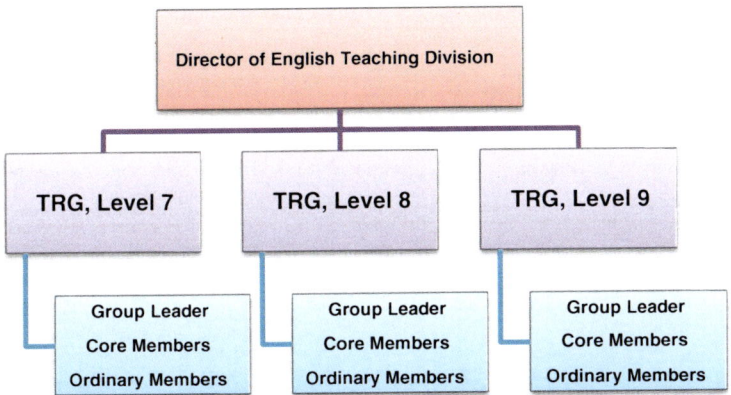

Fig. 3.2 The organizational structure of TRGs (teaching research group) at HES

3.3.3 Five Stages of the Study

As this study addressed educational change, the project was divided into five stages, which were then examined and compared to investigate how changes occurred to the focal informant over the innovation project. Table 3.2, illustrates the basic features of each stage.

3.3.3.1 The Pre-project Stage (May 2009–Aug. 2009)

During four months before the Danyang Project was launched, university researchers paid several visits to HES to carry out preliminary investigation on the teachers, learners, and the institutional context, before an official partnership contract was signed. Essential components of the work list at this stage were the selection of PTs and the provision of a package of initial teacher training courses. The teacher applicants visited SISU to take an intensive teacher training course, consisting of modules on task-based language teaching, syllabus design, material development, and formative assessment. This program for the first time exposed the project teachers to innovative principles that required them to relinquish traditional practices they had long been used to, including, for example, the grammar-translation teaching method and using mandated textbooks.

3.3.3.2 The Top-Down Stage (Sep. 2009–Dec. 2011)

The top-down stage of the Danyang Project featured a radical approach to enacting innovative principles that was a complete departure from the traditional teacher-fronted pedagogy. Three major measures were taken to implement the new,

Table 3.2 Five stages of the study

Stage 1	The pre-project stage	May 2009–Aug. 2009	This is the phase prior to Marian's participation in the DP
Stage 2	The top-down stage	Sep. 2009–Dec. 2011	A radical top-down approach was adopted
Stage 3	The bottom-up stage	Jan. 2012–Mar. 2013	DP was converted into a lenient bottom-up approach
Stage 4	The exam stage	Apr. 2013–Jun. 2013	Students in project classes crammed for the senior high school entrance examination (*zhongkao*)
Stage 5	The post-project stage	Jul. 2013–Jan. 2014	Marian left HES and volunteered to teach at a rural school

school-based curriculum over a 27-month period. The first, which was practically the focus of the DP at the time, involved developing new textbooks and putting them into use. To make the textbooks a cognitive tool for garnering teacher participation and teacher learning, relevant modeling lesson planning and seminars were provided, to make explicit to PTs the steps they were to follow in their teaching. At this stage, teachers were regarded as recipients of new knowledge and innovative practices. Accordingly, the work done by teacher educators was in a transmissive, even spoon-feeding manner.

Marian participated in the DP's teacher education program for one year, before she began teaching a project class in September 2011. The top-down stage covered most of her students' study at Level 7 and the first semester of Level 8.[2]

3.3.3.3 The Bottom-Up Stage (Jan. 2012–Mar. 2013)

The bottom-up stage, informed by the goals and constraints confronted in the previous phase, was intended to instill innovative ideas into teachers' cognition regarding the historical, cultural, and institutional context in which teachers lived, learned, and changed. This stage, as its name suggests, drew more on teacher educators' role as the "guide on the side," instead of the "sage on the stage." Spanning 14 months from January 2012 to August 2013, the bottom-up stage featured teacher educators' facilitative role, and PTs were encouraged to reconstruct teaching practices grounded on innovative rationale. To this end, the teacher education program was gradually diverted to a teacher-directed approach, which mainly covered two modules: classroom-based exploratory action research, and focused classroom observation.

---

[2]Level 7 to Level 9 are in consistent with learners' required levels of proficiency in the national course standard, which are supposed to be achieved through their study in Year 1 to Year 3 respectively at junior secondary schools.

During the bottom-up stage of the DP, Marian's students moved from the second semester of Level 8 to the first semester of Level 9. Level 9 is the last stage of junior secondary schooling in China, during which students are supposed to take the *zhongkao*, the senior high school entrance examination, which is of decisive importance to test-takers and their families. To ensure ample time for exam preparation, the school-based teaching syllabus allocated one month in the second semester of Level 9 to teaching new contents, and three months to exam preparation.

3.3.3.4 The Exam Stage (Apr. 2013–Jun. 2013)

The exam stage per se was purposely set aside for exam preparation. The Level 9 students in project classes were in the last stage of their junior secondary school education. Despite its relatively short duration in comparison with the other four segments, the exam stage provided rich and informative information on how teacher cognition and practices constructed within curriculum innovation collided with the prevailing exam culture.

3.3.3.5 The Post-project Stage (Jul. 2013–Jan. 2014)

After her students graduated from HES, Marian joined in a one-year volunteer teaching program, initiated by the local education bureau, to teach at a rural school, which was around 40 min' drive away from HES. This school, called Yanling for its location, was (by chance) the junior high school where Marian studied when she was young. Yanling School (hereafter YS) had a much smaller population of students and faculty than HES, and included a total of five classes: two classes at Level 7 and Level 8 respectively, and one class at Level 9. The class size was notably smaller than that of HES, with the number of students in each class ranging from 20 to 25. There was a total of 5 English teachers at YS including Marian. She taught a Level 7 class consisting of 22 students.

Now that Marian had entered a new educational setting and was exposed to very limited influence from the Danyang Project, how she conceptualized and carried out language teaching arguably supports whether the DP had sustainable effects on teachers' cognition and practices.

3.3.4   Research Methods

3.3.4.1   Field Notes

The field notes constituted a large part of qualitative and longitudinal data reported in this study. The ethnographic field notes taken during the author's visits to the research venue were 121,533 Chinese words in length, and accounted for 127 anecdotal events from August 2011 to December 2013.[3] To avoid the ambiguity that could be caused by using a second language, all field notes were written in Chinese, which was both the informants' and the researchers' first language and the working language in the research venue. To maintain a detached stance, the field notes were written in the third person, using a narrative style.

   Given the transient nature of ethnographic data, the researcher made every effort to write down what was observed at her earliest convenience, while avoiding the intrusiveness of note-taking in from of informants. She employed the following strategies (LeCompte & Goetz, 1982; LeCompte & Schensul, 1999; Murchison, 2010; Richards, 2003) when keeping ethnographic field notes:

(1) *Be timely.* Due to the fleeting feature of ethnographic data and the illusive trait of human memory, the field notes were taken as soon as an opportunity was found to do so. When permitted, she used a laptop to write down field notes while the observation was in process. In most cases, she did note-taking during her lunch break or on the train back to Shanghai. All the field notes were taken within 24 h after observation.
(2) *Researcher on site.* As mentioned before, this study is part of a larger collaborative project involving other researchers who had co-constructed a communal database for the project. Of the total 108 field note entries entered in the database from May 2009 to December 2012, only those taken by the author were used in this study.
(3) *Intra-group review.* The field notes were sent to fellow researchers and the supervisor in the project group immediately after the first drafting, after which feedback was received regarding project updates and seeking clarification of details in the notes; revisions were then done as needed.
(4) *Detailed and low-inference description.* To avoid vagueness or ambiguity in data coding and analysis, the ethnographer faithfully recorded what she observed in rich detail, with low-inference descriptions. Below are two extracts.

---

[3]The field notes reported here come from a much larger database contributed by the whole research team of the Danyang Project. It is out of research ethical concern that only those field notes written by the researcher were included in the present study.

Extract 1:

Instead of writing:	Julia did not show up in the meeting this morning
It should be described as:	Julia did not show up in the meeting which was held from 9:00–9:40 in PhD Students' Office this morning. Frank told Yan that she was out of school with her students for spring outing. However, Julia did not ask for leave in advance

Extract 2:

Instead of writing:	Julia is a quick learner to use educational technology in teaching
It should be described as:	Yan recommended Julia to use a popular movie-making software program named *Movie Maker*. After two weeks, when visiting Julia's class, Yan found Julia made a fabulous movie clip and embedded it in her PPT. In the post-observation meeting, Julia told Yan she had downloaded the software program and learned how to use it all by herself

(5) *Consistency of wording and formats*. This strategy was employed for the same reasons as the previous one. Specific key words and note-taking formats were formulated and implemented throughout the study. For example, all informants were addressed by their full names, instead of using a "surname + title" format. The observed events and phenomena during a visit were recorded in chronological order, with information provided concerning the time, place, and participants. Moreover, all the word files were saved using a "year/month/ date + DP field notes + note taker's name" file name format.

(6) *Cross-reference links*. As devices were used to facilitate observation in this study, some parts of field notes were associated with videos, audios, or photos. Also, second-hand documents, such as the material used for teacher training, teachers' action research reports, and students' journals, were also collected. These files were either attached as appendices or inserted as super-links in the field notes for cross-reference.

3.3.4.2 Interviews

Two types of interviews—informal/ethnographic interviews and formal in-depth interviews—were conducted in this study, for distinct research purposes. The former, which were conducted constantly between the researcher and informants throughout their ongoing and longitudinal interactions in this study, are a natural and indispensable constituent of ethnography. As Spradley (1979) described, informal interviews are "a series of friendly conversations" (p. 58), and were conducted in an unplanned, casual manner, and were not audio-recorded, in this study. Given the unobtrusive nature and relaxed atmosphere of informal interviews,

Table 3.3 Formal in-depth interviews conducted at the five research stages

Interview 1	The pre-project stage	Semi-structured	2009.05	63 min
Interview 2	The top-down stage	Semi-structured	2011.12	47 min
Interview 3,4	The bottom-up stage	Semi-structured	2012.06	53 min
			2012.12	48 min
Interview 5	The exam stage	Semi-structured	2013.01	42 min
Interview 6	The post-project stage	Semi-structured	2014.01	77 min

informants are more likely to speak without disguise or artifice. In this study, informal interview turned out to be an effective technique for eliciting an informant's opinions, attitudes, and beliefs towards an issue he or she was asked about. Data collected through informal interviews were then incorporated into field notes, in a narrative genre.

While the somewhat fragmentary and discursive information elicited through informal interviews was used to construct cultural and socio-political background knowledge about the field under study, formal in-depth interviews systematically elicited informants' opinions through focused questions at critical points of each stage of the DP. Table 3.3, summarizes the formal in-depth interviews reported in this study. Interviews 1 to 5 were conducted face-to-face with the focal informant in the researcher's office at HES, while interview 6 was conducted by telephone. As is normally done in qualitative data analysis (Borg, 2011; Newby, 2010), the formal in-depth interviews were scheduled cyclically; the interview schedules were informed by an analysis of the informants' responses to previous interviews.

All the interviews conducted in this study were semi-structured. Specifically, a pre-set agenda was designed as points of departure for the interviews, which were not constrained by them (Nunan & Bailey, 2010, p. 313). Most of the questions constructed for these interviews were open-ended. Furthermore, the researcher kept in mind those elements of interview evaluation suggested by Richards (2003, p. 59) when conducting interviews.

3.3.4.3 Teaching Journals

Richards and Lockhart defined the teaching journal as "a teacher's or a student teacher's written response to teaching events" (1996, p. 7), noting that it serves two purposes: recording events and ideas for reflection afterwards, and facilitating the exploratory process of writing itself. Keeping a teaching journal is as means of fostering reflective teaching for teachers, and a source of data for researchers to conduct diary research (e.g., Bailey, 1990; Bartlett, 1990; Boyd & Boyd, 2005; Ho & Richards, 1993; Yuan, 2013).

In the DP, teacher participants wrote teaching journals daily at the early stage of the project, and researchers provided feedback to their teaching journals via emails on a weekly basis. Teaching journals and the feedback also reinforced teacher-researcher connections during the early period of the project; nevertheless, towards the end of the early stage, teachers became increasingly reluctant to keep teaching journals, which was problematic for researchers. Succumbing to teachers' resistance, researchers then suggested PTs instead write reflectively about salient anecdotes from their teaching.

Teaching journal played dual roles in this study—one as a written record of teachers' behavior and beliefs, the other as a cultural artifact capturing the changes in the research setting.

3.3.4.4 Classroom Observations

Classroom observation is an essential method utilized by researchers to investigate teachers' classroom behaviors. In this study, the value of "gathering data during actual language lesson…by watching, listening, and recording" (Nunan & Bailey, 2010, p. 258) was twofold: collecting evidence for school-based teacher training, and keeping strong records as research data. Regarding the ethnographer's insider's perspective, participant observations were conducted. Being a participant meant there were communications between the researcher and the project teachers before or after their lessons were observed.

Given the obtrusiveness of video cameras and logistical considerations, classroom observations were primarily manually recorded at the early stage of the DP. In most cases, the researcher used field notes to collect information during observation. Occasionally, opportunities arose to video-record the observed lessons, and a few video recordings were thereby obtained. Nevertheless, by the later stage of the project, teachers had gradually got used to video cameras, and IT teachers[4] assisted the researcher by taking care of the camera during observation. Therefore, classroom observations at the later stage were both manually and technically conducted.

Overall, two observation approaches were employed at two separate stages of the DP—unfocused and focused observations (see Chap. 1 for details). Unfocused classroom observation was conducted at the early stage, when the researcher had no prior knowledge about the lesson before entering the classroom. The researcher adopted a holistic approach towards the observed lessons, jotting down field notes while observing and provided feedback (mostly negative and corrective) on any salient problems identified during observation.

As its name suggests, focused observation (Shen & Cui 2008; Shen et al., 2007; Zhou & Cui, 2008), was concentrated on a few points put forward by project teachers. It was conducted at the bottom-up stage of the DP. Focused observation comprised three steps: the pre-observation conference; observation; and the post-observation conference. In the first step, the teachers participating in the

---

[4]Special thanks go to Miss Yinfeng Hong and Miss Yufei Zhang at HES for helping with video-recording the observed lessons in this study.

project got together for a meeting, which normally followed the following agenda: (1) the observee briefly introduced his or her lesson planning; (2) the observee proposed one or two aspects of teaching as the focuses of observation; (3) the observers discussed and chose one aspect, or initiated a new aspect as the focus of observation; and, (4) observation schemes were constructed jointly by the researcher and PTs for collecting information during observation. In the second step, observers sat in the back of the classroom and observed the class, which was also video-recorded. As soon as the class ended, the researcher distributed questionnaires to collect students' feedback. In the third step, the observee and observers got together for a post-observation meeting, which also roughly followed a settled procedure: (1) the observee briefly and reflectively reported the implementation of his or her lesson planning; (2) the observers provided feedback on a certain aspect of teaching, based on the information they had gathered using the observation scheme; and, (3) teachers were encouraged to reflect on any salient teaching scenarios that impressed them in the second step, and put forward an alternate solution thereto (i.e., say what they would have done if they had been in the same situation).

Classroom observations were adopted both as a means of in-service teacher training, and to collect research data, and thus were participatory in nature; in other words, observers did not keep a detached stance, but negotiated with teachers on issues emerging from the lessons observed and provided feedback to facilitate PTs' improved teaching.

An essential issue in classroom observation is to ensure its validity; thus, strategies were employed to ensure the truthfulness of the information collected when observing lessons. Despite the distinct approaches adopted at the two stages of the project, one principle followed consistently was to avoid rehearsed lessons; teachers were never informed more than one day in advance of any of the lessons observed in the project. Of the 34 lessons observed by the researcher, 21 were video-recorded, including six lessons taught by Marian, as documented in Table 3.4.

Of all the video-recorded lessons taught by Marian, one representative lesson from each research stage was selected for further analysis, guided by two criteria. One was the consistency of teaching content, i.e., that the lessons dealt with the same language modality. The other consideration was that the lessons were representative of Marian's teaching style at respective research stages. This was achieved by two researchers comparing the selected lessons with other observed lessons taught by Marian at the stage, and reaching consensus on their typicality. Also, Marian's colleagues and the head of the TRG were consulted to ensure the typicality of the selected lessons. These lessons are listed in Table 3.5.

To collect data for triangulation purposes, several non-PTs' lessons at the late-project stage were observed and video-recorded (see Chap. 6). Among these lessons, one lesson teaching the same content was selected to compare with the one taught by Marian at the same stage, to elucidate the differences and similarities between project and non-project teachers' teaching practices after the

Table 3.4 A list of video-recorded lessons

Video code	Teachers	Teaching content	Class	Length of videos (m. s)
20111111JYQ	Julia	Listening and speaking	7–14	34.40
20111111WYP	Grace	Grammar	7–13	39.22
20111111CHJ	Frank	Reading	8–15	44.19
20111111LMD	Marian	Language achievement performance	8–16	38.14
20120320ZWJ	Judy	Revision	9–15	41.27
20120321CHJ	Frank	Listening and speaking	8–15	41.35
20120507LMD	Marian	Reading	8–16	40.20
20120926CHJ	Frank	Listening and speaking	9–16	43.14
20121011LMD	Marian	Listening and speaking	9–15	29.09
20121108JYQ	Julia	Writing	8–14	41.10
20121128CHJ	Frank	Listening and speaking	9–16	51.19
20130109JYQ	Julia	Listening and speaking	8–13	42.30
20130307CHJ	Frank	Listening and speaking	9–15	41.23
20130307LMD	Marian	Listening and speaking	9–16	57.10
20130516JYQ	Julia	Grammar	8–14	39.35
20130530ZWJ	Judy	Listening and speaking	7–18	40.56
20130530ZHF	Helen	Reading	7–16	42.50
20130530LMD	Marian	Revision	9–16	54.41
20131008LMD	Marian	Listening and speaking	7–1	41.56
20130516JCF	Jenny (NPT)	Reading	8–18	40.35
20130307WJB	Jane (NPT)	Listening and speaking	9–6	40.06

Table 3.5 A list of selected lessons taught by Marian at the five stages of the DP

Lesson 1	The pre-project stage	Listening and speaking	11.08
Lesson 2	The top-down stage	Listening and speaking (Language achievement performance)	38.14
Lesson 3	The bottom-up stage	Listening and speaking	57.10
Lesson 4	The exam stage	Exam preparation	54.41
Lesson 5	The post-project stage	Listening and speaking	41.56

implementation of the DP. The comparison between these two lessons will be elaborated on in Chap. 6.

To summarize, this longitudinal study addressed questions about the changes in language teachers' cognition and teaching practices over four years, in five stages. The first provided background information prior to the curriculum innovation project. Stage 2 and Stage 3 were the two major phases constituting the innovation project. Stage 4, the exam stage, provided rich data about the influence of high-stakes standardized tests on curriculum innovation. The last stage, the epilogue of the whole project, revealed what happened to one of the PTs when that

Table 3.6 A summary of research methods at the five stages of the DP

Methods	Pre-project stage	Top-down stage	Bottom-up stage	Exam stage	Post-project stage
Field notes	✓	✓	✓	✓	✓
Formal in-depth interview	✓	✓	✓	✓	✓
Teaching journal	✓	✓	✓	–	–
classroom observation[a]	✓(NP)	✓ (P)	✓ (P)	✓ (P)	✓(NP)

[a]NP stands for non-participant classroom observation; P stands for participant classroom observation

teacher moved to a new educational setting, after the innovation project. Table 3.6 summarizes the research methods used throughout these five stages.

3.4   Transcribing, Coding, and Analyzing Qualitative Data

3.4.1   Transcribing Qualitative Data

All the audio-taped interviews were transcribed verbatim, and double-checked by the researcher and two research assistants.[5] The interview transcripts were then sent back to the informant for member checking (Brown & Rogers, 2003, p. 245); statements Marian was reluctant to have included in the study were excluded, and other wordings were revised according to her suggestions.

3.4.2   Coding and Analyzing Qualitative Data

Following generally acknowledged procedures for working with qualitative data (Dörnyei, 2007; Ellis & Barkhuizen, 2005; LeCompte & Schensul, 1999; Miles & Huberman, 1994; Murchison, 2010; Nunan & Bailey, 2010; Richards, 2003), the researcher went deep into the data by using inductive coding to look for patterns and identify categories and themes therein. In other words, instead of writing "with the data," this study wrote "from the data," which involved iteratively reading ethnographic records and analyzing data in its entirety (Murchison, 2010). As stated by Ellis and Barkhuizen (2005), "[the] 'overall picture' is the aim of any study: to answer the research questions and to reach conclusion" (p. 271). In this study,

---

[5]Many thanks to Miss Xinlu Gu and Miss Hui Shi from Shanghai Normal University for assisting with transcribing and double checking the transcripts.

methods utilized to analyze qualitative data were largely informed by Ellis and Barkhuizen (2005) and Dörnyei (2007), according to the following procedure:

(1) *Choosing a sample of texts and reducing the original data*

The sampling decision was made after thoroughly and recursively scrutinizing the entirety of data gathered throughout this ethnographic study. Among the 10 teachers who participated in the DP, Marian that was selected as the focal informant, partly due to the appropriate typicality she demonstrated in her professional profile, and partly because, of the huge body of data collected over the four years, those involving Marian were most the coherent and the most integral.

Firstly, Marian's participation in the DP covered the whole junior secondary stage, from Level 7 to Level 9. Secondly, the five audio- and video-recordings collected by observing non-PTs' classes included one lesson taught on the same day, using almost the same teaching materials, by a teacher with quite similar demographic and professional background with Marian. What is more, Marian was one two teachers who volunteered to teach at rural schools after completing the teacher education program in the DP; it was of particular interest to see whether the change in her cognition and teaching practices had been developed in a sustainable way when she was positioned in a new educational setting. The sampling decision was made in consultation with the DP supervisors, two fellow researchers and two external project consultants.

Following the sampling decision, data reduction was conducted by extracting data about Marian from the larger database. It was a manageable step dealing with interview transcription, teaching journals, and observation data, as those files followed a "time + teacher's name + data type" naming format. However, when handling ethnographic field notes, considerable discretion was used to excerpt those ethnographic scenarios about Marian from the longer holistic narrative. A principle followed was to extract contextualized descriptions and accounts of events directly or indirectly involving Marian.

(2) *Open coding*

Qualitative data were coded inductively at the initial coding stage. To formulate a codebook, a set of interview data (around 18,000 Chinese characters—approximately 10% of the total data) were inductively coded, and all emergent codes noted by the researcher. Then, the coded file and the list of codes were sent to a research assistant[6] for a second round of coding, in which close attention was paid to checking high-inference data and clarifying ambiguous codes. The researcher and the assistant then met to discuss incongruences, and reach a consensus on all codes and their denotations in the original text. Both coders accepted that the initial codebook was open to revision and expansion due to new codes emerging in

---

[6]Sincere thanks go to Miss Jingwen Wu from the University of Auckland for assisting with coding the data.

subsequent coding, which was a discursive, cumbersome, and (of course), essential step in the study.

A decision was made to use Excel as the coding tool, after trying it out and carefully comparing it with both traditional paper-based colored coding and the computer software program NVivo (v. 10). Excel was selected primarily due to its user-friendly functions for storing, sorting, and retrieving data, in addition to the practical concern that Excel was accessible to both coders.

Approximately 10% of the qualitative data were coded by two coders separately. Given the limited resources the researcher had access to, two rounds of coding were conducted with the rest of qualitative data in this study by the researcher alone, with a two-week interval in between.

Inductive coding of qualitative data in this study generated 137 codes in total, which fell into 11 categories, or coded themes, as listed, below (see Appendix 3 for the codebook for coding qualitative data).

(1) teacher's pressure
(2) easy learning
(3) beliefs about language learning
(4) constraints on curriculum innovation
(5) teacher's professional background
(6) textbook
(7) teacher's beliefs about language teaching
(8) colleague interaction
(9) community of practice and learning
(10) classroom observation
(11) teacher development.

(3) *Pattern coding (axial coding)*

The next stage of qualitative data analysis was to seek relationships or links "between and within categories" (Ellis & Barkhuizen, 2005, p. 268). This step was pivotal to the whole study, for it was during this stage that the analysis and interpretation of data moved to a conceptual level, and thus contributed to theory building. Patterns were discovered by referring to several widely-acknowledged codes of practice in the field, as listed below (Dörnyei, 2007; Ellis & Barkhuizen, 2005; LeCompte & Schensul, 1999).

(1) the occurrence frequency of themes;
(2) the existence of patterns alerted by the informant;
(3) similarity between themes;
(4) the researcher's experience;
(5) in consultation with relevant literature.

The significant of axial coding is evident in the pivotal role it has played in theory building (Miles & Huberman, 1994). However, the very process of axial coding involves the human brain as an instrument, which admittedly makes its so-called 'soft data' vulnerable to criticism (Richards, 2003). To counteract possible researcher bias, in addition to the procedure listed above, the axial coding in this study also involved consultations between the researcher and an external research assistant, who had very little prior knowledge about the project and who read through all the original transcripts and the opening coding before meeting with the researcher to negotiate the patterns she had found. This process resulted in the emergence of nine patterns listed:

(1) Language meaning versus form;
(2) Learner participation and learner autonomy;
(3) Providing corrective feedback;
(4) Using textbooks;
(5) Teacher's prior learning and work experience;
(6) In-service teacher training program;
(7) Social context;
(8) Institutional context;
(9) Teacher's attitudes towards the innovation project.

3.4.3 Transcribing, Coding, and Analyzing Classroom Observation Data

(1) Transcribing and annotating audio-taped lessons

The computer program software ELAN (v.4.6.1)[7] was used to transcribe and annotate classroom observation videos (Pan, 2011; Zhu, 2013). ELAN was selected because it enables researchers to transcribe a video file, and at the same time record the pertaining time data (i.e., the beginning time, end time and time duration of talks, pauses, teaching episodes and teaching activities) of the video-recorded lessons. In addition, it also allows researchers to do transcribing within a pre-constructed framework, called 'tiers' in ELAN. For example, as this study adopted a broad analytical framework to examine different aspects of classroom discourse, before doing the transcribing, various tiers were attached with codes denoting different interlocutors' organizations; utterances were then transcribed into the corresponding tiers.

A screenshot of ELAN, below (Fig. 3.3), displays how it works. The left part at the bottom is a column of 'tiers.' The left part on the top is a video viewer, which plays the lesson video being transcribed and annotated. The block on the right side of the tiers column is a timeline viewer. In this area, an enclosed cell automatically appears when a transcriber stops the time indicator, and the transcriber can type in the transcripts or annotations. Concurrently, what has been transcribed in each tier

---

[7]ELAN, developed by the Language Archive (TLA), is a professional software program for creating complex annotations on video and audio resources. The version used in this study was downloaded and used free of charge from TLA's website: http://tla.mpi.nl/tools/tla-tools/elan/.

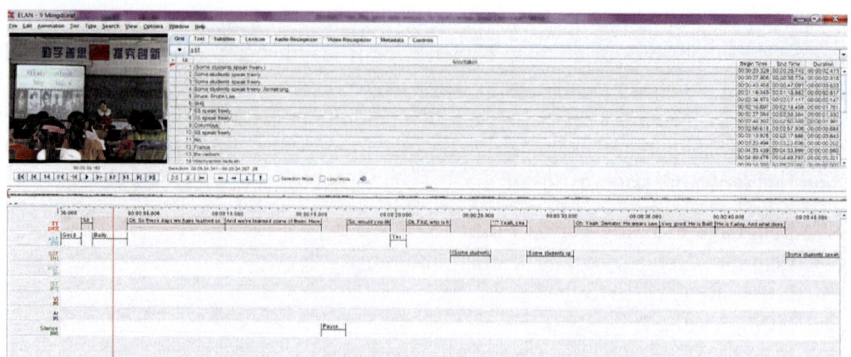

Fig. 3.3 A screenshot of ELAN

is displayed in the grid viewer on the right top, where the beginning time, end time, duration, and utterance of each move is automatically generated.

After transcribing a 43-minute-long video-recorded lesson for pilot analysis, a preliminary protocol of tiers was fine tuned to a system containing eight tiers: teacher talk (TT), all students talk (AST), some students talk (SST), paired students talk (PST), individual students talk (IST), video input (VI), audio input (AI) and silence (Silence). Also, the time format, originally set as 'minutes:seconds' (ms:ss), was changed into 'seconds:milliseconds' (ss:ms), for the sake of convenience in subsequent calculations.

In this study, a broad transcribing scheme was adopted in which teacher and student utterances were transcribed verbatim. Unintelligible parts resulting from classroom activities were annotated in angle brackets, for example, <SS work in pairs>. Incomprehensible or inaudible words were denoted with asterisks '***' and nonverbal behaviors were annotated in parentheses—for example, (A student comes to the front of classroom). The names of students were anonymized, due to ethical concerns. When annotation and transcription were completed, the data in the grid viewer of ELAN were output into an excel file, in which the columns displayed interlocutor, beginning time, end time, duration, and utterance of each move, as shown in Table 3.7.

In the original excel file, as shown in Table 3.7, the data were arrayed in the sequence of interlocutors. In the next step, the data were sorted in ascending order by the beginning time, thus unfolding the classroom interaction in its authentic time sequence, as displayed in Table 3.8.

The transcribing and annotating of audio files was laborious and time-consuming, with the time spent on each audio-recorded lesson ranging from 10 to 23 h. The transcribed files were much larger than expected, ranging from 601 to 1015 moves per lesson. After the time-sequenced classroom discourse data files were generated, they were sent, with the original audio files, to a research assistant for rigorous double-checking; ambiguous parts were negotiated until congruity was achieved. Next, as was done with the interview data, transcripts of the observed

Table 3.7 A sample of original transcript and annotation of observed lessons

Interlocutor	Beginning time	End time	Duration	Utterance
TT	1.22	1.908	0.688	Sit down, please
TT	4.009	9.844	5.835	Ok. So, these days we have learned something about great people, right?
...	...	...	...	...
TT	3427.71	3430.088	2.378	So much for today
AST	0	1.22	1.22	Good morning, Miss Li
AST	1.899	4.009	2.11	Bailey
...	...	...	...	...
AST	157.054	158.384	1.33	<SS speak freely.>
SST	168.392	170.383	1.991	<SS speak freely.>
SST	176.618	177.306	0.688	Columbus
...	...	...	...	...
SST	3308.766	3316.714	7.948	<SS talk freely.>
PST	2384.871	2520.543	135.672	<SS talk in pairs freely.>
...	...	...	...	...
IST	47.356	51.173	3.817	He is a football player
IST	65.55	69.541	3.991	He *** in the World Cup
...	...	...	...	...
IST	3357.832	3358.191	0.359	Yes
AI	961.56	1003.48	41.92	Marie Curie is a famous woman born in 1867. She became one of the greatest scientists in history with 2 Nobel prizes. Let's take a brief look ...
...	...	...	...	...
Silence	15.608	17.104	1.496	(Pause.)
Silence	56.338	60.751	4.413	<The student is thinking.>
...	...	...	...	...
Silence	3359.728	3363.907	4.179	(Wait time.)

lessons were sent back to the informant for member checking, and alterations made accordingly.

(2) Coding classroom discourse data

A draft coding scheme was constructed relating to seven aspects of classroom discourse within the framework of effective teaching principles that informed the DP, as detailed in Chap. 2. A preliminary trial coding was done on a 43-minute long lesson by the researcher and one research assistant separately, after which they met to check and negotiate their coding. As a result, the draft coding scheme was fine-tuned, with high-inference codes being replaced by low-inference ones, and ambiguous denotations addressed and clarified. Table 3.9, below, provides a

Table 3.8 A sample of time sequenced transcript of classroom observation

Interlocutor	Beginning time	End time	Duration	Utterance
AST	0	1.22	1.22	Good morning. Miss Li
TT	1.22	4.009	0.688	Sit down, please
TT	4.009	9.844	5.835	Ok. So, these days we have learned something about great people, right?
TT	9.853	15.605	5.752	And we've learned some of them. Here I have some famous people
Silence	15.608	17.104	1.496	<Pause.>
TT	17.118	19.687	2.569	So, would you like to guess them?
…	…	…	…	…
TT	3428	3430	2.378	So much for today

description of the coding scheme for classroom observation data (see Appendix 4 for a coded classroom transcript).

(3) Quantifying coded classroom discourse data

The inductive coding of classroom observation data made it possible to quantify those indicators under investigation, to examine whether and how changes took place in classroom instruction within the curriculum innovation. The following techniques were adopted to compress classroom discourse into quantifying data:

(1) *Frequency*: calculated by counting the codes allocated to relevant cases.
(2) *Percentage*: calculated by dividing the frequency of a specific code by the total cases of codes in a category.
(3) *Length*: the number of words in a certain category, e.g., teacher talk.
(4) *Average length per move*: calculated by dividing the overall length of a discourse category by the total number of moves in the utterances.
(5) *Speaking speed*: calculated by dividing the total number of words of a discourse category by the overall time spent in completing the discourse category.

Caution should also be exercised when interpreting data in numerical forms, as those forms may undermine the richness of qualitative data by de-contextualizing the interactions in classroom dynamics. Thus, typical sequences in lessons were analyzed within a multi-faceted framework encompassing such factors as pedagogical objectives, instructional materials, teacher talk, student talk, participatory organization, and discourse structure.

Table 3.9 The coding scheme of the classroom discourse

Category	Codes	Denotation
Activity	A + numerical sequence, e.g., A1, A2, etc.	A pedagogical activity
	A brief description of the activity, e.g., 'Students play a jigsaw puzzle in groups.'	Describe what the teacher and students do in this activity
Sequence	S + numerical sequence, e.g., S1, S1, S3	A complete sequence
Exchange	m/f/m&f	Meaning-oriented exchanges/form-oriented exchanges/exchanges combining meaning and forms
	Pre./Nuc./Dep./Emb.	Preparatory exchanges/nuclear exchanges/dependent exchanges/embedded exchanges
	T/S	Teacher-initiated exchanges/student-initiated exchanges
	Combinations of initials indicating interlocutors, e.g., T-AS (the teacher and all students)	The participatory organization of classroom interaction
	IR/IRF	Exchanges with initiation-response pattern/initiation-response-follow-up pattern
Teacher questions	DQ/RQ	Display question/referential question
Learner talk	RL/UL	Restricted learner talk/unrestricted learner talk
Move	I/R/F	Initiation/response/follow-up
Instructional materials	MM/MMTA/TDM/SPM	Mandated materials/mandated material with teacher's adaptations/teacher-developed material/students-provided material

3.5 Summary

This chapter started by introducing the four research questions that motivated the present study. It then situated this study in a naturalistic paradigm by justifying the suitability of ethnography for answering the research questions. Subsequent subsections introduced the research informants, research setting, and five stages of the study, before the research methods were delineated and the data analysis procedure elaborated.

Chapter 4
Changes of Teacher Cognition within Curriculum Innovation

This chapter depicts how changes took place in the focal informant's cognition over four years' participation in the Danyang Project. It draws primarily on the analysis of qualitative data collected through field notes, interviews, and teaching journals, as documented in Chap. 3. In alignment with the five stages in this study, this chapter investigates whether and how changes took place in teacher cognition within each phase, when distinct approaches were adopted to implement curriculum innovation. Furthermore, to support the likelihood and sustainability of change in teacher cognition at the post-innovation stage, this chapter also examines the project teacher's mental life after she moved to a new educational setting.

The inductive analysis of the qualitative data led the researcher to two broad thematic emphases, which functioned as operational lenses to observe the changes in teacher's cognition. Overall, these thematic categories aligned with the broad families of issues proposed by previous research (Borg, 2003; Freeman, 2002)— that is, how the teacher perceived the nature of language teaching, and how she responded to educational change. To be more specific, aspects relating to the nature of language teaching include: (1) meaning versus forms; (2) learner participation and learner autonomy; (3) providing corrective feedback; and, (4) using textbooks. Responding to the call by Borg to examine "the content, structure, and development processes" (2003, p. 91) involved in the process of cognitive change, this chapter's elaborations on the thematic categories formulated by recursive analysis and synthesis of qualitative data are supported with illustrative narrative accounts. A chronological order was followed to report the results over the five stages of the Danyang Project.

© Springer Nature Singapore Pte Ltd. 2018
Y. Zhu, *Language Curriculum Innovation in a Chinese Secondary School*,
https://doi.org/10.1007/978-981-10-7239-0_4

4.1   The Nature of Language Teaching

4.1.1   Meaning versus Forms

As Ellis put it, classroom instruction "needs to ensure that learners focus pre-dominantly on meaning" (Ellis, 2005, p. 211). Regarding the two senses of meaning—i.e., semantic meaning and pragmatic meaning—it is arguably the latter that "is crucial to language learning" (Ellis, ibid); thus, the target language is treated as a tool for meaning-oriented communication. In this sense, how teachers conceptualize the relationship between and the roles played by meaning and forms in language teaching arguably reveals to what extent teacher cognition concurs with innovative principles.

4.1.1.1   The Pre-project Stage

Two major issues regarding the nature of language teaching in foreign language classrooms addressed herein are 'what to teach' and 'how to teach.' An in-depth interview with Marian before the innovative project was launched revealed an ambivalent belief in her cognition. While expecting and embracing the notion of building communicative competence in language learners, she reiterated the indispensable role played by the accumulation of discrete linguistic forms in language teaching. The conflicting coexistence of dichotomous beliefs was also revealed by the repetition of pairs of contradictory key words, such as "reciting for dictation" versus "telling stories," when Marian spoke about the teaching strategies she adopted.

> As the exam is approaching, I've been repeatedly teaching some confusable phrases containing the word "use," such as "used to" and "be used to doing," just in case the students mixed them up. (I09: 31)[1]

> When my students were at Level 7, I devised for them a mini-talk activity in English class, in which they gave a small talk to the whole class every morning one by one, following the order of ID numbers. Their talks were the extension of the topic taught in that week, such as *My Best Friend, Introducing Myself, My Family, My Favorite Activity,* etc. After all, they talked about various topics and in general performed very well. (I09: 68)

The dichotomy between meaning and form in language teaching, with the former at a subordinate position was further revealed by a metaphor Marian used to illustrate how she perceived the role of forms or grammatical rules in language teaching.

---

[1]Data cited in this chapter carry the following codes: I = interview; FN = field notes; TJ = teaching journal; the subsequent number indicates the time when the data were collected; the number after colon indicates the sequential number of the entry in original file. e.g. I09: 31 = entry No. 31 in the interview conducted in 2009.

So far, a belief I've been holding and kept telling my students is that learning a foreign language is just like building a house, of which the basic structure is constructed of steel and concrete. Grammatical rules function as the supporting fundamentals in learning English. (I09: 41)

4.1.1.2   The Top-Down Stage

Compared with the ambivalent perceptions of the nature of language teaching at the pre-project stage, evidence was found revealing the changes in Marian's cognition at the top-down stage of the DP. One apparent change was that more importance was attached to the meaning of language in teaching, as Marian began to depart from traditional teaching strategies underpinned by structuralism. Reflecting on the way she taught vocabulary, Marian observed:

In the past, the only strategy I used to teach new vocabulary was to ask students to read them loudly in chorus following my demonstration. The students read those words repeatedly, and then recited them. Now I seldom deprive a word of its contextual meaning in teaching. I no longer teach discrete vocabulary explicitly or ask students to read after me. Occasionally, of course, I would write down one or two words on the blackboard with corresponding phonetic symbols. However, I ask students to learn pronunciation by themselves.... Also, I let them infer the meanings of new words from contextual clues. (I11: 2)

However, the sign of departure from teaching pedagogy emphasizing linguistic forms was not a strong one, because it was also found Marian held a deeply-rooted belief favoring the effectiveness of traditional grammar teaching, which normally focuses on pre-set target structure(s). Though this attitude was not revealed in the formal interview, it was shown unintentionally in Marian's reflective account of her teaching. For instance, when she recalled a grammar lesson, she wrote in her teaching journal:

[In my class, today] it went smoothly when we practiced patterned drills, for students could practice the structure they've just learned...Because not all students brought their photos today, I allowed those who had photos to move around and ask their classmates questions about their photos. Frankly speaking, I think this activity was not successful, for some students went too far to ask questions that did not contain the target structure. For example, some questions were about age. Those questions were not to the point. (TJ: Sep. 2, 2010)

4.1.1.3   The Bottom-Up Stage

Marian expressed her preference for cooperative meaning-focused teaching at the bottom-up stage, with more signs indicating her uptake of innovative principles. Moreover, she tended to show more initiative and self-maintenance in reconstructing her teaching practices, grounded on innovative rationale. However, she did not show full departure from traditional form-focused pedagogy, which was deeply-entrenched in her cognition as the fundamental core of language teaching. To a certain extent, she saw meaning-focused activities and tasks as serving entertaining and motivating purposes, rather than playing a decisive role in language learning, as the following anecdote illustrates.

> Yan found it a widely-used strategy for the PTs to embed a competition activity in their lesson planning. That is, students were divided into groups to answer the questions asked by the teacher to check their comprehension on given reading or listening materials. When observing Marian's lesson today, Yan found she did the competition activity again. And this time the purpose was obviously not for comprehension check, for there was a precedent question and answer session that served the purpose. Since the lesson observed was claimed to practice listening and speaking skills, Marian said in the post-observation group meeting that she designed the competition step just to double-check learner's comprehension. Yan observed that this double-checking was somewhat redundant given the teaching objectives of this lesson. She also pointed out that teachers tended to use eye-catching fanfare activities in public lessons or teaching contests without examining the effectiveness of those activities. She suggested due caution should be exercised in the project classes. (FN: Mar. 7, 2013)

4.1.1.4   The Exam Stage

While Marian had raised her awareness of and willingness to adopt principles of meaning-focused language teaching, at both the top-down and bottom-up stages, there was an apparent shift of focus from meaning to form(s), at the exam stage. The subordination of the communicative approach to the mainstream traditional, teacher-fronted pedagogy intensified as the high-stakes exams approached, as evidenced Marian's comments after observing one of her mentor teacher's lessons.

> No wonder she is an experienced teacher and our head teacher. She teaches in such a solid style. She presents the language points so clearly. What is more, she makes full use of time and thus teaches so efficiently. Her students can get all the reciting work done in class. Her students have good memories.... Looking back on what I did before, I left my students homework to do reciting after class for the sake of saving in-class time. I could probably be wrong. (I12: 12)

However, when Marian commented on her colleagues' teaching in post-observation meetings, her attitude was much more deviant from traditional form-focused teaching, particularly when the class she observed was not at Level 9; for example, in one post-observation meeting, the researchers and PTs argued about the last activity in the lesson, which was supposed to improve students' listening and speaking skills on the topic, *My Pets*. The Level-7 class was taught by Judy, another project teacher. When she planned the lesson, Judy asked her students to list some tips about taking good care of pets. Marian argued that an activity designed in this way was not communicative. She said,

> Why not provide more contextualized information, thus the activity would be more like what we do in real life. Say, we could describe some scenarios in which someone is taking care of pets inappropriately, and ask students to spot where the problems are. (FN: May 30, 2013)

4.1.1.5 The Post-project Stage

Following giving increased weight to language forms towards the end of the bottom-up stage and, of course, during the exam stage, Marian went back to perceiving the coexistence of meaning and form in classroom instruction, with the latter being the priority. While Marian restated the subordination of accuracy to fluency in authentic communication, she still thought teaching for test scores more important than teaching for communicative competence. However, at this stage, Marian tended not to perceive meaning and form as mutually exclusive, and was more assertive about the effectiveness of meaning-focused teaching pedagogy for learners' acquisition of linguistic forms.

> The first month I came here I suffered a lot from the exam pressure. I had no idea of the students' learning background and thought it was shameful if the class I taught performed worse than other classes…In that month, I printed out the vocabulary list of primary English and asked my students to recite it. Some students were really not good in English; thus, I gave them extra tutoring lessons when they were supposed to attend the PE course. (I14: 49–54)

> I've compared my students' test scores with those of the HES students taught with traditional pedagogy. I found my students did not perform worse than they did, not to say my students' learning background was much poorer than theirs in general. (I14: 58)

4.1.2 Learner Participation and Learner Autonomy

From a socio-cultural perspective, language learning takes place in social interaction; thus, effective classroom instruction should provide learners with opportunities to participate in collaborative activities with others, and foster learners' autonomy to attend to linguistic production and learning strategies that are conducive to language learning. In this sense, learners' are participants who actively construct classroom interaction, rather than recipients who passively master specific learning objectives.

4.1.2.1 The Pre-project Stage

Marian's preferences for teaching linguistic forms in language teaching was evident when she described learners' role as recipients of linguistic knowledge, instead of language users in communication. An illustrative teaching scenario was narrated by Marian when she tried to differentiate "afford" and "affect," by associating the pronunciation of the letter "d" in "afford" with a Chinese character. Arguably, despite the possible effects this teaching strategy (or trick) could bring about in memorizing words deprived of their contextualized pragmatic meanings, resorting to mnemonics is by no means an effective way to improve learners' capacity to use words in authentic communication.

However, as to Marian's cognition, it was found that perceiving learners' roles as passive recipients did not exist exclusively with expecting learners to foster autonomy in language learning. She explicitly stated the divergent attitudes, and attributed them to the variance in learner autonomy among students.

> If I conduct self-directed learning in my classroom, the good students would find no difficulty getting accustomed to the new mode of learning, whereas the poor students, particularly the extremely poor ones, would get lost. Those students do not know how to study at all. If you advise that they should consult the dictionary to learn more about the vocabulary we've learned today, make sentences with those words, or construct a story by using some of them, they would probably ignore the task, or even worse, some of them might even plagiarize others' homework. (I09: 50)

4.1.2.2 The Top-Down Stage

While Marian expressed her willingness to enhance learner participation and foster learner autonomy at the pre-project stage, she now came up with a feasible pedagogical mechanism to involve students in self-directed learning. Marian held the belief that the teacher's role should be transformed from dictating to facilitating, as evidenced by a "little teacher" strategy she employed in grammar teaching.

> I used to teach grammar by explicitly presenting the rules and asking students to take notes. Now, I hand this over to the students. Let them act as little teachers in class. I give my students homework to preview what is going to be learned, with some key points highlighted. Then the students learn by themselves and present what they've achieved in a subsequent lesson. In this way, autonomous learning and cooperative learning are carried out, and both the presenters and the audience benefit from this activity through a deep learning process. I also provide complementary instruction while or after the little teacher teaches his or her parts in the lessons. (I11: 3)

Apart from fostering learner autonomy in learning the content included in the mandated textbooks, Marian also adopted the DP's innovative principles by tentatively starting to teach a newly-designed course entitled *Language Achievement Performance* (shortened as LAP). This course was completely new to the teachers and their students, and encouraged learners to present (in groups or individually) what they learned outside their classrooms. Since there were no settled rules about what should be presented or how presentations should be delivered, students were given much freedom and the flexibility to put on performances, ranging from telling stories to acting out mini-dramas. Despite being supportive of this new course, Marian was by no means dauntless, saying she felt sometimes panic and frustration, because she was worried that the students' language production would be beyond her capacity, and that the linguistic content in the LAP course might be incompatible with the exams (I14: 67).

4.1.2.3 The Bottom-Up Stage

Marian showed a tendency to reconcile innovative principles with classroom practicalities at the bottom-up stage, despite her strong intention to collaborate with her colleagues on shared work plans to promote learner autonomy and disseminate the practices that had proved rewarding in her teaching experience.

For example, due to her conflicting beliefs about the LAP course's benefits in improving learners' proficiency in general, and its potential to reduce learners' performance on standardized exams, Marian compromised by reducing the amount of time allocated to LAP course (FN: Aug. 30, 2012). Towards the end of the third phase of this study, the LAP course was reduced to a sporadic five-minute presentation session in regular classes.

During constant meetings with teacher educators and fellow project teachers, Marian and Frank initiated an extensive reading activity to promote self-directed extensive reading. They jointly worked out a booklist and a specific work plan to let students know what to read, the agenda to follow, and how their reading would be assessed (FN: Feb. 16, 2012; FN: May 4, 2012). Once they found students had benefited from this activity (Marian's and Frank's classes outperformed non-project classes in an end-of-semester reading contest), they showed great willingness to cascade the successful experience to their peers in the TRG (FN: Aug. 30, 2012).

4.1.2.4 The Exam Stage

At the exam stage, Marian perceived autonomous learning as learning something not encompassed in textbooks, and thus thought her students hardly had any time to learn autonomously during the weekdays. For instance, her enthusiasm towards the extensive reading activity, a distinctive activity in project classes, dissipated due to the pressure of exams.

> The students had given up doing extensive reading, except reading for participating in a reading competition. There is going to be a province-wide reading contest in two or three months. The TRG has registered for it on behalf of all the students. There is a list of recommended readings. But I guess they are too busy to read them. (I13: 34)

However, both Marian and Frank were enthusiastic about sharing with their colleagues their positive experiences with and resources for promoting learner autonomy. Shortly after her students took the high school entrance examination, Marian wrote an article entitled *LAP Course: An Effective Way to Foster Younger Learners' Autonomy in Language Teaching*, in which she detailed the rationale and specifications for the LAP course and its teaching (FN: Jul. 11, 2013).

4.1.2.5 The Post-project Stage

Once she began teaching at the new school, Marian's passion to promote learner participation and learner autonomy was rekindled. At this stage, her enthusiasm and expertise were manifested both in-class and out-of-class, and in both teacher-initiated and institution-assigned activities. Marian held the belief that it was her responsibility to help those poor rural students, and saw her teaching career at YS as a mission of dissemination—that is, she felt she ought to pass on what she had learned to her colleagues in the new educational setting.

> Here I can transfer what we've done in the DP to my teaching practices at YS…and work out a mechanism to motivate my students and enhance their involvement in classroom interaction. For example, I keep attending to learners' needs and encouraging them to provide feedback to my teaching. (I14: 17)

4.1.3 Providing Corrective Feedback

Corrective feedback is an important type of teacher talk in response to learners' linguistic production that deviates from the target output, and is an essential part of classroom interaction (Gass et al., 2012). While meta-analytical studies support of the overall positive effect of corrective feedback on language development (Li, 2010; Mackey & Goo, 2007; Russell & Spada, 2006), there is also a general consensus that teachers' choice of different types of corrective feedback should be based on classroom realities and individual learners' affective and cognitive styles (see for example, Ellis, 2009; Yoshida, 2010). However, as Ellis suggested, "teachers should be prepared to vary who, when, and how they correct in accordance with the cognitive and affective needs of the individual learner" (Ellis, 2009, p. 14), therefore teachers' cognition about providing corrective feedback depends on their theory of language teaching and learning.

4.1.3.1 The Pre-project Stage

At the very beginning, Marian was bewildered as to whether and how corrective feedback should be provided in relation to erroneous production by her students. One issue confounding her was whether errors should be treated; while she recognized insignificant errors might not impair the flow of meaning in real communication, she was frustrated when "some students did it all correctly in writing, but made mistakes here and there when they speak it out" (I09: 119). Yet, central to Marian's reflective account about how she provided corrective feedback was the priority she gave to accuracy in learner's production—that is, all errors identified should be corrected. With respect to how corrective feedback was provided, Marian primarily drew on explicit correction and peer correction; however, she realized what she did in teaching was not consistent with how interlocutors behave in real communication.

> In fact, I should admit I've perceived it in a wrong way. When we communicate with foreigners, they understand what I mean all the same despite the mistakes I make. The same is the case when we communicate in our first language. The mistakes won't affect communication. It is to this point that I feel bewildered. When my students give presentations in class, I listen to them carefully and note down all the errors I detect, the grammatical errors, the vocabulary errors, all of them. Then I ask the audience students to point out and correct those errors.... (I09: 120–121)

4.1.3.2 The Top-Down Stage

Regarding providing corrective feedback, changes were found as to whether and how errors were treated in the top-down stage. Marian no longer regarded errors as a monolithic entities, and began to speculate about dealing with students' errors differently. The field notes recount Marian's enquiries about the guiding principles for dealing with treatable and untreatable errors (FN: Nov. 10, 2011), and she began to correct erroneous parts of learners' production implicitly. A reflective episode about how she treated students' written corrective feedback exemplifies the finding:

> I gave my students a writing assignment after finishing Unit 1. I did the first marking by underlining and correcting all the errors I detected. Then I handed the compositions back to students for the second writing. When I began to do the subsequent marking, I had a sense that I should ask students to correct the errors by themselves. This time I underlined the errors without correcting them and required some students to do the correction in front of me. They could do it. (I11: 54)

While she tried to change the ways she used to correct learners' errors, Marian still found it challenging to decide when, how, and what to correct, particularly with errors in learners' free oral production. As a tradeoff, she either controlled learners' output or found more correctors in class.

> Marian asked her students to recite a passage and correct their errors...When students gave presentations, Marian encouraged the audience to spot and correct the errors. She created a Woodpecker award for the students who did well in correcting classmates' errors. (FN: Aug. 21, 2011)

4.1.3.3 The Bottom-Up Stage

At this stage, Marian became hesitant about providing corrective feedback on learners' errors. In one of her public lessons, she did not correct any errors in learner production; in the subsequent reflective discussion with the researcher, Marian said she "was not sure whether she should correct learners' errors or not" (FN: March 3–7, 2012). Moreover, Marian tended to initiate pre-emptive error correction before the students gave task performances in class—that is, she would meet with those students before they gave presentations, to make sure they got "everything correct before they stepped onto the stage" (TJ: Mar. 7, 2012). She perceived learners' errors as undesirable and to be eliminated, as she thought such utterances were indicative of low quality language production and not conducive to learning.

With respect to written corrective feedback, Marian increasingly resorted to learners' self-correction, and was keen on using pedagogical incentives to prevent learners from getting bored in the process. An exemplar teaching practice was that Marian formulated a writing activity consisting of three procedures: the students did a writing assignment, the teacher revised their writing homework, and students revised their writing based on the feedback from the teacher and designed a poster to present their writings, which would be hung up on the classroom walls. (FN: Feb. 16, 2012; TJ: Feb. 28, 2012)

4.1.3.4   The Exam Stage

In general, corrective feedback was provided in an explicit and mechanic manner at this stage. The majority of interaction between Marian and her students was about the incorrect answers the latter gave on a marked test paper; Marian provided standardized correction forms, which were quite rigid in that little or no variance from the provided answers was permitted. In most cases, only those forms contained in the mandated textbooks were accepted as the "right" answers. To consolidate what had been corrected, all Marian's students kept an error correction notebook in which they took down their erroneous exercise items for later review. Marian thought this way of providing corrective feedback was effective in improving students' exam performance.

However, when Marian commented on one of her colleague's teaching, she said the feedback provided "was too rigid," asserting that "corrective feedback should have been given in a more flexible way." (FN: Mar. 21, 2013)

4.1.3.5   The Post-project Stage

In the last stage, Marian gradually grew more interested in published classroom-based studies on corrective feedback. She read a few research articles on corrective feedback, and came to the researcher with several questions. When the researcher carried out a quasi-experimental study on immediate and delayed feedback at HES, Marian observed the whole process, and was curious about the findings. At this stage, her cognition included a sophisticated scheme about whether and how to provide corrective feedback to learners' errors. In retrospect, Marian said she was aware of the change that took place in how she perceived learners' errors should be corrected.

> In the past, I was so impatient as to repeat my questions without giving students any wait time, or would explicitly tell students the correct answers. I was worried that I did not have enough time to cover the contents I prepared to teach. Now when a student uttered a correct answer to my question, I would respond with "good" or "very good." If they gave an incorrect answer, I would repeat a part of or the whole sentence, or responded with a hint indicating something was erroneous in his or her answer…If the speaker was a very poor student, I would leave more wait time for him or her. (I14: 85–87)

Another change found in Marian's cognition regarding providing corrective feedback was that she drew more on peer correction to deal with learners' written errors. This aligned with her belief that learner autonomy should be fostered and instilled in language teaching. As to the three-step writing task she conducted in the bottom-up stage, Marian now substituted a peer-correction step for the self-correction one. The same inclination was revealed when she reported a newly-constructed assessment task that turned out to work well in her class.

> The homework I gave to my students for the last weekend was to design a test paper… Yesterday, I asked them to exchange their test papers with their desk mates, work out the exercises and negotiate with their desk mates to check their answers. If there were questions they could not solve, they would ask me for help. Wow, I was so busy answering their questions yesterday…but I was very happy. (I14: 69)

4.1.4   Using Textbooks

As stated in Sect. 2.1.5, how textbooks were used was regarded as an indicator of PTs' cognition relating to the nature of language teaching. A major objective in the teacher education program of the DP was to cultivate in PTs the confidence and competence to adapt, abridge, supplement, or substitute the contents in mandated textbooks to better suit teaching objectives. Thus, it was an essential component of the teacher education program to develop PTs' knowledge for and expertise in designing tasks.

4.1.4.1   The Pre-project Stage

Marian virtually had no awareness of how to examine critically the value and effectiveness of the mandated textbooks before she participated in the DP. The textbooks provided a comprehensive repertoire of linguistic forms prescribed in the national course standard, and (given their authoritative status in the educational setting) were closely associated with almost all types of achievement exams in basic education. It was not surprising the mandated textbooks were practically a hidden syllabus, and the basis of teaching for Marian at the time. Notwithstanding her obvious reliance on the mandated textbooks and lack of confidence in adapting their content, Marian said she occasionally adjusted the sequence and time allotment of some sections in a unit.

The reading section was positioned before the grammar section in the mandated textbook. But when I was teaching the unit containing passive voice, I rearranged the order and put grammar ahead of reading, because the target structure (passive voice) was too difficult for the students. Teaching grammar first would help them understand the reading passage better….I normally spend more time than required in the reading section, for it is the core of the whole unit, just like what the intensive reading section was in my English course when I was in college. As to the other sections, such as integrated skills and the main task, probably I won't spend as much time as required. (I09: 75)

4.1.4.2 The Top-Down Stage

At the top-down stage of the DP, a series of school-based textbooks developed by researchers were recommended to be used in project classes, as a substitute for a set of provincially-mandated textbooks. Underpinned by the principles of the Danyang Project and the innovative principles of the National Curriculum, the newly complied textbooks featured authentic language input and task-based language teaching. Despite the assumed superiority of the new textbooks, however, Marian lacked the confidence to completely abandon the provincially-mandated textbooks; a similar diffidence was found with other project teachers. After using the new textbooks exclusively for one academic year, Marian gradually adopted an eclectic strategy of using the mandated textbooks as core teaching materials, and the experimental textbooks as subsidiary instructional materials.

Deciding what to use, of course, by no means captured the whole picture of her perceptions concerning the textbooks. If we go deeper to examine what she perceived as the optimal way to use textbooks, it can be seen that, by the second stage, Marian had gained some confidence in adapting the mandated textbooks. For example, when talking about her lesson planning for a teaching contest, Marian said she planned to adapt the lead-in section in the mandated textbooks into an activity entitled 'watch, listen and say,' which was quite like a corresponding section in the experimental textbooks. In this way, Marian showed her willingness to transplant innovative elements into her teaching practices, irrespective of the vehicle of the instructional content. (I11: 40)

4.1.4.3 The Bottom-Up Stage

While in the second stage, Marian thought it desirable to adapt the mandated textbooks by incorporating them it a relevant part of the experimental textbooks. In the bottom-up stage of the DP, she began to develop instructional materials by adapting existing materials and constructing new tasks to suit her teaching objectives. An illustrative example, below, shows how she raised her awareness and gradually learned to design a dictogloss task, over two teacher training sessions.

In a pre-observation group meeting, Marian was reporting her lesson planning. Yan found a task Marian had designed was not compatible with her teaching objectives. Thus, Yan suggested that she change it into a dictogloss task. Having no idea about what a dictogloss was, Marian was curious about this new stuff and asked Yan to elaborate on the specifications to design and the procedures to implement a dictogloss task. However, Marian did not change her lesson planning by using a dictogloss that day. (FN: Mar. 7, 2013)

In a post-observation group meeting, Yan and several PTs were providing feedback to a lesson taught by Judy. Reflecting on her teaching, Judy said she thought a certain activity in her teaching was not good enough. Hearing Judy's complaint, Marian advised her to use a dictogloss task next time. (FN: May. 30, 2013)

4.1.4.4   The Exam Stage

The experimental textbooks were completely cast out by Marian and her colleagues in this stage in favor of the mandated textbooks, supplemented with worksheets synthesizing key points likely to appear in the exam. Marian considered it of no use to add supplementary materials not directly associated with the exam. In one meeting with the researcher, Marian told her,

> The assignment is a 16k size worksheet in which all exercises are relating to the exam. The worksheet is designed by the TRG and it is impossible to us to give students extra homework. (FN: Mar. 7, 2013)

Marian was curious about how instructional materials were used by her colleagues when she observed their classrooms at this stage. During a focused classroom observation, she chose to use an observation scheme and noted down whether and how the teacher adapted the mandated textbooks. In the post-observation meeting, Marian asked how to develop extended activities based on materials in the mandated textbooks. (FN: Mar. 21)

4.1.4.5   The Post-project Stage

Marian's passion for and expertise in adapting the mandated textbooks were sustained and consolidated by independently making pedagogical decisions of adding, abridging, or rearranging their components. She largely relied on herself to collect extended teaching and learning materials to supplement the mandated textbook, occasionally turning to the researchers for help. Meanwhile, Marian also reflectively drew on her prior teaching practices to reconstruct tasks. For example, she told the researcher she had made a video and used it to conduct an activity in a public lesson, several years before the DP was launched. At that time, she had no idea what a task really was; she did it just to liven up the classroom. Now that she teaching the same content to her students at YS, she redesigned the activity to make it more like a task; this time, she was sure she was using a task, and could state the rationale for using it as "providing students with authentic communicative context in which the target structure is used." (I14: 77)

> I felt I should use a task to teach the singular and plural nouns, so I searched in the bulk of teaching materials I had used before. Then I found a video I had made with the foreign teacher a couple of years ago. The story was that he was shopping for a Christmas party. The students watched this video clip and retold the stuff he had bought in the grocery store. (I14: 74)

4.2   Attitudes Towards the Innovation Project

4.2.1   The Pre-project Stage

Marian was optimistic the innovation program would change deeply-entrenched, exam-oriented educational concepts and practices into a brand-new model of "easy teaching and happy learning" (I09: 3). She explicitly stated,

> Perhaps due to the current educational mechanism, the exam-oriented teaching frustrates me with unbearable workload. Working nonstop every day with lesson planning, teaching, checking assignments, etc., there seems to be endless work to do. (I09: 1–2)

To sum up, Marian was supportive of the innovation project at the very beginning, irrespective of the conception that the changes it entailed would cause a huge workload for her. With limited information about the specifications of the project, she intuitively made an assessment that the project was a remedy for some long-standing problems in English language classrooms. In general, she was optimistic about the outcome of the project, if "the collaboration is good." (I09: 142)

4.2.2   The Top-Down Stage

Starting with a supportive attitude towards and an optimistic vision of the innovation project, towards the end of the top-down stage of the DP, Marian's beliefs were characterized by an interactive, dynamic, and dialogic relationship with specific components thereof. She figuratively regarded her learning experience within the project as a "third leg" to walk with, indicating it provided her with new space for professional development. The aspects Marian perceived as conducive to her changes in cognition included:

(1) Regular meetings with the other fellow PTs to discuss issues about teaching.

> We talked about our students and classes, things like what is going on with them, and how to deal with new problems. Mostly we discussed our lesson planning and useful teaching strategies and tried to keep up with a common tempo within the same TRG. All in all, we enjoy talking about the teaching stuff. (I11: 55)

(2) Seminars organized by researchers, covering topics ranging from task-based language teaching to classroom-based research.

> I quite like a talk given by Yan last time. The seminars taught by PhD students give us theoretical and practical guidance. But it would be better if the gap between theory and practice could be bridged, for we are at the forefront of teaching most of the time. (I11: 70)

(3) Instant on-line or face-to-face support from teacher educators; e.g., providing resources and suggestions for improving teaching, offering feedback on lesson planning, reviewing research proposals and articles, etc.

> It is so good that you always respond promptly to my inquiries via emails and QQ chats. You also give me a lot of help by reviewing my articles and giving me valuable suggestions. (I11: 78)

(4) Target language input from teacher educators, and the materials they provided, which helped Marian improve her pronunciation.

> For long I've been thinking my pronunciation is not good enough. Not really good. But during this period, I listened attentively to your pronunciation and the listening materials in the experimental textbooks as well. I like the listening materials very much, and imitated it spontaneously or intentionally sometimes. It gradually helped me improve [my pronunciation]. (I11: 90)

> My mentor teacher said my pronunciation had improved a lot after she observed my lesson last time. (I11: 91)

> And I was assigned the task to make audio recordings for school-wide listening tests administered by the TRG. Ha-ha, I did not realize I was that good. (I11: 92)

(5) Increased awareness of reading academic books and journal articles on second language research.

> As a matter of fact, I had no clear idea about those academic books and journals shelved in the school library before. It was until you told us that I got to know *Foreign Language Teaching in Primary and Secondary Schools*[2] is an influential and useful journal. (I11: 120)

Despite the DP's advantageous effects on teacher learning and the consequent changes in cognition, Marian expected researchers would do more to bridge the gap between theory and practice, and relate the teacher education program more closely with context-specific realities.

> I hope you could come here more frequently, to get us together, to know more about what is going on with us,…to cater to our practical needs, and then we can get improved. (I11: 71)

---

[2]*Foreign Language Teaching in Primary and Secondary Schools*, published by Beijing Normal University, is one of the leading academic journals specializing in language teaching and research in basic education in China.

4.2.3   The Bottom-Up Stage

In addition to the components listed in Sect. 4.2.2 perceived to be beneficial to her professional development, Marian's perceptions of the innovation project and the teacher educators during the bottom-up stage can be summarized as follows.

(1) The teacher training program aroused in Marian's awareness of conducting classroom-based exploratory research for improving teaching and learning. She was scaffolded by relevant methods and resources provided by teacher educators, and benefited from modeling studies conducted by some teacher educators.

> I have been sort of irritated by some students who got more and more reluctant to speak in my class. Though I have repeatedly reminded them to speak out, they were still very quiet. The PhD students suggested that conducting action research might help me solve this problem. And I read a book they recommended about how to carry out action research in language classrooms. Thus, I got started. This is the first time I did action research in my classroom. (TJ: Mar. 18, 2012)

> Marian told Yan she would like to conduct a study to address a problem with which she felt annoyed. It was about how to improve learner participation in classroom interaction. Yan had a meeting with her to formulate a preliminary research agenda. Through their discussion Yan found Marian had learned some fundamental principles of conducing action research. What is more, she was willing to accept the suggestions given by Yan. At the end of the meeting, Yan promised she would facilitate Marian with her study by offering suggestions and necessary resources. (FN: Mar. 7, 2012)

(2) Marian demonstrated more inclination to reference academic publications when preparing for and carrying out her research.

> I read *English Teachers' Action Research: From theory to practice* (Wang, 2012) last summer. And I also read some other books on how to improve teaching…I should do more reading in the future and get my teaching practices informed by theories in those books. (TJ: Feb. 16, 2012)

> I subscribed *Foreign Language Teaching in Primary and Secondary Schools* last year. Those articles in it were quite useful. Sometimes I selectively read some articles before sleep. (I13: 40)

(3) Marian agreed that conducting focused classroom observations was conducive to directing observers' and observees' attention to specific aspect(s) of classroom teaching practices, and evoked their search for solutions for detected problems.

> We've never done the focused classroom observation before. In fact, who would tell us how to improve a specific aspect like, for example, how to use and adapt the textbooks and how to provide corrective feedback? Indeed, we did it in a rather vague and holistic manner before. (I14: 101)

(4) Marian became critical of the principles and practices suggested by teacher educators with whom she was occasionally involved in academic disputes at this stage. However, the disputes turned out to be constructive, as she was

either convinced of the rationales provided by the latter, or was frankly told there was no universal agreement because the issue under dispute was under-investigated.

> I wonder if it could be better if we revised the classroom observation scheme we've used. Sometimes I found the boundaries between those categories are quite blurring. I felt perplexed when I took observation notes with the scheme. (I13: 10)

(5) Marian was developing a willingness to diffuse innovative principles and practices within her institutional context. However, she had no aspiration of becoming an opinion leader. The head of the TRG played a decisive role in collecting rewarding practices from PTs and disseminating them among non-project teachers.

> The head of the TRG attended the group meeting today. She inquired at length about how Marian and Frank conducted the extensive reading activity last semester, and she decided later to cascade the good practice down to non-project classes. (FN: Aug. 30, 2012)

4.2.4 The Exam Stage

Over the exam preparation period, which lasted around one semester, Marian had little or no intention of enacting innovative principles in her teaching. In conformity with the teaching syllabus designed by the TRG, she believed and adopted the so-called "exercise-stuffed teaching method," bombarding her students with numerous model tests papers recommended by the TRG. The same was true of Frank. Before they took the senior high school entrance exam, the students sat two city-wide mock tests that were administered to help schools, teachers, and parents collect data to inform the ensuing teaching for exams.

Within this short time span, Marian was obsessed with exams and students' academic performance. Most contacts she initiated with the researchers were to find answers to confusing grammatical exercises, or to report how her students had done on a certain exam. Marian did not withdraw from the DP at this stage; instead, she still participated in the project quite actively by observing her peers' lessons and attending group meetings. What is distinct about her teaching practices at the time is that the feedback she gave her colleagues who were teaching Level 7 and Level 8 was still quite communicative-oriented and consistent with innovative principles.

4.2.5 The Post-project Stage

At the last stage of this study, the researcher went abroad for a long-term academic visit, and therefore had very limited contact with the project teachers. Despite the absence of teacher educators on site, Marian managed to keep regular communication with them via instant messaging tools, letting them know what was going on in her life and asking questions occasionally. In retrospect, Marian was nostalgic for the days of the DP. She stated the role researchers had played in her professional life at the time as academic guides, craft facilitators, and resource providers. Moreover, she also held that university researchers were novice practitioners, in the sense that they had learned much context-specific culture and practices in basic education.

(1) Academic guide: the innovative principles

Marian repeatedly said in the interview that she had learned quite a lot "advanced" ideas from the researchers that had played a guiding role in her decision-making and practices. However, it was beyond her capacity to summarize those principles, and instead named a few discrete points, such as mapping form and meaning, fostering learner autonomy, training learners to use learning strategies, and improving the quality of teacher' feedback. However, it is worth pointing out that Marian felt the innovative principles were a bit intangible for her and her colleagues at the very beginning of the DP, and that they were on the horns of a dilemma at the time.

(2) Craft facilitator: the innovative practices

Marian said she had accumulated a large repertoire of pedagogical strategies through her learning in the DP. She thought the learning took place as teacher educators scaffolded her by proposing, modeling, observing, and commenting on her teaching practices. She found the guidance provided by teacher educators was principled, consistent, and systematic, unlike the help she obtained through attending the TRG meetings, which was largely governed by "old doctrines."

> My mentor teachers in the TRG gave me feedback after observing my teaching. But they just commented on those trivial and superficial points, and sometimes showed me how to follow a collectively prepared teaching plan when I was preparing for a teaching contest. I think something in it was out of date and within the old framework. In the DP, I found I came out of the boundary. The PhD students helped me jump out and move to a higher level. (I14: 101)

(3) Resource provider: to preserve and to expand

In Marian's eyes, university researchers were her "teaching resource database" or her "treasure trunk," and enriched her teaching career by providing individually tailored resources. The bulk of teacher training materials to which PTs had free access was left by teacher educators to help preserve innovative principles, and ensure sustained teacher learning. What is more, the on-line provision of new resources was conducive to consolidating learning.

> Last time when I was helping my students preparing for the speech contest, I searched from a document entitled *Modeling English Pronunciation* in our resource bank. I used it before and know it was good. But this time I needed an mp3 file attached to it, which would be helpful for the students to imitate the speaker's pronunciation and intonation. I contacted An Lin for help. She was so efficient that she sent me the file in a few minutes. (I14: 104)

4.3 Summary

Drawing on qualitative data from in-depth interviews, field notes, and teaching journals, the analysis presented in this chapter has provided evidence of how changes took place in teacher cognition over the five stages of this study, to answer the first research question: What changes took place in the Danyang teacher's cognition?

The change in teacher cognition was a dialogic, interactional, non-linear, and longitudinal process. Teacher learning took place at two levels: explicit cognition and implicit cognition. The teacher's explicit cognition was converted into implicit cognition when what she had learned in the teacher education program became automated. Such automatization was likely catalyzed by reflective practices, particularly rewarding experiences in her and her colleagues' community of practice. The following is a brief synthesis of the major findings in this chapter:

(1) Changes occurred in Marian's cognition over the five stages of her participation in the Danyang Project, with distinctive features of change in each stage. The idiosyncrasies of teacher cognition at each stage were influenced by personal, institutional, and socio-political factors.

(2) At the top-down stage, Marian's cognition about innovative principles tended to be explicit. There was an emerging awareness of assimilating innovative ideology, whereas her beliefs about traditional pedagogy were intrinsically deeply-rooted and resistant to change, which hindered her explicit cognition from becoming implicit cognition.

(3) At the bottom-up stage, the transformation from explicit cognition to implicit cognition began to take place, catalyzed by Marian's and her colleagues' personally rewarding experience pertaining to the Danyang Project. Her reflective practices of trying out innovative principles and gradually incorporating them into her belief system was essential to the conversion from explicit cognition to implicit cognition.

(4) Ethical and ideological factors played dominant roles in Marian's cognitive world. The standardized exam, with its immense influence on students' life, activated the ethical components in Marian's cognition system, and in turn inhibited her from up-taking innovative principles.

(5) At the post-project stage, automaticity took place, as Marian spontaneously drew on innovative principles without the scaffolding of teacher educators. It was found that the implicit cognition could be latently developed.

Chapter 5
Changes of Teacher and Student Behaviors in Project Classrooms

One way to evaluate the effectiveness of curriculum innovation is to examine whether any changes took place in classrooms over the period when the innovative approach was implemented. Within the framework proposed in Chap. 2, this chapter examines whether and how changes took place in Marian's classrooms because of the curriculum innovation. Five representative lessons were selected and inductively analyzed to describe the differences and similarities between Marian's teaching practices at the five stages of curriculum innovation. As teacher and student behaviors are inseparable, how students acted and interacted with peers and the teacher is also described. Table 5.1 documents the background information of these five lessons. As elaborated in Chap. 3, the stated teaching objectives of the five lessons were the same. Excerpt for the last lesson, which was offered by Marian at the rural school, the students who learned the other four lessons were the same group (with one student dropped out at the exam stage).

In alignment with the theoretical framework of this study, seven aspects crucial to the effectiveness of language teaching are examined: (1) time allotment to different activities of a lesson; (2) choice of instructional materials; (3) teacher talk—quantity/types of questions asked; (4) student talk—amount/average length per move; (5) participatory organization; (6) focus on meaning verses form; and, (7) discourse structures, including IRF and student-initiated exchanges.

5.1 The Pre-project Stage (May 2009–August 2009)

When Marian applied for the teacher education program of the Danyang Project in early 2009, she video-recorded an 11-minute segment of her teaching, and enclosed it with the application documents she submitted to university researchers. In this study, this video was used as baseline data on Marian's teaching behaviors before the Danyang Project was launched. Though the video footage accessible to the

© Springer Nature Singapore Pte Ltd. 2018
Y. Zhu, *Language Curriculum Innovation in a Chinese Secondary School*,
https://doi.org/10.1007/978-981-10-7239-0_5

Table 5.1 The five lessons under investigation

Lesson	Stage	Stated teaching objectives	Duration (m.s)	Level of students	Number of students
Lesson 1	Pre-project stage	Listening and speaking	11.08	Level 7	55
Lesson 2	Top-down stage	Listening and speaking (Language achievement performance)	38.14	Level 8	55
Lesson 3	Bottom-up stage	Listening and speaking	57.10	Level 9	55
Lesson 4	Exam stage	Exam preparation	45.05	Level 9	54
Lesson 5	Post-project stage	Listening and speaking	41.56	Level 7	22

researcher documented only part of a lesson, it shed light on how Marian instructed and interacted with her students at the pre-project stage.

5.1.1 Time Allotment to Different Activities of a Lesson

Table 5.2, shows the time allotment for different activities in Marian's lesson before she participated in the Danyang Project. In this teaching episode, the activity that occupies the largest time segment is role-play; however, one would have reservations about calling this activity a task, since what students did was to imitate and recite mechanically dialogue that was presented as listening material, with virtually no information or opinion gap on which communication could be built (Ellis, 2003, 2012). Thus, this activity was by no means communicative, despite it appearing to be learner-centered.

The other activity to which Marian allocated a notably large proportion of time was the third one: students reading a dialogue that was delivered as listening input

Table 5.2 The time allotment to different activities at the pre-project stage

Activity description	Time allotment	
	Duration (s.ms)	Percentage (%)
1. Lead-in.	99.73	15.78
2. Students listened to a dialogue and answered one question.	60.52	9.57
3. Students read the dialogue in the textbook and answered some questions. Marian taught the pronunciations of selected words.	198.97	31.48
4. Role-play: students rehearsed the dialogue that was taught in A2 and A3 in pairs. And two pairs of students did the role-play.	221.14	34.99
5. Explicit instruction of two phrases.	51.73	8.18
Total	632.09	100.00

in the preceding session, and then answering questions to check their comprehension of the dialogue. By reading the dialogue in the textbook, the aural language input was reinforced in a visual form. Embedded in the question and answer session were Marian's occasional instructions to consolidate students' pronunciation. This activity, one could argue, was also form-oriented.

Though there is no universal criterion for time allocation for form-focused activities in the evaluation of a language class's communicativeness, it was found that none of the activities in this teaching episode was communicative-oriented. Thus, it can be observed that, before she joined the teacher education program in the Danyang Project, Marian taught in a non-communicative manner, as evidenced by her activity design and the proportion of time allocated to form-oriented activities.

5.1.2 Choice of Instructional Materials

Marian's teaching decisions were highly reliant on the mandated textbook before she participated in the Danyang Project. There were hardly any adaptations to the mandated textbook in her teaching. In the fourth step shown in Table 5.2 Marian designed a role play activity that was strictly based on the language material prescribed by the textbook. To a certain extent, Marian's teaching practices were governed and directed by the mandated textbook, which almost dominated her teaching decisions, in terms of the input to which her learners were exposed.

5.1.3 Teacher Talk

As Table 5.3 shows, teacher talk accounted for 51.52% of the teaching episode, and the percentage of words uttered by the teacher was 66% of its length. At this stage, Marian's speaking speed was around 103.2 words per minute and she spoke 5.32 words per move on average. During the 11-minute lesson, Marian asked 16 questions, of which four were referential questions and 12 were display questions, with the latter making up a dominant percentage (75%).

Table 5.3 Teacher talk at the pre-project stage

Time proportion		51.52%
Length proportion		66.00%
Average length/move (words/move)		5.32
Speaking speed (words/second)		1.72
Types of questions asked	Display questions	16 (75.00%)
	Referential questions	4 (25.00%)

5.1.4 Learner Talk

As demonstrated in Table 5.4 learner talk accounted for 45.67% of the teaching episode, with 24.37% of the learner talk being students' choral responses to the teacher's questions. On average, learner talk constituted 28.41% of the whole classroom talk. When individual students spoke, the average length was 5.55 words per move, and most of the utterances (76.67%) were restricted—i.e., students were seldom given the opportunity to speak freely in Marian's class at this stage.

5.1.5 Participatory Organization

Table 5.5 lists the frequency and percentage of different participatory structures, in descending order. The three most salient participatory organization patterns were constructed by the teacher and all students, the teacher and individual students, and the teacher and some students, respectively. Among these three types of participatory patterns, the interaction between the teacher and individual students accounted for the smallest percentage.

5.1.6 Focus on Meaning versus Form

Table 5.6 displays the frequency and percentage of exchange types, in terms of their focus on either meaning or form. Form-focused exchanges outnumbered

Table 5.4 Learner talk at the pre-project stage

Time proportion	45.67%	
Length proportion	28.41%	
Types of learner talk	Restricted	39 (86.67%)
	Unrestricted	6 (13.33%)
Average length/move of individual learner talk (words/move)	5.55	

Table 5.5 Participatory organization at the pre-project stage

Participatory organization pattern	Frequency	Percentage (%)
T-AS	12	31.58
T-IS	11	28.95
T-SS	10	26.32
Total exchanges	38	100.00

(T—teacher; AS—all students; IS—individual student; SS—some students)

Table 5.6 Meaning- and form- oriented exchanges at the pre-project stage

Meaning versus form	Frequency	Percentage (%)
Meaning-focused	14	36.84
Form-focused	16	42.11
Meaning + Form	8	21.05
Total exchanges	38	100.00

meaning-focused ones, and constituted nearly half (42.11%) of all the exchanges in this teaching episode.

5.1.7 Discourse Structures

As shown in Table 5.7 the IR pattern far outnumbered the IRF pattern in this teaching episode, accounting for 68.42% of the total discourse patterns. Also, teacher-initiated exchanges accounted for 84.21% of all discourse patterns, revealing that the teaching episode examined was teacher-fronted.

5.1.8 Analyzing a Selected Episode

Episode 5–1 was selected from the teaching transcript of this stage to exemplify the attributes of Marian's classroom instruction before she participated in the Danyang Project. This teaching episode took place after Marian required her students to read a dialogue from the textbook. The episode consisted of two sequences, with moves 1 to 10 constituting the first sequence, and moves 11–19 constituting the second. In each sequence, there was a preparatory exchange in which Marian initiated a question and students bid to answer it. Then followed a nuclear exchange, in which the nominated student answered the question and Marian gave evaluative feedback. Following this nuclear exchange, were two successive dependent exchanges aiming at consolidating the linguistic forms Marian deemed important. Students were quite sensitive in identifying their teacher's intention to request repetition, and were highly willing to do so (they repeated each phase twice).

Table 5.7 Discourse patterns at the pre-project stage

Discourse patterns	Frequency	Percentage (%)
IR	26	68.42
IRF	12	31.58
Teacher-initiated exchanges	32	84.21
Student-initiated exchanges	6	15.79
Total exchanges	38	100.00

From this episode shows classroom instruction at this stage of Marian's professional life was largely dominated, organized, and led by the teacher. Learners played a subsidiary role and contributed to classroom discourse in a controlled and limited way. There was an apparent focus on form-focused teaching, and a tacit agreement between the teacher and students to learn linguistic forms by memorization.

Episode 5–1

1	T	<Clap hands. > Ok, be quiet	Preparatory exchange
		So, what does Hobo ask Eddie to do?	
		<pause>	
		What does Hobo ask Eddie to do?	
		<pause>	
		Ok, put up your hands.	
2	SS	<Some students raise hands.>	
3	T	S's name.	Nuclear exchange
4	IS	He asks Eddie to support…him.	
5	T	Very good. Sit down, please.	
6	T	Now, read after me. Support.	Dependent exchange
7	AS	Support. Support.	
8	T	S-u-p-p-o-r-t, support.	Dependent exchange
9	AS	S-u-p-p-o-r-t, support.	
10	AS	Support him. Support him.	
11	T	Next one, what does Eddie think about the charity?	Preparatory exchange
		What does Eddie think about the charity?	
12	SS	<Some students raise hands.>	
13	T	<point to a student.>	Nuclear exchange
14	IS	He thinks it is meaningful to support the charity.	
15	T	Very good.	
16	T	Now, together. It is meaningful to do sth.	Dependent exchange
17	AS	It's meaningful to do sth. It's meaningful to do sth.	
18	T	It's meaningful to support charities.	Dependent exchange
19	AS	It's meaningful to support charities. It's meaningful to support charities.	

In sum, analysis of the transcribed video-recording of the teaching episode at the pre-project stage reveals that Marian's teaching practices tended to be teacher-fronted, form-oriented, and non-communicative before she participated in the curriculum innovation. Specifically, her pedagogical activity designs and the time allocated to each activity indicated she was in favor of traditional teacher-fronted, form-oriented pedagogy, strictly based on the mandated textbook. In addition, Marian spoke more than her students did, and asked more display questions, which are more likely to lead to restricted students' responses. She interacted more with all or some of her students than she did with individual students. Most interactions in her class at this stage were form-oriented and followed the IR sequence. Student-initiated exchanges constituted a very limited proportion in her classroom instruction.

5.2   The Top-Down Stage (September 2009–December 2011)

The top-down stage of the Danyang Project featured a series of innovative courses designed in alignment with innovative principles. The Language Achievement Performance (LAP) course, as the name suggests, was a complete departure from regular courses, in the sense that students were required to present what they achieved through out-of-class language learning. Normally, the teacher gave students a theme for their presentation one or two weeks in advance, and students prepared to perform in class by drawing on learning resources other than regular classroom instruction. The teacher acted as organizer and facilitator when teaching this new course. At this stage, LAP courses were offered monthly, with each lesson lasting around 80 min.

5.2.1   Time Allotment to Different Activities of a Lesson

As the teaching procedure displayed in Table 5.8 suggests, the LAP class examined here consisted of a string of student performances on the theme of famous people. The performances varied in form from monologues to mini-plays, and were obvious student-centered. The allocation of time was decided by the students rather than by the teacher, and the activities were primarily meaning-oriented. Those activities

Table 5.8 Time allotment to different activities of a lesson at the top-down stage

Activity description	Time allotment	
	Duration (s.ms)	Percentage (%)
1. Introduction.	101.44	4.36
2. A group of students performed a short play written by a famous Chinese writer named Lu Xun.	441.90	19.01
3. A group of students presented the biography of Lang Lang, a famous Chinese pianist.	358.65	15.43
4. One student presented the life story of Steve Jobs.	295.22	12.70
5. A student recited a famous poem written by Li Bai and two students acted out a story about the poet in his childhood.	594.86	25.59
6. Three students acted out a story of Napoleon.	373.54	16.07
7. The teacher gave comments on students' performance.	158.70	6.83

dominated by the teacher (i.e., Activities 1 and 7) occupied a relatively smaller proportion of time than did students-led activities. Thus, it could be argued that the LAP class was student-centered in terms of time allotment and activity arrangement.

5.2.2 Choice of Instructional Materials

As mentioned in the previous sub-section, the instructional materials were collected, adapted, and presented by students via accessible resources. The rationale for self-directed learning material development is that it exposes learners to unlimited language input, and is thus conducive to fostering learner autonomy. Table 5.8 also shows the rich selection of learning materials collected by learners; what it does not show, is that these materials were presented on PPT slides, which supplied visual and audio input to classroom instruction at the same time.

5.2.3 Teacher Talk

It can be observed from Table 5.9 that, at this stage, the percentage of teacher talk largely declined, compared to the lesson at the pre-project stage. The average length of move Marian uttered when teaching the LAP class was higher than in her pre-project class (7.15 > 5.32). She also spoke slightly faster (2.11 > 1.72), and utilized many more referential questions than display questions (42.86% > 25.00%).

5.2.4 Learner Talk

The decrease in the amount and proportion of teacher talk led to an increase in learner talk, as shown in Table 5.10. Learner talk accounted for 79.19% of the

Table 5.9 Teacher talk at the top-down stage

		The top-down stage	The pre-project stage
Time proportion		16.34%	51.52%
Length proportion		20.81%	66.00%
Average length/move (words/move)		7.15	5.32
Speaking speed (words/second)		2.11	1.72
Types of questions asked	Display questions	8 (57.14%)	16 (75.00%)
	Referential questions	6 (42.86%)	4 (25.00%)

Table 5.10 Learner talk at the top-down stage

		Top-down stage	Pre-project stage
Time proportion		79.19%	45.67%
Length proportion		79.19%	28.41%
Types of learner talk	Restricted	142 (44.38%)	39 (86.67%)
	Unrestricted	178 (55.62%)	6 (13.33%)
Average length/move of individual learner talk (words/move)		9.33	5.55

whole classroom talk, an obvious increase from the pre-project stage (45.67%). The increase was in accordance with the rising length proportion of learner talk (79.19% > 28.41%), and the notably larger percentage accounted for by individual learner talk (76.91% > 8.13%). As the amount and duration of learner talk increased, the percentage of unrestricted learner production also became higher (55.62% > 13.33%), as did the average length of individual learner talk (9.33 > 5.55).

5.2.5   Participatory Organization

Table 5.11 illustrates the participatory organization pattern in Marian's lesson at the top-down stage, in comparison with the preceding stage. The most prominent types of participatory organization patterns at this stage were those involving students, whereas all the salient participatory organization patterns at the pre-project stage involved the teacher. As the LAP course was student-centered in nature, the percentage of student-student interaction accounted for 68.66% of classroom talk, virtually dominating the class. Of the two salient types of student-student interaction, the percentage of exchanges uttered between individual learners was the highest, featuring exuberant one-to-one interaction.

Table 5.11 Participatory organization at the top-down stage

The top-down stage			The pre-project stage		
Participatory organization pattern	Frequency	Percentage (%)	Participatory organization pattern	Frequency	Percentage (%)
IS-IS	52	38.81	T-AS	12	31.58
IS-AS	40	29.85	T-IS	11	28.95
T-AS	20	14.93	T-SS	10	26.32
Total exchanges	134	100.00	Total exchanges	38	100.00

(T—teacher; AS—all students; IS—individual student)

5.2.6 Focus on Meaning versus Form

In can be observed from Table 5.12 that the percentage of meaning-focused exchanges in Marian's instruction at the top-down stage nearly doubled that at the pre-project stage (77.61% > 36.84%), and that the percentage of form-focused exchanges largely declined (8.96% < 42.11%). Also, a declining trend was found for exchanges combining meaning and form (13.43% < 21.05%). The statistics regarding meaning-focused exchanges provide empirical evidence for the communicativeness of LAP courses, as students were engaged in classroom interaction that simulated communication in authentic contexts.

5.2.7 Discourse Structures

Table 5.13 shows that the percentage of IRF pattern grew moderately at this stage (44.78% > 31.58%), and that there were far more student-initiated exchanges at the top-down stage (77.61% > 15.79%). As the LAP course was designed to generate learner engagement and learners' target language production, that objective was achieved.

Table 5.12 Meaning- and form-focused exchanges at the top-down stage

Meaning versus form	The top-down stage		The pre-project stage	
	Frequency	Percentage (%)	Frequency	Percentage (%)
Meaning-focused	104	77.61	14	36.84
Form-focused	12	8.96	16	42.11
Meaning + Form	18	13.43	8	21.05
Total exchanges	134	100.00	38	100.00

Table 5.13 Discourse structures at the top-down stage

Discourse patterns	The top-down stage		The pre-project stage	
	Frequency	Percentage (%)	Frequency	Percentage (%)
IR	74	55.22	26	68.42
IRF	60	44.78	12	31.58
Teacher-initiated exchanges	30	22.39	32	84.21
Student-initiated exchanges	104	77.61	6	15.79
Total exchanges	134	100.00	38	100.00

5.2.8   Analyzing Selected Episodes

Episode 5–2 from the LAP class clearly shows the instructional activities and interaction featuring classroom instruction at the top-down stage of the Danyang Project. The teaching episode started with an activity in which a group of students acted out a story written by Lu Xun, a famous Chinese writer. The first sequence of this episode consisted of moves 1–15, with a presenter teaching new vocabulary to his classmates. Then, in the second sequence (moves 16–17) the presenter raised two questions, to which the answers were to be found through watching the upcoming performance. From move 18, the presenter began to introduce background information of Lu Xun, halting intentionally to interact with his classmates by checking comprehension, offering clarification (moves 20–21), and asking questions (moves 26–30 and moves 31–33).

A prominent feature of this episode was that it involved no teacher participation. In addition, this episode reveals another attribute of the LAP course—that is, it is up to the students to decide what to learn and how to learn, which is a departure from traditional teaching pedagogy, which emphasizes teacher's authority and covering textbooks.

Notwithstanding the notable shift, Episode 5–2 also indicates learners were not fully ready to take an active part in an LAP course. Despite students' observably enhanced participation in this episode, a closer examination shows that the fronted 'teacher' was still there, as the student presenter was imitating his teacher by presenting knowledge, asking questions, and eliciting and evaluating answers, particularly when it comes to vocabulary repetition (e.g., moves 5–6).

Episode 5–2

1	IS1	Hello, everyone. Today, I will introduce a famous people to you.	Preparatory exchange
		His name is Lu Xun. Lu Xun.	
2	AS	<Listen attentively.>	
3	IS1	Err, first, I will show you some new words.	Nuclear exchange
		Please read after me.	
4	AS	(silence)	
5	IS1	Essay.	Dependent exchange
6	AS	Essay, essay.	
7	IS1	Translation works.	Dependent exchange
8	AS	Translation works, translation works.	
9	IS1	Moustache.	Dependent exchange
10	AS	Moustache, moustache.	
11	IS1	Politician.	Dependent exchange
12	AS	Politician, politician.	
13	IS1	Crowd.	Dependent exchange
14	AS	Crowd, crowd.	

(continued)

(continued)

15	Silence	<pause>	
16	IS1	Now, there are some questions for you.	Nuclear exchange
		You can find the answer in our show.	
		The first one, what was Lu Xun's moustache like?	
		Why was Kong Yiji's leg broken?	
17	AS	(Silence) <The teacher prepares PPT.>	
18	IS1	Now, let's begin.	Nuclear exchange
		Lu Xun was born in Shaoxing, Zhejiang.	
		He was famous for, he was famous for his pen name.	
		His moustache is just like one in Chinese.	
19	AS	<Listen attentively.>	
20	IS1	Can you find that?	Embedded exchange
21	SS	Yes.	
22	IS1	His works included essays, translation works and short stories.	Nuclear exchange
23	AS	(Silence) <prepare PPT.>	
24	IS1	Do you know some works in our Chinese books? We have learned some.	Preparatory exchange
25	AS	(Silence) (wait time)	
26	IS1	S's name	Nuclear exchange
27	IS2	*** ?	
28	IS1	Yes, you did well.	
29	IS1	(pause)	
30	IS1	Very well.	
31	IS1	S's name.	Nuclear exchange
32	IS3	《从百草园到三味书屋》。	
33	IS1	Yes, thank you.	
34	IS1	(pause)	Nuclear exchange
35	IS1	Lu Xun was not only a writer, but also a politician.	
		Today, two of my partners will act a short story about his novel.	
36	IS1	(Pause) Let's begin.	
37	AS	(Silence) <The presenter prepares PPT.>	

Episode 5–3 sheds light on the transformation of Marian's role in the LAP course; this episode is the concluding part of the same activity illustrated in Episode 5–2. After students finished performing the story, Marian joined them to provide corrective feedback on some errors in the learner production. The corrective strategies she used were mainly indirect; for instance, she tended to invite another student or the rest of the class to judge and identify the erroneous part of the learner production before providing the correct form (for example, moves 8–12). After dealing with linguistic errors, Marian moved on to make comments on the content of students' performance, entailing two meaning-focused exchanges (moves 19–25). This

indicated changes in Marian's teaching practices towards the communicativeness underpinning the innovative principles of the Danyang Project.

However, we could also find from this episode that Marian's English language proficiency frequently impeded her from expressing herself in a fluent and accurate manner. There were linguistic and pragmatic errors that made the teacher talk awkward.

Episode 5–3

1	T	Now, wait a moment. I would say something. Just now, Peter's group acted very well, right?	Preparatory exchange
2	AS	Yes.	
3	T	I think so. But actually, they made some small mistakes. Can you find them? Ok, who notice it? *** If you know, please put up your hands. Don't be nervous.	Preparatory exchange
4	SS	\<Some students raise their hands.>	
5	T	Ok, just relax yourselves. Amy.	Nuclear exchange
6	IS	I think Peter. He should say anything, but he …	
7	T	Not everything, right? Yes, very good.	
8	T	And Steve just now said, "I won't give you everything." Is he right?	Nuclear exchange
9	SS	No.	
10	T	No, you should say, I won't give you… anything.	Dependent exchange
11	SS	Anything.	
12	T	Right.	
13	T	And Steve made another small mistake. "That is a famous people." Is it right?	Nuclear exchange
14	SS	No. Famous people.	
15	T	Yes, good, very good.	
16	T	And I want to ask one student. Em, Nick. Stand up. Do you like be a man like Kong Yiji?	Nuclear exchange
17	IS	Oh, no.	
18	SS	(laughter)	
19	T	Ok, and what do we learn from him?	Dependent exchange
20	IS	Don't. Don't steal others' things.	
21	Silence	(pause)	
22	T	Anything else?	Dependent exchange
23	IS	And be an honest man.	
24	T	Ok, very good, thank you. We shouldn't steal others' things. Right? We should work hard, and depend on ourselves, right? And should we, we should be honest.	
25	T	Very good. Ok, go on.	

To conclude, when Marian was teaching at the top-down stage of the Danyang Project, she shifted from the traditional to the communicative way of teaching, by giving up her role as the conduit of linguistic knowledge. The transformation of her role entailed a change in classroom activities, and involved more learner participation in and contribution to classroom talk. At this stage, Marian spoke faster and produced longer utterances per move, but contributed fewer utterances. Correspondingly, the students spoke more, produced more unrestricted utterances, and initiated more interactions. Moreover, there were more meaning-oriented exchanges in the LAP course.

However, caution should be exercised in claiming that teaching a new course grounded in innovative principles indicates teaching behaviors are more effective, which depends on the teacher's expertise in implementing the innovative principles as expected. Learning to teach this new course, Marian asserted, was a challenging and stressful experience, and she sometimes found it beyond her competence to deal with students' unpredictable production in classroom interactions. As such, Marian's feedback to student talk was rather mechanical and unsystematic; after the first student's performance, she pointed out some grammatical errors and gave corrective feedback implicitly, but did not provide feedback on learners' language after the other groups performed.

5.3   The Bottom-Up Stage (January 2012–March 2013)

Towards the end of the top-down stage, the Danyang Project was caught in a dilemma, as there emerged a strong resistance to the experimental textbooks and the innovative courses. This resistance intensified when PTs found their students' scores in traditional standardized tests were not advantageous, compared with students in non-project classes. To address the resulting anxiety, doubt, and even criticism, a compromise was made to convert the Danyang Project from a top-down to a bottom-up approach, and tacit consent was given to teachers' intent to resort back to mandated textbook and traditional courses. Despite the hardships in implementing curriculum innovation, however, the teacher education program still facilitated PTs' adoption of innovative principles, regardless of their textbook and course selections. The lesson analyzed in this section is one of the regular lessons Marian taught at this stage.

5.3.1   Time Allotment to Different Activities of a Lesson

Table 5.14 provides an overview of a regular lesson taught by Marian at the bottom-up stage. This is a listening and speaking lesson, using the mandated textbook. The table shows Marian followed a teaching agenda consisting of 15 activities, which can be further segmented into two main parts. The first part,

Table 5.14 Time allotment to different activities at the bottom-up stage

Activities	Time allotment	
	Duration (s.ms)	Percentage (%)
1. Greeting and opening remarks.	1.91	0.06
2. Led in and warmed up.	222.96	6.44
3. The teacher presented the topic and taught the pronunciation of some new words.	204.25	5.90
4. Students read a passage about Marie Curie freely and answered questions.	172.11	4.97
5. Students read the text again and worked out a gap-filling exercise in textbook.	320.40	9.25
6. Students listened to a passage and worked out part of the second gap-filling exercise.	474.32	13.69
7. Students worked out the rest part of the gap-filling exercise in textbook.	353.44	10.20
8. The teacher taught the pronunciations of new words again and students read the passage aloud freely.	86.96	2.51
9. Q&A competition.	150.70	4.35
10. Students listened to a dialogue and answered some questions.	124.72	3.60
11. Students read the dialogue synchronously following the tape.	93.01	2.69
12. Students read the dialogue aloud freely.	98.72	2.85
13. Pair work: students made their own dialogues by using sentence structures in samples given by the teacher.	509.95	14.72
14. Debate.	648.72	18.73
15. Concluding remarks.	2.38	0.07
Total	3464.54	100.00

comprising the first 12 activities in Table 5.14 contained a succession of pedagogical steps centered on listening exercises from the textbook. These steps were generally comprehension-based, and the teacher played a major role in presenting new knowledge and controlling the teaching procedure. The part followed a traditional model of presenting, practicing, and consolidating linguistic knowledge. The second part, which consisted of pair work (Activity 13) and a debate (Activity 14), was more production-based. In these two activities, students were required to engage in tasks designed by Marian.

As to the time allotted to the two parts, the second part, or the more communicative one, comprised around 1/3 of the overall time of this class. Given a notable decline in the amount of classroom time allocated to communicative tasks, the newness of classroom instruction did not completely fade out with Marian's resistance to some components of the curriculum innovation.

5.3.2   Choice of Instructional Materials

Table 5.15 synthesizes how Marian used the mandated textbook at the bottom-up stage. Among the 13 activities involving instructional materials, 10 were based exclusively upon the mandated textbook, two were involved her adaptations of the mandated textbook, and one was based on teacher-designed instructional materials. One could conclude that, at the bottom-up stage, there was a return to the mandated textbook, and that this was likely the case in Marian's practices in the comprehension-based teaching. Despite a heavy reliance on the mandated textbook, there was evidence of Marian's confidence and expertise in adapting and designing teaching materials, which she primarily did in conducting production-based teaching.

5.3.3   Teacher Talk

Table 5.16 illustrates how changes took place in various aspects of teacher talk at the bottom-up stage. An obvious increase can be found in the percentages of both time and length of teacher talk, compared to the previous stage. The increasing proportion of teacher talk, in terms of both quantity and duration, indicates Marian reverted to teacher-fronted teaching pedagogy at this stage. There was a slight increase in the average length per move in teacher talk from 7.15 words to 7.72

Table 5.15   Choice of instructional materials at the bottom-up stage

Activities	Materials
A1	N/A
A2	Mandated textbook with teacher's adaptations
A3–A12	Mandated textbook
A13	Mandated textbook with teacher's adaptations
A14	A task designed by the teacher
A15	N/A

Table 5.16   Teacher talk at the bottom-up stage

		The bottom-up stage	The top-down stage
Time proportion		40.67%	16.34%
Length proportion		58.43%	20.81%
Average length/move (words/move)		7.72	7.15
Speaking speed (words/second)		1.88	2.11
Types of questions asked	Display questions	51 (73.91%)	8 (57.14%)
	Referential questions	18 (26.09%)	6 (42.86%)

words; however, Marian spoke somewhat more slowly at this stage (1.88 < 2.11), and the percentage of referential questions declined from 42.86% to 26.09%.

5.3.4   Learner Talk

As shown in Table 5.17, both the time taken up by and length of learner talk decreased at the bottom-up stage, illustrating Marian's reversion to traditional teacher-fronted pedagogy; this can also be seen in the slight decrease in learners' unrestricted oral production, from 55.62% to 41.57%. What is more, students tended to give shorter utterances on average, compared with the previous stage.

5.3.5   Participatory Organization

Table 5.18 compares the three most frequent participatory organization patterns at the bottom-up and top-down stages, respectively. At the bottom-up stage, all participatory organization patterns listed involved the teacher, revealing a regressions toward the teacher's role as dominator of the class.

Table 5.17 Learner talk at the bottom-up stage

		The bottom-up stage	The top-down stage
Time proportion		39.76%	79.19%
Length proportion		24.90%	79.19%
Types of learner talk	Restricted	97 (58.43%)	142 (44.38%)
	Unrestricted	69 (41.57%)	178 (55.62%)
Average length/move of individual learner talk (words/move)		6.43	9.33

(T—teacher; AS—all students; IS—individual student; SS—some students)

Table 5.18 Participatory organization at the bottom-up stage

The bottom-up stage			The top-down stage		
Participatory organization pattern	Frequency	Percentage (%)	Participatory organization pattern	Frequency	Percentage (%)
T-AS	78	40.41	IS-IS	52	38.81
T-IS	78	40.41	IS-AS	40	29.85
T-SS	23	11.92	T-AS	20	14.93
Total exchanges	193	100.00	Total exchanges	134	100.00

5.3.6 Focus on Meaning versus Form

Table 5.19 illustrates the considerable decrease of the percentage of meaning-focused exchanges, and of those exchanges combining meaning and form at the bottom-up stage; meanwhile, the percentage of form-focused exchanges notably increased from 8.96% to 40.93%. This change reveals that Marian had partially given up on implicit, meaning-focused teaching, and drew more on explicit form-focused teaching at this stage.

5.3.7 Discourse Structures

As shown in Table 5.20 the percentage of IRF patterns slightly decreased from 44.78 to 40.41% at the bottom-up stage. More than 90% of the exchanges are initiated by the teacher at this stage, providing more evidence Marian's teaching at this stage was teacher-fronted.

5.3.8 Analyzing Selected Episodes

Episode 5–4 was selected from the lead-in activity of this lesson. In attempting to activate students' background knowledge relating to the topic, *Famous People*, Marian had prepared some PPT slides with pictures of celebrities. She intentionally covered a part of each picture, and let her students figure out who the person in the

Table 5.19 Meaning- and form- focused exchanges at the bottom-up stage

Meaning versus form	The bottom-up stage		The top-down stage	
	Frequency	Percentage (%)	Frequency	Percentage (%)
Meaning-focused	103	53.37	104	77.61
Form-focused	79	40.93	12	8.96
Meaning + Form	11	5.70	18	13.43
Total exchanges	193	100.00	134	100.00

Table 5.20 Discourse structures at the bottom-up stage

Discourse patterns	The bottom-up stage		The top-down stage	
	Frequency	Percentage (%)	Frequency	Percentage (%)
IR	115	59.59	74	55.22
IRF	78	40.41	60	44.78
Teacher-initiated exchanges	178	92.23	30	22.39
Student-initiated exchanges	15	7.77	104	77.61
Total exchanges	193	100.00	134	100.00

picture was. In this episode, the teacher asked a question (move 3) that was responded to by all the students in class; though the answer was obviously correct, it did not result in a closure of interaction. Instead of moving on to the next picture, Marian asked how the student got his answer (move 6), then urged the student to tell more about the football star, entailing four meaning-focused dependent exchanges (moves 12–21).

Compared with the lesson at top-down stage, this lesson was apparently teacher-led. However, there was an obvious change in the quality of teacher talk. First, Marian was more adroit at accommodating her questions to contextual and personal realities in the classroom. As her intent in devising this activity was not to seek answers, but to elicit more learner production on the topic, she manipulated her questioning strategies to achieve her instructional objective, and adjusted her questions in accordance with students' responses. The first question (move 3) she asked was an easy one, but was followed by two questions that were slightly more challenging (move 6 and move 12). When she asked an even more demanding question (move 17), she realized from the student's reticence that it was beyond his capacity to articulate, and so transformed it into an easier one (move 19).

Episode 5–4

1	T	Ok. So, these days we have learned something about great people, right? And we've learned some of them. Here I have some famous people. (Silence) <Pause> So, would you like to guess them?	Preparatory exchange
2	AS	Yes.	
3	T	Ok. First, who is he?	Nuclear exchange
4	AS	(Noise) <Some students speak freely.>	
5	T	*** Yeah, yeah, yeah.	
6	T	How do you know?	Dependent exchange
7	AS	(Noise) <Some students speak freely.>	
8	T	Oh. Yeah. Sweater. He wears sweater.	
9	T	Right?	Embedded exchange
10	SS	Yes.	
11	T	Very good. He is Bailey. He is Bailey.	
12	T	And what does he do? What does he do?	Dependent exchange
13	AS	(Noise) <Some students speak freely.>	
14	T	James.	Dependent exchange
15	IS	He is a football player.	
16	T	Ah, very good.	
17	T	And anything else? Can you describe him?	Dependent exchange
18	IS	(Silence) <The student is thinking.>	
19	T	Did he do anything grea…do anything great?	Dependent exchange
20	IS	He *** in the World Cup.	
21	T	Ah, very good. Thank you. Sit down, please.	

In a nutshell, Marian reached a compromise between the innovative principles and contextual realities in her teaching practices at the bottom-up stage of the curriculum innovation. She resumed her role as the center of classroom instruction, and played a dominant role in classroom talk, and returned to explicit form-focused teaching. Changes in her behaviors resulted in learners' decreased engagement in classroom instruction.

However, despite the obvious reversal in the organizational pattern of instruction, there was substantial progress in Marian's teaching expertise, as evidenced both quantitatively and qualitatively by her: (1) producing longer utterances; (2) willingness and capacity to adapt mandated textbook and design new task; and, (3) being more sensitive to learners' cognitive variances in classroom interaction, and adapting her questioning strategies accordingly.

5.4   The Exam Stage (April 2013–June 2013)

An exam preparation lesson taught by Marian was audio-recorded as the senior high school entrance examination was approaching. As numerous mock exams occupied students' school time at this stage, their English classes were largely given over to either mock exam administration or post-test feedback. The lesson analyzed in this sub-section was given after Marian had scored her students' mock tests and planned to give feedback on their performance. Given the apparent disparity in pedagogical objectives between this lesson and the others in this chapter, it is presumably non-equivalent to examine the quantitative differences or similarities between them; thus, a brief qualitative description of this exam-preparation lesson is given to provide a glimpse of Marian's classroom practices in this special period of the Danyang Project.

5.4.1   Different Activities of a Lesson

When teaching this lesson, Marian started by announcing student's scores on the mock exams, and commenting on those students who had made salient progress or who had performed unsatisfactorily. Then, section by section, she gave students the right answers to the test items, asked students to correct their errors, and sporadically selected students to justify how they got the right answers. The writing section was dealt with somewhat differently; a student who had performed well in the writing section was called on to read her composition.

5.4.2   *Choice of Instructional Materials*

In this lesson, the only instructional material used was the test paper, to which there was no adaptation made by the teacher. As mentioned earlier in this thesis, in standardized tests of this kind, the answers supposed to be "correct" are always those linguistic points found in the mandated textbook. If a student by chance supplies answers that are correct, but outside of the scope of their textbooks, he or she is likely to be penalized for not giving the "exactly correct" answer. Thus, a safe strategy to take is to rely exclusively on the mandated textbook when cramming for the senior high school examination. Consider the following test item:

My father _____ in the park every morning last year. (jog)

Students were supposed to fill in the blank with the simple past tense of the verb in the bracket; thus, "*jogged*" was considered to be the correct answer. However, some students in the project class had learned the phrase "*used to do*," which was also a suitable alternative answer to this test item; they were not given credit for using this construction (i.e., "used to jog"), because it did not appear in the mandated textbook.

5.4.3   *Teacher Talk*

Teacher talk accounted for the preponderance of discourse in this exam preparation class. Moreover, Marian almost entirely used L1, except when reading test items in L2.

5.4.4   *Learner Talk*

Students also talked primarily in L1. They mostly talked when asked to translate one or two sentences in a test paper, elucidate a grammar rule they drew on to work out a test item, or justify a strategy they had used. There was much less student engagement in classroom talk at this stage.

5.4.5   *Participatory Organization*

Classroom interaction occurred mainly between the teacher and the whole class, and between the teacher and individual students. Apart from the writing section, there was hardly any student-student interaction in this exam-preparation class.

5.4.6 Focus on Meaning versus Form

This lesson was predominantly form-oriented, and there was very little meaningful information exchanged as would have happened in communicative tasks, such as information or opinion gap. Per the pedagogical purpose of this class, the instruction was aimed at improving accuracy in linguistic forms on the achievement test.

5.4.7 Discourse Structures

As can be seen, the exam preparation lesson was predominantly teacher-fronted, as Marian initiated almost all the exchanges of classroom discourse.

5.4.8 Analyzing a Selected Episode

Episode 5–5 might evoke in most Chinese EFL learners memories of the exam cramming classes that dominated the months before high-stakes examinations. In this class, the teacher was dealing with problematic items on the test. Here Marian was addressing a multiple-choice question on subject-verb agreement. Metalanguage and learner's L1 were primarily used, and the negotiation focused on solving a grammatical problem. The constituent structure of classroom discourse was much simpler, as there were no dependent exchanges attaching to the nuclear exchange.

Episode 5–5

1	T	好, 继续。还有14题, 是吧?	Preparatory exchange
2	SS	11。	
3	T	哦,11题。The half of the class ____ down most of the work; the rest of the work ____ rather difficult. 好, 这一题, Amy, 你来讲。	Nuclear exchange
4	IS	那个…class 是指那个…嗯…学生, 学生是可数的, 所以"一半学生", 后面的谓语动词应该用复数, 所以先把B和D排除掉, 然后后面 work 是不可数的, 所以谓语动词要用单数, 所以选A.	
5	T	Ok. Sit down, please. 答案选择A。Class, 我们讲,它是一个集体名词对吧?它可以作单数,指班级,如果强调的是班级成员, 班级里的学生, 那谓语动词就是复数啦。"half of the class" 指 "班级里的半数的学生" 已经完成了大部分的功课,所以用 have, 用复数形式, 而后面的"the rest of the work," work是不可数名词, "剩余的部分工作", the rest代替的是工作, 不可数, 所以用单数, 答案选择A。接下来, 我们看14题。……	

In sum, the exam stage was a special phase in the Danyang Project. As the upcoming exam was predictably form-oriented and stressed accuracy in learners' production, teacher and student behaviors at his stage reverted to traditional approaches.

5.5   The Post-project Stage (July 2013–January 2014)

At the post-project stage, Marian left the teacher education program of the Danyang Project, and moved to a new educational setting in which there were few exigent requirements for teachers to initiate or implement curriculum innovation. Now that she was in a new school, it was up to Marian to make pedagogical decisions. The lesson analyzed here, one of the regular lessons she gave to Level 7 students at the rural school, was audio-recorded by Marian herself. To ensure comparability between lessons, this lesson was selected because its teaching objectives (listening and speaking) were equivalent to those of the other lessons in this chapter.

5.5.1   Time Allotments to Different Activities of a Lesson

Table 5.21 shows a list of activities Marian carried out in this lesson. Surprisingly, there was a revival of innovative principles, or communicativeness, as most activities featured students' contributions, engagement, and meaning-oriented interaction. Activity 9, for example, was a guessing game like what young learners at this age played in their daily life, and complied with the basic principles of task-based language teaching.

The succession of activities recounted below show that Marian tended to draw on iconic episodes from her prior teaching experience, and incorporate them into her current teaching practices. Activity 2, for instance, was an exact reproduction of a typical presentation activity from the LAP course. The presenter was given the topic in advance, and there was a task planning process in which the learner drew on accessible linguistic and cognitive resources, before coming to the stage and giving the presentation, followed by feedback from her teacher and peers. Also, Activity 8 simulated the second activity of the lesson analyzed at the bottom-up stage – a guessing-game task with partially-covered PPT slides creating an information gap.

Table 5.21 Time allotment to different activities at the post-project stage

Activities	Time allotment	
	Duration (s.ms)	Percentage (%)
1. Greetings.	16.98	0.68
2. A student gave a presentation to introduce herself.	143.39	5.71
3. Lead-in. The teacher showed some pictures of sport stars on PPT slides, asked the students some questions and teaches several useful phrases.	225.46	8.98
4. Students worked out an exercise in the textbook and then the teacher checked their answers.	100.37	4.00
5. The teacher asked some students about their favorite sports. Next students worked in pairs to practice the dialogue. Then students were asked to perform the dialogue in groups.	197.17	7.85
6. The teacher asked the students to listen to a conversation and completed an exercise in the textbook. Then the teacher checked students' answers, asked them to read the conversation and invited some students to present the conversation in pairs.	278.00	11.07
7. The teacher demonstrated a conversation with one student, asked students to construct their own conversations in pairs and then called some pairs of students to present their conversations.	232.41	9.26
8. The teacher played a guessing game with the students. She showed on PPT slides some pictures about playing sports, with parts of the pictures intentionally covered and asked the students to guess what sport was being played.	268.29	10.69
9. The teacher organized a guessing game in which one student mimed to play a certain sport, another student who stood with his or her back towards the performer guessed the sport by asking some questions to the rest of the class.	461.92	18.40
10. The teacher presented two questions on a PPT slide. She asked the students to find the answers after listening to a dialogue. Then she taught some grammatical points in the dialogue, asked the student to read and acted it out in pairs before some students were called on to perform the dialogue.	310.04	12.35
11. The teacher initiated a free discussion with the student on the issue "the meaning of playing sports" and then presented some proverbs about playing sports.	208.08	8.29
12. The teacher gave a brief review of what's been learned in this class by asking the students to work out a blank-filling exercise, and then she assigned the homework.	68.05	2.71
Total	2510.16	100.00

5.5.2 Choice of Instructional Materials

Regarding the choice of instructional materials, Table 5.22 shows Marian's reliance on the mandated textbook was replaced by her confidence and expertise in adapting it to suit the teaching objectives of the lesson, and the specific requirements of each activity. Activity 3, for example, was designed as a warm-up activity to activate learners' background knowledge about the topic. Marian collected pictures of some popular athletes to supplement relevant content in the mandated textbook; in so doing, she overcame the drawbacks of the textbook, by adding updated information that was presumably more appealing to learners.

5.5.3   Teacher Talk

As shown in Table 5.23, teacher talk accounted for a larger percentage of classroom talk, in terms of both time and length. The average length per move in Marian's utterances slightly decreased (from 7.72 to 5.12 words), but her speaking speed increased from 1.88 to 2.19 words per second, indicating she spoke shorter sentences at a higher speed. The percentage of referential questions greatly increased at this stage.

5.5.4   Learner Talk

Learner talk comprised a lower time percentage and a higher length percentage at the post-project stage than at the bottom-up stage, as illustrated in Table 5.24. What is more, the amount and percentage of unrestricted moves in students' utterances increased to a large degree. The average length of individual learner talk decreased from 6.43 to 4.45 words per move.

Activities	Materials
A1	N/A
A2	Student-provided materials
A3	Teacher-designed materials
A4	Mandated textbook with teacher's adaptations
A5	Teacher-designed materials
A6	The mandated textbook with teacher's adaptation
A7	Teacher-designed materials
A8	Teacher-designed materials
A9	Teacher-designed materials
A10	The mandated textbook with teacher's adaptation
A11	Teacher-designed materials
A12	Teacher-designed materials

Table 5.22 Choice of instructional materials at the post-project stage

Table 5.23 Teacher talk at the post-project stage

		The post-project stage	The bottom-up stage
Time proportion		48.67%	40.67%
Length proportion		70.89%	58.43%
Average length/move (words/move)		5.12	7.72
Speaking speed (words/second)		2.19	1.88
Types of questions asked	Display questions	41 (51.25%)	51 (73.91%)
	Referential questions	39 (48.75%)	18 (26.09%)

Table 5.24 Learner talk at the bottom-up stage

		The post-project stage	The bottom-up stage
Time proportion		33.42%	39.76%
Length proportion		27.63%	24.90%
Types of learner talk	Restricted	116 (43.12%)	97 (58.43%)
	Unrestricted	153 (56.88%)	69 (41.57%)
Average length/move of individual learner talk (words/move)		4.45	6.43

5.5.5 Participatory Organization

Table 5.25 lists participatory organization patterns that accounted for more than 10% of classroom talk in Marian's class. As shown, the percentages of interaction between the teacher and all students, and between the teacher and individual students declined; the percentage of interaction between the teacher and some students remained almost unchanged; and there was an observable increase in the amount of student-student interaction.

Table 5.25 Participatory organization at the bottom-up stage

The post-project stage			The bottom-up stage		
Participatory organization pattern	Frequency	Percentage (%)	Participatory organization pattern	Frequency	Percentage (%)
T-AS	96	35.96	T-AS	78	40.41
T-IS	72	26.97	T-IS	78	40.41
T-SS	32	11.99	T-SS	23	11.92
IS-IS	28	10.49	–	–	–
Total exchanges	267	100.00	Total exchanges	193	100.00

(T—teacher; AS—all students; IS—individual student; SS—some students)

5.5.6   Focus on Meaning versus Form

The lesson was more meaning-oriented at the post-project stage, as the percentages of meaning-focused exchanges and those changes combining meaning and form both increased (see Table 5.26). Only a small proportion of classroom talk focused on linguistic forms, which was a large decrease from the preceding stage.

5.5.7   Discourse Structures

In comparison with the bottom-up stage, the percentage of IR discourse pattern greatly increased in this lesson, as shown in Table 5.27. At the post-project stage, the number of classroom interactions in an IR pattern nearly doubled from that seen at the bottom-up stage, and its percentage increased from 59.59% to 80.52%. The apparent increase could be attributed to the fact that students mostly supplied correct answers in response to Marian's questions, and she responded to their answers with positive non-verbal feedback such as eye contact, gesture, nods, etc.

Similarly, student-initiated exchanges also increased notably in terms of both quantity and percentage, indicating more student engagement in classroom interaction.

Table 5.26 Meaning- and form-focused exchanges at the bottom-up stage

Meaning versus form	The post-project stage		The bottom-up stage	
	Frequency	Percentage (%)	Frequency	Percentage (%)
Meaning-focused	177	66.29	103	53.37
Form-focused	48	17.98	79	40.93
Meaning + Form	42	15.73	11	5.70
Total exchanges	267	100.00	193	100.00

Table 5.27 Discourse structures at the bottom-up stage

Discourse patterns	The post-project stage		The bottom-up stage	
	Frequency	Percentage (%)	Frequency	Percentage (%)
IR	215	80.52	115	59.59
IRF	52	19.48	78	40.41
Teacher-initiated exchanges	213	79.78	178	92.23
Student-initiated exchanges	54	20.22	15	7.77
Total exchanges	267	100.00	193	100.00

5.5.8 Analyzing a Selected Episode

Episode 5–6 was selected from the first activity of this class. Here, a girl had finished giving a presentation entitled *Introducing Myself*, which was responded to with applause (moves 1–2). When the presenter was about to return to her seat, Marian stopped her, and reminded her to ask the audience some questions (moves 3–5), after which the presenter initiated two questions (moves 6 and 15). What makes the question-related exchanges interesting, is the role played by the teacher; she was neither an internal organizer (as in the first stage) nor an external spectator (as in the top-down stage) of classroom interaction, but she played a facilitative role by monitoring, prompting, and scaffolding to keep the flow of interaction moving and correct learners' errors. This shows a fusion of her and her students' roles in classroom interaction.

In addition, this episode shows Marian was more skilled in making interactive decisions at the appropriate time to give corrective feedback. In move 6, when the presenter was asked to elicit questions, she made two errors, which were not corrected by Marian. However, one error was corrected with a recast by another student, when she provided an answer (move 9). Moreover, Marian adopted an implicit strategy to correct students' errors in moves 18–20. When the student made an error in move 17, she repeated the erroneous part with a short pause indicating there was an error; this prompt was succeeded by the correction (move 19) uttered by all the students. Marian did not provide corrective feedback in a monolithic manner, and tended to involve other students in error correction.

Episode 5–6

1	T	Ok, thank you. <Clap hands.>	Dependent exchange
2	AS	<Clap hands.>	
3	T	Stop here. Stop here.	Preparatory exchange
		Do you have any questions to ask them?	
4	IS	Yes.	
5	T	Yes.	
6	IS	What my hobby? What are my hobby?	Nuclear exchange
		(silence)	
7	T	Yes? Yes?	
8	IS	Tom.	
9	IS	Your hobbies are swimming and reading.	
10	IS	Em, no… ***	
		(silence)	
11	T	Some others.	dependent exchange
		(silence)	
		Linda. Ok. Say.	

(continued)

(continued)

	IS	Listen to music and the chess.	
13	IS	Yes.	
		(Silence)	
14	T	Yes, ok, so any questions?	Nuclear exchange
15	IS	Em. How many people are my family?	
		(silence)	
16	IS	Ivy.	
17	IS	Your grandparents, parents, sister and your...	
18	T	Yes, and your...	Embedded exchange
		And...	
19	AS	you.	
20	T	Yes, ok. Thank you. Very good.	
21	AS	<Clap hands.>	Dependent exchange
22	T	Very good.	

To sum up, Marian's teaching practices switched back to a communicative manner when she went to a new educational setting. Overall, most classroom time was allocated to meaning-focused interaction, and Marian manipulated her teaching with more confidence and craft. Marian's re-adoption of the innovative principles entailed changes in students' classroom behaviors, as evidenced by increased learner participation in and initiation of classroom interactions.

5.6 A Synthesis of Quantified Changes

An overview of the teacher's behaviors in classroom instruction, as well as the observable verbal behaviors of her students throughout the five phases of this study, sheds light on our exploration of Marian's changes in teaching practices. The variance of behaviors, both qualitatively and quantitatively, underpins our recognition of the concrete evidence of changes taking place within the school-based curriculum innovation. This sub-section synthesizes the overall picture by tentatively sketching the changing trajectory of the investigated dimensions previously quantified.

5.6.1 Teacher Talk

Figure 5.1 describes how percentages of teacher talk changed from the pre-project stage to the post-project stage, in terms of time and length. There was a downward trend in these two indicators at the top-down stage; however, the statistics moved

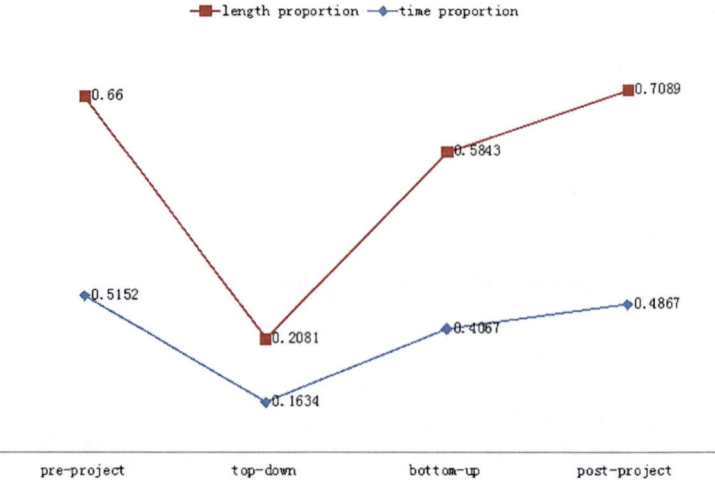

Fig. 5.1   The change of the quantity of teacher talk

upward continually at the two subsequent stages. At the end of the study, the percentages rose to values that differed insignificantly from those at the pre-project stage. These two indicators may vary in accordance with the intensity of innovative measures over the whole process.

While Fig. 5.1 addresses concerns about changes in the quantity of teacher talk, viz. how much Marian's utterances contributed to the whole classroom talk, Fig. 5.2 depicts how she talked over four stages of this study. There was a slight fluctuation in speaking speed over time, and the average length of move, which is more related to teacher talk complexity, increased steadily from the first to the third stages, before dropping to a value lower. While the average length of move in learner talk tended to vary in alignment with learners' levels of proficiency, the teacher's speaking speed was likely to vary with the communicativeness of the lesson.

The percentage of teacher-posed referential questions rose remarkably at the top-down stage, and then plummeted back to the starting point at the bottom-up stage, as shown in Fig. 5.3. After that, the value increased notably, surpassing that of the second stage. It could be found that the percentage of referential questions tended to correlate positively with the extent of communicativeness of class.

5.6.2   Learner Talk

Figure 5.4 shows how learner talk changed over time, in terms of its percentages of time and length. The values of these two indicators peaked at the top-down stage, and decreased sharply at the bottom-up stage, before levelling? off towards the end

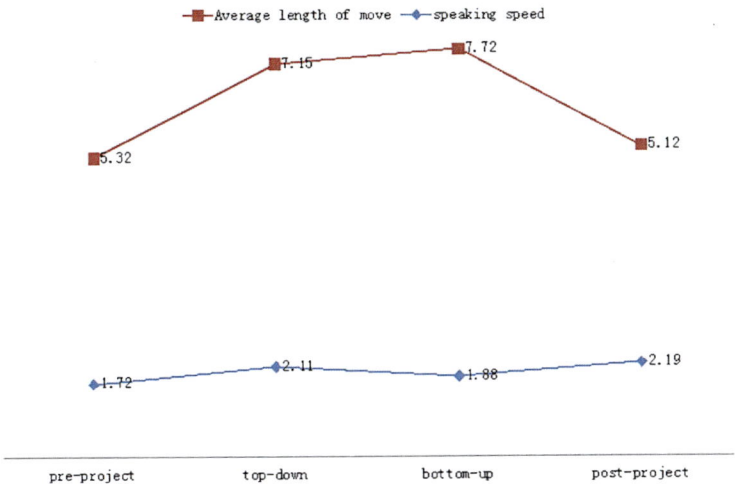

Fig. 5.2 The change of the length and speaking speed of teacher talk

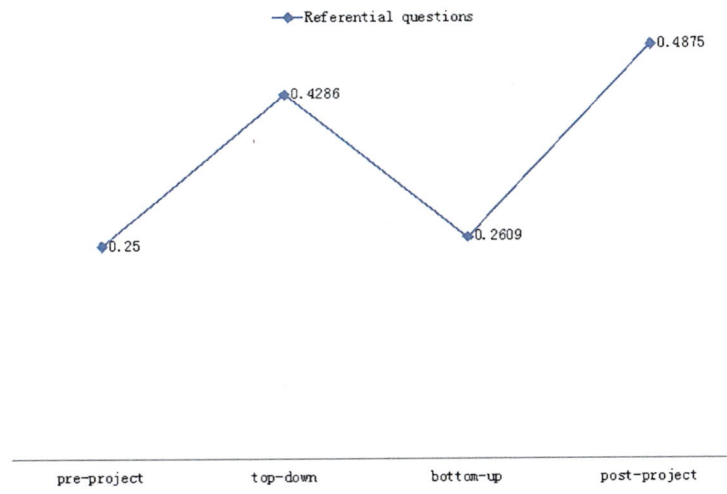

Fig. 5.3 The change of the percentage of referential questions

of the study. Thus, we could say these two indicators depended on the intensity of the innovation project, rather than on the communicativeness of the class.

As shown in Fig. 5.5 there was an uprising trend in the percentage of learners' unrestricted talk over the innovative project, with a slight dip at the third stage. It could be speculated that the changes could be attributed more to Marian's teaching capacity and the communicativeness of the lesson, than to the innovativeness of the teaching initiative.

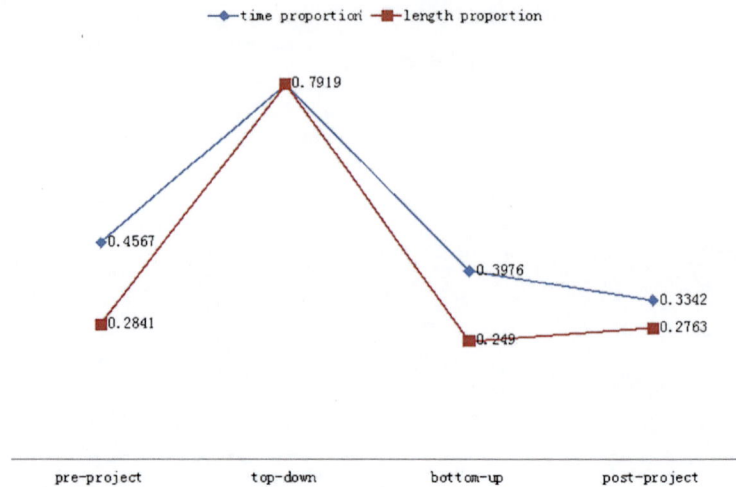

Fig. 5.4 The change of the quantity of learner talk

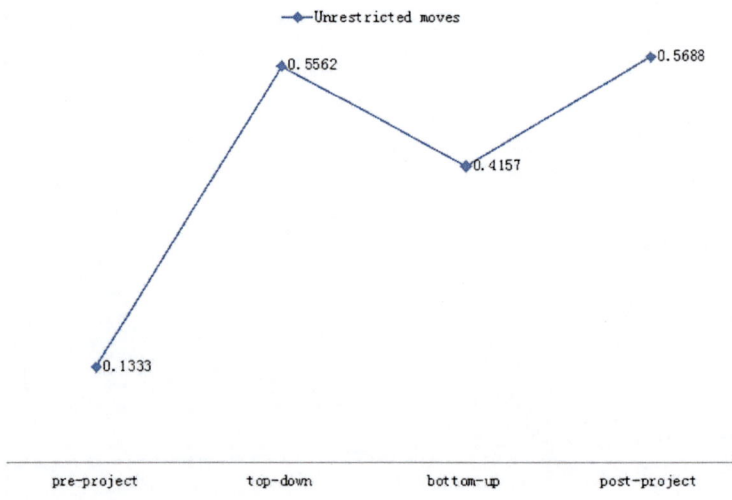

Fig. 5.5 The change of the quantity of unrestricted learner talk

Over the four phases under investigation, the average length per move of learner talk peaked at the top-down stage, and then decreased steadily until the end of the study (see Fig. 5.6). Given learners were deeply involved in well-planned performances at the second stage, it is not surprising they uttered longer phrases. Thus, it is likely the complexity of learner talk was more correlated with the design of task and learners' level of proficiency.

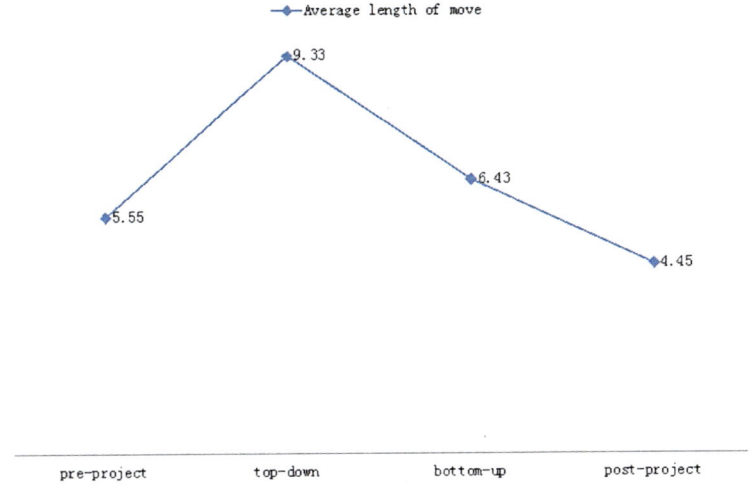

Fig. 5.6 The change of the average length per move of learner talk

5.6.3   *Participatory Organization*

As can be seen in Fig. 5.7 the percentage of student-initiated exchanges rocketed to its peak value at the top-down stage, and then dropped to around the same value as the percentage of the pre-project stage. Towards the end of the study, it bounced back to 25.08%, which was much higher than the value at the pre-project stage. Thus, it could be argued that the percentage of student-student interaction likely changed in accordance with the communicativeness of the class (Fig. 5.8).

5.6.4   *Focus on Meaning versus Form*

The percentage of form-focused exchanges was 42.11% at the pre-project stage, and decreased dramatically at the top-down stage, when innovative principles were enacted in a radical manner. As the project entered the bottom-up stage, the proportion of form-focused exchanges rose again, to 40.93%. In the last lesson planned independently by Marian, the percentage dropped to 17.98%. Thus, it is likely the percentage of form-focused exchanges varied with the communicativeness of the class.

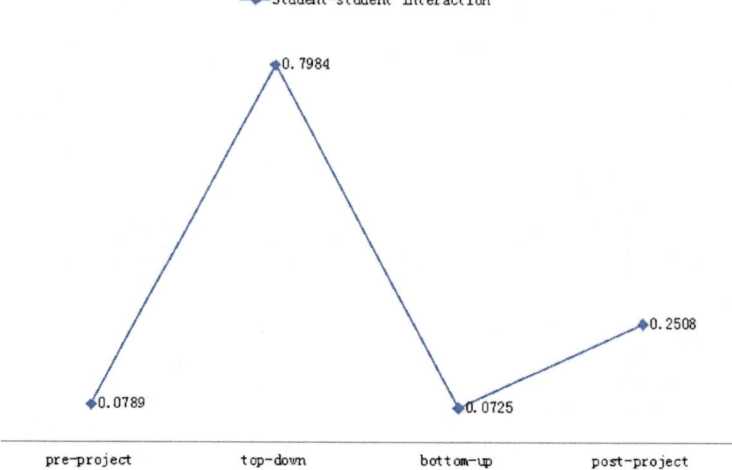

Fig. 5.7 The change of the student-student interaction

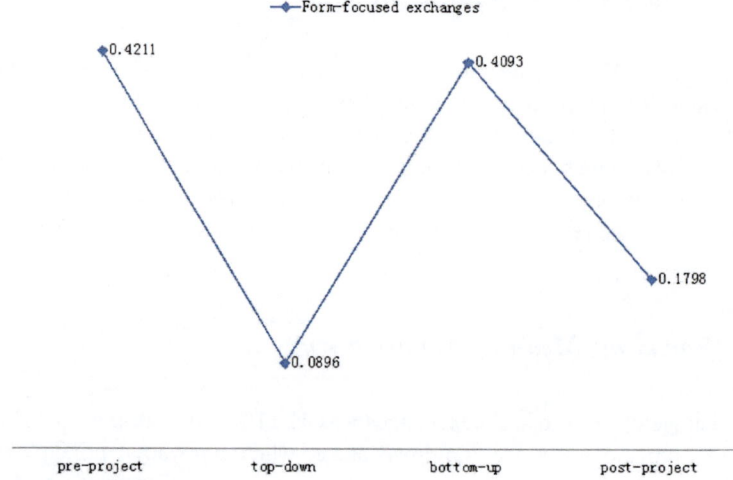

Fig. 5.8 The change of the form-focused exchanges

5.6.5 *Discourse Structures*

Figure 5.9 shows that the percentage of IRF discourse patterns did not vary greatly from the top-down to the bottom-up stage. However, in the last lesson examined, the figure dropped to 17.98%, which was much lower than the percentage in Marian's pre-project lesson. As was analyzed earlier in this chapter, the large

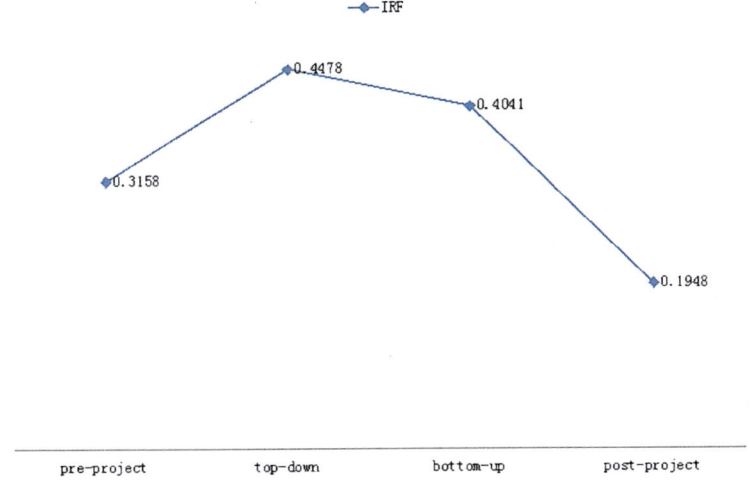

Fig. 5.9 The change of the IRF discourse patterns

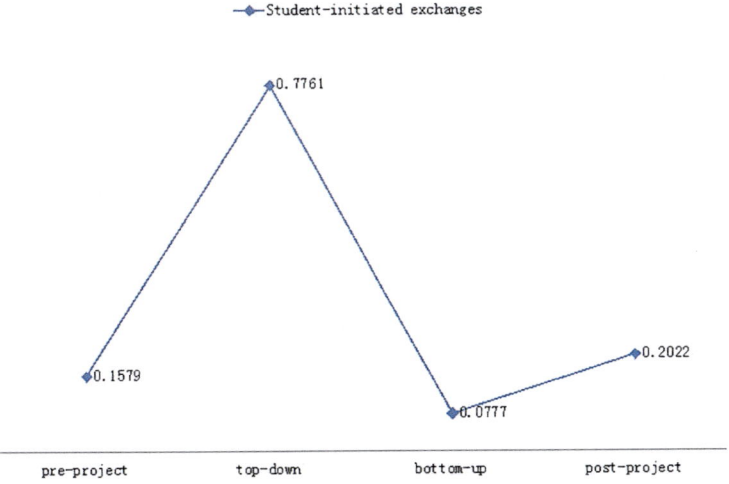

Fig. 5.10 The change of the student-initiated exchanges

decrease might have been caused by Marian's providing more non-verbal feedback to students' responses.

The fluctuating line in Fig. 5.10 indicates the percentage of moves initiated by learners. The figure reached its highest point at the top-down stage, and slightly recovered at the end of the project, after a dramatic decrease at the bottom-up stage. Thus, it could be found that student-initiated exchanges are likely to change in relation to the communicativeness of the class.

5.7 Summary

A synthesis of the path tracking the changes in Marian's and her students' classroom behaviors reveals four prominent patterns:

(1) At the top-down stage, curriculum innovation had prominent effects on almost all aspects of classroom behavior.

(2) The bottom-up stage witnessed reduced implementation of innovation, evidenced by the backward changes in all indicators, except the average length per move in teacher talk. Nevertheless, this phase was a silent period in which the innovation principles were internalized, rather than a passive retreat by a teacher resistant to change.

(3) The post-project stage provides evidence of the sustained effect of the Danyang Project, as evidenced by the reviving trends in most aspects of classroom behaviors.

(4) Among the ten indicators under investigation, four did not vary in accordance with the intensity of innovation, including the quantity of teacher talk, the length and speaking speed of teacher talk, average length per move of learner talk, and IRF discourse patterns. Therefore, it could be argued that Marian's and her students' classroom behaviors were not exclusively influenced by the implementation of innovative principles; rather, they were also affected by other factors, including the attributes of tasks, the levels of learners' proficiency, the teacher's expertise to make interactive pedagogical decisions, etc.

Chapter 6
Teacher Cognition and Practices: Project versus Non-project and Consistency versus Inconsistency

To triangulate what has been found so far, this chapter compares the cognition and practices of Marian and Jane (a non-project teacher) towards the end of the DP. While examining the differences in Marian's teaching practices over the five stages within curriculum innovation reveals the path of change over the time she participated in the innovative project, it might be argued that those changes observed in Chap. 5 might not be exclusively attributable to the implementation of the DP. The argument is plausible, given that this school-based innovation project was not an insular context in which PTs lived, learned, and interacted. Thus, there is an obvious necessity to compare teacher cognition, as well as teacher and student behaviors in project and non-project classrooms, to triangulate evidence to justify the influence of the DP on the project teacher's cognition and teaching practices.

In this chapter, a selected dyad of lessons taught by the project teacher (PT) and a non-project teacher (NPT) towards the end of the Danyang Project are comparatively analyzed. In-depth post-observation interviews were conducted to examine the similarities in and distinctions between the two teachers' cognition on different aspects of classroom instruction. To map teachers' cognition with their teaching practices, the analysis of classroom observation data are followed by interview data.

In addition, this chapter also examines the relationship between project teacher's cognition and classroom practices, by juxtaposing what has been found so far about the changes in these two entities.

6.1 Background and Sampling of Project and Non-Project Teachers and Classrooms

6.1.1 Background

In the spring semester of 2013, the TRG (Teaching Research Group) of HES school organized an activity in which teachers gave public lessons for peer observation within the group. In this activity, as its name "same lesson, different planning" (*tongke yigou*) suggested, the same content was assigned to teachers, while allowing them to do their own separate lesson planning. Marian and other project teachers, with their colleagues in the TRG, participated in the activity as both observees and observers. The TRG provided teachers in the group guiding lesson and planning materials, including recommended teaching agenda, PPTs, worksheets containing key language points, and exercises. The teachers who participated as observers used a classroom observation scheme (see Appendix 11) formulated by the school's Office of Academic Affairs (*Jiaowu Chu*). As the observation form was originally designed to be used by teachers of all subjects, it was global and unfocussed—that is, no specific aspects of classroom instruction were addressed. Post-observation feedback, normally provided by the head of the TRG, was directed at any salient scenarios that interested the observers.

As the researcher had built a rather harmonious rapport with people in the setting, she was invited to join in the activity during her visits to the school. Her request to video-record some lessons and conduct post-observation interviews with the involved teachers was supported. By maximizing available logistical resources, a total of seven lessons were video-recorded by the end of the semester. The teachers who gave the public lessons were only informed one day in advance, to ensure the authenticity of the observed lessons, by largely excluding the possibility the lessons were rehearsed. Of the recorded lessons, two were selected for analysis, based on the comparability of the teachers' demographic and professional background, and the equivalence of the contents taught.

6.1.2   Sampling of Project and Non-Project Teachers and Classrooms

Marian's demographic and professional background led the researcher to select Jane as a representative non-project teacher. Jane was also born in 1974, and was thus the same age as Marian. She graduated from the same provincial teachers' college where Marian had studied with an education diploma before she started teaching in 1996. Jane's first teaching position was also at a county-level secondary school, where she had worked for twelve years, during which period she received her Bachelor of English through attending a correspondence program (from 1997 to 2001). Since 2006, Jane had been working at Huanan Experimental School.

Thus, both Marian and Jane were female, of the same age, and had similar education experiences. When their lessons were observed and recorded, Marian had been teaching for twenty years and Jane, nineteen. Both teachers came to teach at HES in 2006, taught the same level of students, and worked in the same the TRG. A major difference between these two teachers was that Marian had been participating in the Danyang Project for nearly four years at the time. Table 6.1, documents the background information of the lessons taught by Marian and Jane, respectively.

Consistent with the framework within which the analysis was conducted in Chap. 5, observable student and teacher behaviors in these two lessons were

Table 6.1 Background information of Marian's and Jane's lessons

Teacher	Lesson			
	Target language skills	Date	Duration (m. s)	Number of students
Marian (PT)	Listening and speaking	Mar. 07, 2013	57.10	55
Jane (NPT)	Listening and speaking	Mar. 07, 2013	40.06	54

inductively analyzed and compared to examine similarities and differences, in seven aspects: (1) time allotment to different activities of a lesson; (2) choice of instructional materials; (3) teacher talk—quantity/types of questions asked; (4) student talk—amount/average length per move; (5) participatory organization; (6) focus on meaning versus form; and, (7) discourse structures, including IRF and student-initiated exchanges.

As shown in Table 6.1, the total amount of teaching time for these two lessons was different. Given the epistemological underpinning of this study, it was speculated that artificially truncating the longer lesson would impair its entirety and natural attributes; thus, the unit of comparison in the quantitative data analysis was percentage, to ensure equivalence of comparison.

6.2   Comparing a Dyad of Classrooms

6.2.1   Time Allotments to Different Activities of a Lesson

Time allotments were examined in this study as indicators signaling how activities carried out in a lesson contributed to the achievement of instructional goals. Table 6.2 displays the teaching activities and their time allotments in both lessons. This table shows that Marian and Jane roughly followed a sequence of *'presenting topic—explicit instruction—practice—performance,'* with some cyclic steps in between to reinforce what was taught. This major similarity could be explained by the fact that both teachers had access to and largely relied on guiding materials provided by the TRG while doing their lesson planning.

However, one recognizable distinction existed in the penultimate activities in this pair of lessons—i.e., Activity 14 in Marian's, and Activity 15 in Jane's lessons. In Jane's lesson, she spent 7.45% of total time (Activity 15) summarizing important language forms, while requiring students to underline those words and phrases in their textbooks for rote learning. However, at the equivalent stage in Marian's lesson, there was a debate task (Activity 14) in which students were assigned into two groups arguing on an issue related to the topic they had just learned. This task accounted for 18.73% of the total time. In a sense, this part was a departure from traditional pedagogy, as enacting a debate task is communicative, rather than explicit, instruction of discrete language forms.

Table 6.2 Time allotment to different activities in the two lessons

Marian (PT)			Jane (NPT)		
Activities/Episodes	Time allotment		Activities/Episode	Time allotment	
	Duration (s.ms)	Percentage		Duration (s.ms)	Percentage
(1) Greeting and opening remarks.	1.91	0.06%	(1) Greeting and opening remarks.	5.91	0.25%
(2) Lead-in and warm-up.	222.96	6.44%	(2) Lead-in and warm-up.	57.01	2.36%
(3) The teacher presented the topic and taught the pronunciations of some new words.	204.25	5.90%	(3) The teacher presented the topic and taught the pronunciations of some new words.	252.51	10.47%
(4) Students read a passage about Marie Curie freely and answered some questions.	172.11	4.97%	(4) Students read the passage about Marie Curie in chorus and the teacher taught the pronunciations of new words again.	62.80	2.60%
(5) Students read the text again and worked out a gap-filling exercise in textbook.	320.40	9.25%	(5) Students read the passage freely, worked out a gap-filling exercise and then the teacher checked the answers.	206.37	8.56%
(6) Students listened to a passage and worked out part of the second gap-filling exercise.	474.32	13.69%	(6) Students listened to a passage twice and filled in the rest of the gaps of the exercise	444.59	18.43%
(7) Students worked out the rest part of the gap-filling exercise in the textbook.	353.44	10.20%	(7) Students read a text in the textbook, worked out the second gap-filling exercise, and then the teacher checked the answers.	213.81	8.87%
(8) Students learned the pronunciation of new words again and students read the passage aloud freely.	86.96	2.51%	(8) Students read the passage with filled gaps aloud freely.	69.48	2.88%
(9) Q&A competition.	150.70	4.35%	(9) Q&A competition.	156.47	6.49%
(10) Students listened to a dialogue and answered some questions.	124.72	3.60%	(10) Students listened to a dialogue and answered some questions.	126.48	5.24%

(continued)

Table 6.2 (continued)

Marian (PT)			Jane (NPT)		
Activities/Episodes	Time allotment		Activities/Episode	Time allotment	
	Duration (s.ms)	Percentage		Duration (s.ms)	Percentage
(11) Students read the dialogue synchronously following the tape.	93.01	2.69%	(11) Students read the dialogue following the tape sentence by sentence	105.08	4.36%
(12) Students read the dialogue aloud freely.	98.72	2.85%	(12) Students were divided into 2 groups and each group read one role's part in the dialogue in chorus	56.86	2.36%
(13) Pair work: students made their own dialogues by using sentence structures in samples given by the teacher.	509.95	14.72%	(13) Students read the dialogue in pairs freely	141.67	5.87%
(14) Student performed a debate task.	648.72	18.73%	(14) Students made their own dialogues following the pattern	330.70	13.71%
(15) Concluding remarks.	2.38	00.07%	(15) The teacher pointed out some important language points and students underlined them in the textbook	179.70	7.45%
			(16) Concluding remarks	2.40	0.10%
Total	3464.54	100.00%	Total	2411.84	100.00%

The following section further examines this part in the lesson planning guide offered by the TRG. Teachers were advised to prepare and present a news report at the end of the class, in which students were required to read a passage about some famous people in Chinese (learners' L1), construct a related news report, and present it to the whole class. From the alignment of activities in both lessons, neither teacher followed the guiding agenda at this stage. To probe into their decision-making processes, post-observation interviews were conducted with Marian and Jane, respectively. When asked, immediately after finishing teaching, to reflect on this activity, Jane thought it an indispensable step that highlighted important lexical and grammatical items. However, Marian told the researcher she had been quite skeptical about the communicativeness of this news report task, and expressed her concern that it could be transformed into an interpretation exercise, as students had access to the Chinese text while giving their oral presentation. As she had experience in successfully conducting a debate task, she decided to do it again, as a substitute for the mandated news report task.

A second major difference emerged when the overall time proportion of activities, in terms of different modalities, was counted. As both Marian and Jane claimed the target language skills of their lessons to be "listening and speaking," it was interesting that, in Jane's class, only 13.71% of the time (Activity 14) was focused on speaking; in addition, the 'speaking' was simply practicing patterned drills presented by the teacher on PPT slides. Apart from this activity, the only other chances for students in Jane's class to speak English involved either chorusing the teacher's or the audio input, or reading a given text aloud. In the post-observation interview, when asked to elaborate on her conception of speaking skills, Jane's response indicated a strong inclination to restricted oral production, with a strong emphasis on accuracy; she was rather frank in admitting that she kept examinations in mind while preparing her lessons and making interactive decisions during teaching.

In Marian's lesson, however, two activities (Activities 13 and 14) involving developing students' speaking skills consumed more than one-third of class time. What is more, there was a transition from focused to unfocused language production in these two activities. In the post-observation interview with Marian, when talking about designing tasks to elicit oral production, she used phrases like "express meaning," "get meaning across" quite a few times, and no phrases related to "forms" or "exams."

As to listening, Activities 6 and 10 were organized by both teachers to develop students' listening skills, and no significant difference could be found in their respective time allotments. In Marian's lesson, the overall time spent in Activities 6 and 10 was 599.04 s, which accounted for 17.29% of the overall time. In Jane's lesson, the time span of these two activities was 571.07 s, accounting for 23.68% of the time. Nevertheless, a closer look at what happened in these two listening-focused activities unveiled a notable difference at the pre-listening stage, in which Marian conducted listening strategy training, whereas Jane did not. In the post-observation interview, when asked to reflect on the activities involving listening practice in their lessons, Jane's response indicated little knowledge or awareness about strategy training. In contrast, Marian explicitly stated why and how she trained her students to read the text seeded with blanks, and then predict what could probably be heard before students were exposed to the listening material.

6.2.2 Choice of Instructional Materials

Table 6.3, shows how Marian and Jane used instructional materials in distinct ways. In Activity 2, Activity 13, and Activity 14, Marian made adaptations to the mandated textbooks. Specifically, when undertaking Activity 2, both teachers roughly followed the TRG's teaching guide, in which some pictures of famous

Table 6.3 Choices of instructional materials in the two lessons

Marian (PT)		Jane (NPT)	
Activities	Materials	Activities	Materials
A2	Mandated textbook with teacher's revision	A2–A15	Mandated textbook
A3–A12	Mandated textbook		
A13	Mandated textbook with teacher's revision		
A14	Teacher designed a task		

Table 6.4 Teacher talk in the two lessons

		Marian (PT)	Jane (NPT)
Time proportion		40.47%	36.13%
Length proportion		58.43%	48.02%
Average length/move (words/move)		7.72	5.19
Speaking speed (words/second)		1.88	1.72
Types of questions asked	Display questions	51 (73.91%)	22 (100.00%)
	Referential questions	18 (26.09%)	0 (0.00%)

people were used to introduce the topic of the lesson with a guessing game. While Jane strictly stuck to the provided material design, Marian adapted the PPT by adding extra pictures, and intentionally covering certain parts of the pictures she used, to make the task "more challenging" by enlarging the information gap (Table 6.4).

In Activity 13, students were required to work in pairs and construct dialogues, using two structures they had learned in earlier sessions of the lesson. This activity was designed by the TRG in a very restricted way, as the target dialogue with some blanks was presented on a PPT slide. Also in the slide were several pictures of famous people; students were required to choose one, and use background information about that person to make a dialogue. The six famous people in the mandated PPT slide included Bill Gates, Yang Chen-Ning, Deng Xiaoping, Mother Teresa, Yang Liwei and Yao Ming. Extract 6.1, is the dialogue recommended in the TRG's teaching guide.

Extract 6.1

1 A: Who do you think is the greatest person that has ever lived?
2 B: _____. I admire him/her the most.
3 A: What did _____ do?
4 B: He's/She's _____.
5 A: Why do you admire him/her?
6 B: Because_____.

When organizing this activity, Jane strictly followed the teaching guide; when Marian's lesson adapted this part of the teaching materials into the following dialogue (shown in Extract 6.2). What is more, Marian also telescoped the given materials by reducing the number of pictures in the slide from six to three.

Extract 6.2
1 A: Who do you think is the greatest person that_____?
2 B: I admire _____ the most.
3 A: What did he do?
4 B: He is _____.
5 A: Why do you admire _____?
6 B: Because _____.
7 A: What do you want to be in the future?
8 B: I want to be a _____ like _____.
9 A: What will you do to realize your dream?
10 B: I will _____.

As can be seen from the adapted conversation, Marian added four moves (7–10) to the suggested materials in her teaching planning. As the famous people displayed on the PPT slide were well-known to most students, there was no meaningful information gap in the original dialogue. In the post-observation interview, Marian expressed her concern that the activity guide might have been too unchallenging for the students; thus, she adapted it to suit students' cognitive and linguistic competence better. The moves she had added were likely to elicit unpredictable information, and thus involve students in negotiation of meaning. Nevertheless, in the post-observation interview with Jane, she expressed no awareness of changing the activity design recommended by the TRG.

6.2.3 Teacher Talk

The differences in teacher talk in Marian's and Jane's lessons are illustrated in Table 5.4. Teacher talk accounted for a larger proportion of time in Marian's lesson than in Jane's (40.47% > 36.13%). As to the overall length of teacher talk, the percentage of Marian's talk exceeded that of Jane's (58.43% > 48.02%). Moreover, Marian uttered relatively longer clauses than Jane, as her average length per move was longer (7.72 > 5.19), and she spoke at a slightly higher speed (1.88 > 1.72).

Marian asked a large percentage (26.09%) of referential questions in her class, whereas no referential questions were found in Jane's. In the post-observation interview, when asked how to address the claimed teaching objectives of the lessons just taught, Marian stressed learner participation, while Jane emphasized accuracy, as it indicated students were "grasping the content in the textbook."

6.2.4 Learner Talk

Table 6.5 shows Marian's and Jane's lessons did not differ much in learner talk in terms of the percentages of time and length. However, a major distinction was found in the percentage of unrestricted learner talk, which accounted for 41.57% of

Table 6.5 Learner talk in the two lessons

		Marian (PT)	Jane (NPT)
Time proportion		39.76%	40.53%
Length proportion		24.90%	30.64%
Types of learner talk	Restricted	97 (58.43%)	120 (90.91%)
	Unrestricted	69 (41.57%)	12 (9.09%)
Average length/move of individual learner talk (words/move)		6.43	8.39

classroom talk in Marian's class, was much higher than that in the lesson taught by Jane. Learners in Jane's class tended to utter longer clauses, probably because most their moves were repetitions of sentences spoken by the teacher or the audio tape, entailing longer learner production.

6.2.5   Participatory Organization

Table 6.6, lists the frequencies of the major participatory organization patterns and their percentages in Marian's and Jane's lessons. The data are arrayed in descending order. One major similarity was that the dominant participatory organization patterns in both teachers' lessons were teacher-student interaction, with interaction between the teacher and all students comprising large percentages of both lessons. Despite this primary similarity, two main differences were explicit between the two lessons. In Marian's lesson, there were fewer cases of interaction between the teacher and all students, and more cases of interaction between the teacher and individual students, and between the teacher and some students. As to student-student interaction, the percentage was also higher in Marian's class.

In the post-observation interview, when asked about their attitude towards classroom interaction and learner engagement in teaching, Marian expressed a

Table 6.6 Frequencies of participatory organization patterns in the two lessons

Marian (PT)			Jane (NPT)		
Participatory organization pattern	Frequency	Percentage	Participatory organization pattern	Frequency	Percentage
T-AS	78	40.41%	T-AS	65	48.51%
T-IS	78	40.41%	T-IS	36	26.87%
T-SS	23	11.92%	T-SS	12	8.96%
S-S	15	7.77%	S-S	3	2.24%
Total exchanges	193	100.0%	Total exchanges	134	100.00%

(T—teacher; S—student; AS—all students; IS—individual student; SS—some students)

positive conception of students' participation in classroom instruction, whereas Jane valued the teacher's role as a conduit of knowledge.

6.2.6 Focus on Meaning versus Form

To examine the communicativeness of the two lessons, exchanges were inductively coded. The data fell into three categories: meaning-focused exchanges; form-focused exchanges; and meaning + form exchanges. Table 6.7 displays the frequency and percentage of the three types of exchanges in both teachers' lessons. The frequency and percentage of meaning-focused exchanges in Marian's lesson far outnumbered those in Jane's, indicating Marian's lesson was more communicative and meaning-oriented. By comparison, Jane's lesson, which largely drew on linguistic forms, was quite traditional.

In the post-observation interview, the researcher asked each of the two teachers to reflect on a selected instructional step that dealt with a gap-filling exercise in the mandated textbook, requiring students to listen to a short passage and fill in the blanks. In the textbook, this exercise was the second of two exercises based on the same listening material; the first was designed to check learners' comprehension. The arrangement of these two exercises was arguably problematic, for it repeatedly emphasized improving listening skills, while giving little attention to speaking practice. When teaching this part, Jane gave students some time to fill in the blanks, and then checked their answers one by one.

Reflecting on this teaching scenario, Jane said she did "exactly what the textbook writer required us to do," and she did it following the lesson plan jointly prepared by all the teachers in the TRG. She also told the researcher that "limited time was allocated to this activity because there was a haste to cover the content in the mandated textbook." Thus, Jane's decision was largely influenced or even governed by 'authoritative' factors, viz. the textbook and the TRG, in this setting. When a teacher's aim is to follow a pre-planned teaching agenda or mandated textbook without fully understanding and accepting its rationale, it is unlikely that he or she can teach for the purpose of fostering effective learning.

Marian did some adaptations, by adding a retelling task to this exercise—that is, asking students to fill in the blanks according to what they had heard, and then formulate a presentation retelling the passage. However, this was not satisfactorily done, for most students read the passage, rather than retelling it. In the post-observation interview, when asked to reflect on this instructional step, Marian thought her instruction could be improved by re-designing the task to "give students more chances to speak instead of reading." She also proposed changing the blank-filling exercise into a dictogloss task, as introduced by teacher educator in an earlier seminar. Given the observed self-criticism and reflection, it was found that Marian had moved away from passively following the mandated textbook or recommended teaching agenda, and was gradually formulating her personalized theory

Table 6.7 Meaning- and form-focused exchanges in the two lessons

Meaning versus form	Marian (PT)		Jane (NPT)	
	Frequency	Percentage	Frequency	Percentage
Meaning-focused	102	52.85%	28	20.90%
Form-focused	80	41.45%	90	67.16%
Meaning + Form	11	5.70%	16	11.94%
Total exchanges	193	100.00%	134	100.00%

of teaching, by undergoing a spiral upgrading process of testing, reflecting on, criticizing, and re-testing teaching theory.

6.2.7 Discourse Structures

Table 6.8, shows how classroom discourse structure differed between the two lessons. The percentage of IRF in Marian's lesson slightly outnumbered that in Jane's lesson, as did the percentage of student-initiated exchanges. Given the total number of exchanges in Marian's lesson was notably higher, the amount of IRF and student-initiated exchanges was much larger. The quantitative distinction indicated that Marian, the project teacher, was more likely to provide feedback to learners' responses and create opportunities for learners to initiate classroom talk.

Taking a close look at the distribution of student-initiated exchanges in each activity, shows most student-initiated exchanges existed in activities in which students were performing tasks (Activities 13 and 14, shown in Table 6.9), as "task-based teaching affords opportunities for student-initiated discourse" (Ellis, 2012, p. 92).

In the post-observation interview, when asked about their attitudes towards tasks in language teaching, Jane thought she would consider designing "one or two interesting activities" if she had "enough time"; otherwise, she would rather "make full use of classroom time to consolidate linguistic forms." In contrast, Marian thought the task was an effective way to liven up a lesson, motivate learners, and enhance learner engagement; however, she did not show any preference between

Table 6.8 Discourse structures in the two lessons

Discourse patterns	Marian (PT)		Jane (NPT)	
	Frequency	Percentage	Frequency	Percentage
IR	115	59.59%	86	64.18%
IRF	78	40.41%	48	35.82%
Teacher-initiated exchanges	178	92.23%	129	96.27%
Student-initiated exchanges	15	7.77%	5	3.73%
Total exchanges	193	100.00%	134	100.00%

Table 6.9 Student-initiated exchanges in PT's lesson

Activity	Initiator	Frequency	Total exchanges
A13	PS	2	13
A14	IS	7	26
	AS	1	
	SS	1	

(PS—paired student; IS—individual student; AS—all students; SS—some students)

task-based teaching and traditional explicit instruction. Regarding the two teachers' cognition about task-based teaching, Marian could be arguably positioned closer to the communicative end.

6.2.8 Analyzing Selected Episodes

Episodes 6.1 and 6.2, were selected from Marian's and Jane's lesson, respectively. The first episode documents part of the interaction in the lead-in activity, which was designed to activate learners' background knowledge relating to the topic. As analyzed in Sect. 5.5.8 of Chap. 5, the constituent structure of Marian's classroom discourse was more complex, containing more bound exchanges. Here, Marian was pointing to a picture on a PPT slide and asking a student named Celina (pseudonym) to guess who the person in it was (move 1). While the first answer given by Celina (move 2) was incorrect, Marian did not judge its correctness explicitly; instead, she hinted the probable error in Celina's answer with hesitation (Err…) and a rhetoric question (Really?), which prompted the learner to rethink her answer and come up with another (move 4). Again, Marian did not make judgment of the answer, and instead handed the task to the whole class (move 5), entailing the engagement of more students. What is more, the right answer alone did not draw this episode to an end; moves 8–10 constituted a dependent exchange entailing extended, meaning-focused, and unrestricted learner production.

In contrast, Episode 6.2, selected from Jane's lesson, took on a much simpler, enclosed pattern. Here, Jane was checking students' answers to a listening comprehension exercise. This episode consisted of an array of sequences, but contained only one IRF nuclear exchange. The follow-up moves in these exchanges were rather mechanical and rigid, regardless of learners' response. Her moves following learners' responses normally contained full or partial repetition of the student's answer, evaluative feedback, and acknowledgement. There was no justification, clarification, or exemplification to involve learners in negotiation of form or meaning.

In comparison, the constituent structures of the two lessons differed largely between the two teachers' lessons. Bound exchanges (dependent exchanges and embedded exchanges) in the episode taught by Marian outnumbered those in the one taught by Jane. It was in the bound exchanges that negotiation of meaning occurred, which, in turn, was likely to entail language learning.

Episode 6.1 (PT)

1	T	Ok. Next one. Next one.	Nuclear exchange
		Who is he? Who is he? Or who is she?	
		Celina, try to guess.	
2	IS	*** (inaudible)	
3	T	Err…Really?	Embedded exchange
4	IS	(Silence) <The student is thinking.>	
		Elvis Presley.	
5	T	Elvis Presley.	Embedded exchange
		Let's see. Yes or no?	
6	AS	Yes.	
7	T	Yes. Very good.	
8	T	So, can you describe him?	Dependent exchange
9	IS	He is a singer. He is the king of rock and roll.	
10	T	Good.	
		He is the king of rock and roll.	

Episode 6.2 (NPT)

1	T	Peter, please.	Nuclear exchange
		(Silence)	
2	IS	Columbus discovered the American people.	
3	T	Columbus discovered the America.	
		Thanks. Please.	
4	T	(Silence)	
		Ok. Now, next one.	
5	IS	***	Nuclear exchange
		<S answers the question not very fluently.>	
6	T	Penny.	
		Thank you. Good.	
7	T	Amy. Please.	Nuclear exchange
8	IS	Bruce Lee made a ***	
9	T	Err, Bruce Lee.	
		Thank you. Sit down.	
10	T	Next one. <Point to a student.>	Nuclear exchange
11	IS	Maria Currie discovered the radium.	
12	T	En. Maria Currie.	
		Thank you. Very good.	

6.3 Summary of Similarities and Differences in PT's Lesson and NPT's Lesson

To conclude, the major similarities in the two teachers' lessons are as follows. First, the lessons delivered by both teachers roughly followed a PPP procedure, as recommended by the TRG. Second, both the project teacher and the non-project teacher primarily relied on mandated textbooks. Third, no significant disparity was found in teacher talk in either lesson, in terms of time duration and percentage of moves. Fourth, the most frequent participatory patterns in both lessons were exchanges between the teacher and all students, the teacher and individual students, and the teacher and some students. Fifth, IRF patterns dominated classroom discourse in both lessons, and more than half of the exchanges in each lesson took an IR pattern. Sixth, student-initiated exchanges accounted for a minor proportion of classroom discourse in both teachers' lessons.

Despite these resemblances, there were also evident distinctions between the lessons. First, there was more congruence between the time proportion to different activities or tasks and the stated instructional objectives in Marian's lesson. Second, the way Marian adapted the mandated teaching materials and tasks, combined with the beliefs underpinning her teaching behaviors, revealed she was more autonomous in making pedagogical decisions. Third, judging from its overall length and average length per move, teacher talk was more complex in Marian's lesson than in Jane's. Fourth, there was more paired and individual student talk in Marian's lesson, resulting from more pair and group work her class. Fifth, the participatory organization patterns in Marian's lesson had greater variations; there were more types of participatory organization patterns involving her in her lesson, indicating a better integration between the teacher and students. Sixth, Marian's lesson was more communicative-oriented, because the frequency and percentage of meaning-focused exchanges therein far outnumbered those in Jane's lesson. Seventh, the constituent structure of Marian's lesson was comparatively more elaborate, with more types of exchanges and a larger average number of exchanges per sequence. There were also noticeably more IRF exchanges in her lesson, and she was more adept at manipulating the feedback move to cater to contextual realities and individual learners' cognitive and socio-cultural attributes.

6.4 Summary of Similarities and Differences in PT's Cognition and NPT's Cognition

Comparing Marian's and Jane's cognition shows a rough consistency in their cognition and teaching behaviors. Both teachers' cognitions on the nature of language and language teaching were largely influenced by their education background and prior work experience. Their beliefs about foreign language teaching were basically traditional and structure-oriented, stressing grasping discrete linguistic components. Moreover, the contingent environment they were exposed to, particularly the interaction with the TRG and other colleagues at school, exerted direct influence on the decisions they made in classroom instruction.

Despite these similarities, differences were also found in Marian's and Jane's cognitions. In comparison with Jane, Marian espoused communicative teaching more and manifested more autonomy in designing and using instructional materials. She valued the task and classroom interaction it brought forth, regarding it as an effective way to facilitate language learning. Though still influenced by traditional recognition about language teaching, Marian was more communicative-oriented than her counterparts in non-project classes.

6.5 Relationship between Teacher Cognition and Classroom Practices: Consistency versus Inconsistency

So far, trajectories of changes over the innovation project have been delineated regarding Marian's cognition and classroom practices, in comparison with a non-project teacher with similar demographic and professional background, to gather triangulated evidence. Now, we can answer the third research question: What relationship is there between the changes in the teacher's cognition and changes in his/her classroom practices?

6.5.1 The Pre-project Stage

Before Marian participated into the Danyang Project, her cognition was consistent with her classroom practices. She had a limited understanding of FLT theory and innovative principles, and what she perceived to be right with teaching was largely based on intuition that emerged from her learning and teaching experience. Her classroom behavior was traditional, remaining intact before the project was initiated.

6.5.2 The Top-Down Stage

However, at the top-down stage, divergent themes were found relating to Marian's cognition. That is, though she willingly accepted the innovative principles and tried out the new pedagogy in classroom instruction, she still embraced the effectiveness of a traditional grammar-focused and teacher-fronted teaching approach. Marian's classroom practices showed a strong tendency toward communicative, student-centered, meaning-oriented classroom instruction. Thus, Marian's cognition did not completely conform to her teaching practices, at the top-down stage.

6.5.3 The Bottom-Up Stage

When the Danyang Project moved to the bottom-up stage, Marian's cognition favored an eclectic approach combining communicative teaching with classroom realities, as did her practices. Therefore, Marian's cognition was consistent with her practices at the third stage.

6.5.4 The Exam Stage

When Marian and her colleagues were preparing for the high-stakes exam, she firmly believed that exam scores were the "lifeline" for her students, and her teaching practices were exam-oriented. However, when Marian was involved in work concerning teaching and learning at Level 7 and Level 8, her stated beliefs were congruent with the innovation project. Thus, the relationship between Marian's cognition and classroom practices was inconsistent at this stage.

6.5.5 The Post-project Stage

At the post-project stage, though her cognition was still influenced by traditional pedagogy and the exam culture, Marian was supportive of the innovative principles, and thought communicative language teaching was effective for improving learners' communicative competence. She incorporated in her teaching such communicative elements as tasks and games, and initiated activities to promote learner autonomy at the rural school. Hence Marian's cognition at the post-project stage was compatible with her teaching practices.

6.5.6 Summary

To conclude, consistency between teacher cognition and classroom practices was found at the pre-project, bottom-up, and post-project stages. However, at the top-down and exam stages of the Danyang Project, the changes in Marian's cognition did not conform to the changes in her classroom practices.

Chapter 7
Factors Influencing the Implementation of the Danyang Project

In the present study, inductive analysis of qualitative data relating to the factors influencing the implementation of the Danyang Project identified five themes: (1) the teacher's prior experience; (2) in-service teacher training programs; (3) the social context; (4) the institutional context; and (5) attributes of the innovation project.

7.1 Prior Experience

Marian was born into a farming family in a small county in Danyang, which she had never left for long. As mentioned in Chap. 3, Marian was 35 years old when she joined the Danyang Project, by which time she had been teaching for 13 years, including three years at HES. Amiable, companionable, and warm-hearted, Marian was very popular with her colleagues at school. Marian's husband was a doctor at a local hospital. Her son and only child was also at HES when the DP was launched, but was not assigned to a project class, all of which were randomly selected.

Marian received her Bachelor of English Education in 2004 through a four-year correspondence degree program held by a provincial teachers' college. For Marian, the Danyang Project was the first and longest school-based in-service teacher education program she had joined in her career. When Marian entered in the Danyang Project in 2009, her professional level was at Grade-1; in 2010, she was promoted to be a high-grade teacher.[1]

---

[1]The professional levels (*Zhicheng*) for secondary teachers in China range upward from Grade-3, Grade-2, Grade 1, High-grade, to Special-grade. The prestige of a special-grade secondary teacher, which is categorized into the senior professional level (*Gaoji Zhicheng*), is equivalent to that of an associate professor at tertiary schools in China.

© Springer Nature Singapore Pte Ltd. 2018
Y. Zhu, *Language Curriculum Innovation in a Chinese Secondary School*,
https://doi.org/10.1007/978-981-10-7239-0_7

7.1.1 Prior Learning Experience

Marian began to learn English in her first year of junior high school. She thought her learning experience during her secondary education was quite successful, as she performed exceptionally well on exams. "My teacher thought highly of me, for I got 100 or 99 out of 100 points in almost all the exams," she proudly noted, "and I often told the feat to my students." As the classroom instruction to which she was exposed at the time was dominantly teacher-fronted, Marian said what she did in her English class was to follow her teacher attentively and take notes. "I was a fast note-taker," she said, "and after class I relied on my notes to review what I'd learned." Apart from note-taking, Marian also said she was confident of her pronunciation, for she had devised an innovative strategy to learn phonetics.

> I imitated my teacher when I began to learn English. However, what challenged me was that the phonetic symbols were not taught at that time. I found a way out by annotating the words with Chinese phonetic alphabet. It worked well for me. (I09: 33)

Recalling her learning experience at senior high school, Marian said she benefited from self-directed learning by using two reference books to expand what she learned inside the classroom.

> Two books were my Bibles in English learning when I was at senior high school. One was entitled *Contextualized Communication in English*. I bought it. The other was a grammar book written by Zhang Daozhen,[2] which was borrowed from my teacher. I used the first book as reference when I reviewed the notes I took in class, and I learned the grammar book quite intensively by underlining those parts I did not understand and inquiring about those questions with my teacher. I always remember that grammar book, with a yellow cover. I read it too often, and several pages had been torn out. (I09: 55)

In retrospect of her college time, Marian talked about two teachers who influenced her greatly—Mr. Sun and Mr. Yi. To Marian, the intensive reading course taught by Mr. Sun was quite impressive; she recalled that "the instruction was basically teacher-fronted and Mr. Sun meticulously analyzed the passage sentence by sentence" (I09:44). In Mr. Yi's course, however, students were encouraged to learn autonomously; "There is an obvious contrast between these two teachers." Marian said.

> More often than not, Mr. Yi told us to learn by ourselves, and suggested that we use a dictionary, go to the library, and discuss with classmates. We studied the vocabulary and most of the content in the textbook through self-directed learning. (I09: 44–45)

To sum up, as a language learner, Marian was exposed to a traditional language teaching context, featuring teacher-fronted, form-focused instruction. There was a depletion of target language input outside the classroom. Along with the pedagogy

---

[2]Professor Daozhen Zhang (1926–2009) was a distinguished Chinese scholar specializing in English grammar, translation and FLT curriculum innovation. One of his books *A Practical English Grammar* was widely published and highly valued by Chinese EFL learners, teachers and researchers over decades.

her teachers adopted, Marian developed her own learning strategies, including note-taking, reviewing, and reciting, which were later consolidated due to the self-efficacy Marian thought they brought about in her study. In senior high school, Marian began to do some self-directed learning by consulting reference books, with her teacher's guidance when necessary. Marian benefited from both teacher–and self-directed modes of learning; hence, in college, she embraced the contrastive teaching styles of her two favorite teachers.

7.1.2 Prior Work Experience

Marian experienced a one-month internship teaching at a public school in Zhenjiang, a city at a higher administrative level than Danyang, before she got her first job at a rural school. Her tutor, Ms. Dai, was "quite good at motivating students and creating a lively climate while teaching." In apparent admiration for her tutor teacher, Marian said it was "[no] wonder she had a teaching position in Zhenjiang. Her teaching skills deserved the reputation of that city." (I09: 84)

Marian had been teaching at a rural secondary school for around 10 years before she was transferred to HES, what she called an "idling" decade in her career. While she used to be praised by her colleagues after teaching public lessons at the rural school, she was astonished by her new colleagues' teaching expertise when she first came to observe their lessons at HES. Her life at the rural school, she realized, had been leisurely and pressure-free.

> At that time, I taught by strictly following the prescribed items in a guiding syllabus. The students there were underachieved, without much aspiration for success in learning, and there was not much pressure from their parents or the society, either. (I09: 63, 65).

To conclude, Marian's tutor teacher during her internship was the role model after whom she patterned her teaching. However, she did not find her 10 years' teaching experience at the rural school beneficial to her professional development when she left that school for a new educational setting.

7.2 In-Service Teacher Training Program

When she was teaching at the rural school, Marian was eager for in-service teacher training programs, and her desire for self-development was evident when she sat, but failed a graduate enrolment examination in 2004.

> The local education bureau provided some overseas teacher training programs to Australia and England years ago. But it was practically very difficult for rural teachers to get the opportunities. As a matter of fact, we had long been waiting for a chance to get in-service training. (I09: 126)

> It was a pity that I lost the chance (to pursue graduate study) that year. However, I would be hesitant if I were given such an opportunity now. I am 36 years old. And the time span of a graduate program would be too much for me due to my heavy workload at the moment. (I09: 128–129)

The dilemma Marian was facing sprang from the collision between her desire for further education, and the lack of in-service teacher training programs that fit her professional and constitutional realities. Though there were chances for Marian and her colleagues to attend conferences, seminars, or workshops held by the local education bureau, local schools, or other external organizers, the benefits she might get were limited, as most of the training sessions had large numbers of participants, and were expert-fronted in nature. It was barely possible for individual teachers to communicate with invited experts or other attendees about specific issues relating to classroom instruction. To some extent, Marian regarded the training sessions outside school as opportunities to "get some time off" and "see famous experts in person." Four PTs had an opportunity to attend a TESOL conference held in Beijing in July 2011; the author recalled in her notes:

> For most of the project teachers, it was the first time for them to attend an academic conference in Beijing. Some of them felt much content for getting the school-sponsored chance. And two teachers even brought their family members with them to Beijing. During the TESOL conference at Beijing Normal University, I chatted with some PTs after a few presenters gave their talks. However, I found what interested them most were those superficial aspects of presentations. (FN: Jul. 18, 2011)

In sum, Marian and her colleagues embraced in-service teacher training programs in general, even though the effectiveness of these programs was unknown.

7.3   Social Context

Two recurrent themes emerged from data analysis relating to social contextual factors affecting the implementation of the Danyang Project—standardized tests, and parents' expectations of their children's academic performance.

7.3.1   Standardized Tests

7.3.1.1   The Pre-project Stage

Standardized tests were frequently administered at HES before the Danyang Project was launched, infusing the whole school with a stressful atmosphere.

> The education here is exam-oriented. In general, there is one informal test for the students every two weeks, one grade-wide formal test every month, one city-wide mid-term exam, and one city-wide final exam. The formal tests resemble the senior high school entrance exam. And all the classes at the same level are ranked by the mean scores. (FN: Jun. 25, 2009)

Before participating in the Danyang Project, Marian quite overtly stated her concerns about the possible negative impact of the innovative project on students' performance on standardized tests. Being assured of the high points normally brought about by a well-enacted test preparation procedure at HES, she was quite doubtful about the impact of the forthcoming changes in pedagogy on students' exam scores.

> They (the students) must get high scores so that they could be enrolled by a key senior high school, right? In fact, the exam-oriented teaching turns out to be quite effective at present. The students won't fail in English exams. What if they are assigned to the project class but fail in the senior high school entrance exam? I feel quite uneasy thinking about this. (I09: 157)

7.3.1.2 The Top-Down Stage

At this stage of the Danyang Project, Marian and Frank had the freedom to evaluate students' learning outcome with exams developed exclusively for students in project classes. The students could be exempted from taking the school–or city-wide standardized exams when they were at Levels 7 or 8; however, the exams for project students did not resemble the standardized tests, and formative assessment measures, including learning portfolios and student learning journals were implemented to associate teaching more closely with the process of learning.

> ...I think it feasible for the students to make a weekly plan, for I can know whether they carry out their plans or not [in a short time]. Once the students have learned how to make and carry out a week plan, I will show them how to make a monthly plan, and then an annual plan. (TJ: Sep. 6, 2010)

> I finished reading students' learning journals today.... Quite a few students wrote in their journals that they found it challenging to differentiate confusable syllables when they did the listening exercises.... They hope they could learn more about phonetic alphabets. (TJ: Sep. 16, 2010)

Nevertheless, towards the end of the top-down stage, Marian and Frank gradually began to worry about their students' performance on standardized tests. As they could not compare their students' learning outcomes with those of students in the non-project classes, they were uncertain about the effectiveness of the Danyang Project. In a meeting with researchers, Marian expressed her concern about this issue.

> Marian said the items contained in the senior high school entrance examination were about the small details in the mandated textbook. For example, one of the items in the test of this year was about the phrase "leave sth. off/on." But this phrase does not appear in the experimental textbooks and tests. If our students were given this test paper, they would probably lose some points in this item. (FN: Aug. 21, 2011)

7.3.1.3 The Bottom-Up Stage

When the first group of students in project classes moved to Grade 9, they took the standardized test for the first time. However, they did not outperform their counterparts in non-project classes. The results were astonishing to almost all the people involved in the project, for they had long been expecting significantly higher scores from the project classes. Many people immediately became dubious about the project, and some non-PTs even criticized the PTs and researchers. Though Marian's class was at the Grade 8 level, she was not free from criticism. Marian told the researcher that she was bombarded with questions like, "What is the use of the innovation?" and "Why bother?" (FN: Sep. 22, 2011):

> During her visit, Yan got to know that students had finished the mid-term exam and she wanted to have a look at the scores of all the project and non-project classes. She went to an office and asked a teacher in a low voice where she could get the data. Suddenly, a teacher in the other corner of the office asked her in a sarcastic tone, "You are the PhD student, aren't you? You wanna know the scores? Aha, do you plan to do some research on this?" (FN: Sep. 23, 2011)

Marian's and Frank's students were at Level 8 at the time. Now that these two teachers were alert to the 'failure' they would probably experience in one year, they decided to 'work hard and catch up with their peers.' Then, when their students were at Level 9, their performance was better than that of the first group of project students.

> Mr. Wang told Yan that Frank's class was ranked 4 and Marian's class was ranked 14 among 18 classes of the grade. He said these two classes performed satisfactorily in the mid-term exam. (FN: Nov. 28, 2012)

7.3.1.4 The Exam Stage

At this stage, *zhongkao*, the senior high school entrance examination was the hot topic in Marian's life and in the whole school. The only purpose of teaching was to improve students' overall scores; thus, English teachers frequently met with teachers of other subjects, regarding how to collaborate to explore students' 'unexplored potential':

> The TRG of Level 9 organized meetings regularly to find out those promising students, whose scores in the mock test should be above a pre-set benchmark. Only those students who got high overall scores could be selected into the list. Though students in Marian's and Frank's classes performed well in English, most of their overall scores were not good enough. Consequently, the students who were selected were not the best performers in the English test. There were only 19 days left before the test. Frank was quite anxious to help them improve their English. (FN: May 30, 2013)

7.3.1.5 The Post-project Stage

When Marian began teaching at the rural school, she felt stressed, due to the uncertainty about her students' performance on tests. She said quite frankly that one of her objectives at the new setting was to "be the first one." Only when students' test scores were good enough would she be brave enough to "do other things."

> At the beginning, I had no idea about the students' English proficiency. I did not know how poor they could be. The only idea in my mind at that time was to improve their test performance, to be the first one. I must be ahead of my colleagues here, otherwise it was too humiliating to face my old friends there. (I14: 49)

In sum, the standardized test played an essential role in Marian's life throughout all the five stages of the Danyang Project, even though, in the formulated blueprint, students' test performance was not a decisive factor indicating the effectiveness of the project. However, scores spoke much louder than achievements that were invisible or unaccountable.

7.3.2 Parents

7.3.2.1 The Pre-project Stage

Parents were a salient factor influencing the changes in Marian's cognition. She thought parents selected HES because of its good academic reputation, and that they had high expectations to which a teacher should aspire. This tacit commitment was fueled with self-blame when she talked about the possible failure her students might experience in high-stakes examinations by participating in the innovative project. She said, "In that case, the parents would blame us. They would blame the school administrators as well" (I09: 156).

7.3.2.2 The Top-Down Stage

At the second stage, Marian's perceptions began to change, and she began to perceive parents as collaborators in her teaching practices. She built connections with parents through sending out letters, meeting with individual parents, and organizing parent conferences. At this stage, the major role played by parents was to assist her by overseeing students' language learning at home. Marian offered a detailed account about how this collaboration was conducted.

> I listed items of the stuff that must be recited in a form and suggested the parents hang it up in their children's rooms. If their children finish reciting one item, there will be a tick in the form. I am not sure whether the parents would follow my advice or not, but some of them are very cooperative. (I11: 33)

7.3.2.3 The Bottom-Up Stage

Marian continued to interact with her students' parents at the bottom-up stage, and gradually built up a mechanism of regular communication with them. She sent letters to parents reporting on updates of teaching and learning in her class every Friday, and received parents' feedback on the following Monday. At this stage, the collaboration between Marian and parents deepened, as the latter took initiative to negotiate with Marian by sending her long letters, which, in Marian's words, was "a big surprise":

> Peter's mom sent me a long letter yesterday. Her son suffers from ADD (Attention Deficit Disorder). What a poor mom. She is doing whatever she can to help her son. She took a detailed account of Peter's daily routine in her letter. Just let me know and care more about her son. I replied her letter by adding some feedback and advice in it. Hope what I've done would be helpful to Peter and his mom. (TJ: Feb. 20, 2012)

7.3.2.4 The Exam Stage

No major changes were found in the mechanisms by which Marian worked with parents, although there were more parents-initiated contacts with her, particularly when parents were informed of exam results.

7.3.2.5 The Post-project Stage

As a larger proportion of students Marian taught at the rural school were "left-behind" children, it was difficult to keep in contact with their parents.[3] Compared with the parents in cities, who greatly valued education and were willing to interact with teachers to catch up with their children's performances at school, the parents in rural areas were much less educated and less cooperative. What is worse, quite a few students now in Marian's class were from so-called problematic families—i.e., families suffering from marital conflicts or disastrous losses. The teacher-parent liaison Marian used to work with did not exist in her new school, and Marian sometimes played parental roles for her students. During her visit to the rural school, the researcher noticed Marian had prepared some blouses and dresses for two female students in her class. Marian told the researcher one student's story:

> She is a poor girl. Her mother was from Sichuan Province,[4] and her father was local people. Unfortunately, her father died when she was very young. Shortly after her father's death, her mother remarried and left her with her aunt. Now she lives with her aunt's family. Such

---

[3]In rural areas in China, there are millions of children left behind by their parents who went to cities as emigrant workers. These children are under the care of their relatives, mostly grandparents with little or no education and limited income, family friends, or having to take care of themselves.
[4]Sichuan Province is located in Southwest China.

a poor girl, but she is very diligent and interested in learning English. She is good at speaking. You've seen her performance in the Speech Contest, right? That's why I organize this activity. These poor kids, I want to help them. I brought these clothes for them to put on for public speaking. (FN: December 25, 2013)

In conclusion, parents were pivotal factors influencing Marian's making over the five stages of the Danyang Project. As in many other Asian countries influenced by Confucian culture, beliefs that valued education, teachers, and exams were deeply ingrained among Chinese parents. Parents' beliefs indirectly influenced the implementation of the Danyang Project through the interactive and dialogic relationship among parents, students, and teachers.

7.4 Institutional Context

7.4.1 Learners

7.4.1.1 The Pre-project Stage

Marian's students began to learn English much earlier than their teacher had as a language learner. She expressed concern about the earlier starting time, as "students' native language is not fully developed, and the early start causes some problems in secondary classrooms, one of which is the diversification of students' language proficiency and motivation" (I09: 21–26). With respect to the early start issue, Marian also said the English proficiency level of her students was much higher than before; "The textbooks I use to teach now are much more difficult than what I used when I was a student" (I09: 27).

7.4.1.2 The Top-Down Stage

Marian's concern about learners' diversification caused by an early start age of English learning at the first stage was consistent with her complex perceptions towards outstanding and under-achieved students. After the innovation project had been enacted for over one year, a proportion of students in her class made observable progress in their language proficiency and learning strategies as well. Therefore, Marian was from time to time bombarded with unexpected challenging questions raised by those students. She confided feeling anxious when confronted with good students' questions.

The good students are making progress in learning so rapidly. Sometimes I even have a sense that they outperform me. Yes, there is no doubt. I feel some students are better than me. (I11: 14)

I find those students improve more rapidly than I expect. I think I am not competent enough [to teach them]. I must learn more and develop my expertise. Otherwise I won't be qualified to teach them. (I11: 49–50)

Along with the pressure and, in turn, awareness of self-development caused by challenging good students came Marian's unceasing concern about the under-motivated and under-achieving students in her class. She thought those students' lack of confidence and motivation was caused by their relatively weak command of fundamentals in their prior learning experience, and regarded it her responsibility to help them out. However, she had no clear idea what strategies were effective for doing so.

This group of students deserves our concern and care. What can I do to motivate them? If I help them consolidate the fundamentals of their linguistic knowledge, they could probably perform better in future exams. Otherwise they might become less and less interested in learning due to their low scores. (I11: 15)

7.4.1.3   The Bottom-Up Stage

Different from the stress caused both by outstanding and under-achieved students in the previous stage, Marian held more sophisticated beliefs and knowledge about students' academic performance at the bottom-up stage. With on-going training and reflective practices, she was more curious to probe into the cognitive and affective factors contributing to learners' classroom behaviors. She came to realize she should conduct classroom-based exploratory research to address learners' individualized needs and attributes, which would in turn inform her teaching practices. What is more, she found the teacher education program of the DP facilitative to her research.

Now I find to improve teaching skills alone is not enough to result in effective teaching. The more important thing is that we should know students' real needs and work out a feasible work plan that caters to their needs. Perhaps I can collect some useful data by conducting a questionnaire survey. But I don't know how to design those questions. I'd like to ask those PhD students for help. (TJ: Feb. 16, 2012)

7.4.1.4   The Exam Stage

At the exam stage, Marian's knowledge about her students was largely derived from how they performed on exams. She frankly said she had to care more about those good students, because they were more likely to be admitted by a key senior high school in the city; HES evaluated a teacher's teaching by counting the number of students who got offers from that school. That's why it was a common decision made by most teachers to give up on under-achieved or (in their words) "hopeless" students at this stage.

7.4.1.5   The Post-project Stage

When Marian went to teach at YS, her pedagogical decisions tended to be more student-oriented, as she incorporated learner factors as vital components in her schema of language teaching. She still identified the gap between outstanding and underachieved students, but could manage the pressure it entailed by analyzing individual learner difference and formulating feasible work plans. At the very beginning of the semester she stayed at YS, she contacted the researcher and asked how to design a students' needs analysis questionnaire, and she also asked the researcher for a teaching feedback form to collect students' evaluative responses to her teaching.

Marian's concern for students was further evidenced by her belief that language education should empower students to learn sustainably. She thought she did it as some students she taught before in the project class made phone calls to her and told her what was happening to them after they entered senior high schools.

> Those students told me they were in advantageous positions in their classes now. They said it was quite easy for them to understand their teachers as the instruction was conducted primarily in English. (I14: 96)

In a word, learner factors exerted great influence on Marian's cognition and practices within the curriculum innovation. To her students, Marian was a caring teacher who was concerned about the full development of students over the five stages of the project. The emerging problems relating to students, i.e., the polarization between students, and the extremely good/poor students, motivated Marian to learn more. Her interaction with the students gave impetus to Marian's professional development.

7.4.2   Peers

7.4.2.1   The Pre-project Stage

A salient theme emerging from the interview data reveals how teacher learning took place within the domain of the TRG (teaching research group). Marian admitted she was astonished by the superb teaching skills of her colleagues when she first came to HES. She said, "I found I was lagging far behind my colleague here. Their teaching expertise was fabulous, really excellent" (I09: 87–89). What impressed Marian even more was how her mentor teacher in the TRG provided feedback after observing her class, emphasizing the necessity to improve the transitional language she used in teaching.

> She told me that the language I used to link one pedagogical step with another was too plain. She said I should make efforts to improve the transitional language, and in turn enrich the lesson I am teaching. (I09: 91)

In retrospect, this sort of evaluative feedback, combined with a monthly routine of peer classroom observation at HES, provided Marian with a lot of opportunities to learn from peers and improve her teaching skills.

7.4.2.2 The Top-Down Stage

Distinct from Marian's overt admiration for her colleagues' teaching when she first came to teach at HES, she had adopted a reflectively critical perspective of it towards the end of the second phase. To put it specifically, there were two layers of thinking in her mental life after observing a peer's lesson. One was the imaginary teaching scenario, that is, she envisioned in her mind the pedagogical decision she would make to re-teach a particular episode she had observed. The other was the tacit comment, which involved providing feedback to the lesson she had observed silently. Marian thought this mental process related more with scrutinizing those concrete aspects in teaching than forming a vague impression on the lesson as a whole. The possible reasons why she remained tacit at this stage could be the presence of her mentor teachers in the TRG, who were the opinion leader in the institutional context.

> In the past, classroom observations were conducted just for the sake of observing. I knew a lesson I observed was good, but could not tell the exact factors contributing to its goodness. It was after the mentor teachers gave their feedback that I realized where the points were… Now I speak to myself privately about the good points and drawbacks of a lesson I observed. Of course, my comments are not comparable with those provided by the mentor teachers in the TRG. They are the experts, really giving comments that strike home. I need to learn from them. (I11: 60)

7.4.2.3 The Bottom-Up Stage

A prominent change found at the bottom-up stage of the DP was that Marian gained more confidence to comment on her colleagues' lessons. She could reconstruct with reference to, provide alternative decision to or even criticize a specific teaching scenario she had observed with well-grounded reasons. She made comments on her colleagues' lessons reflectively and on concrete aspects, tacitly and overtly comparing similar parts taught by her and her colleagues with different lesson planning. She could judge whether the lessons she'd observed were innovative or not.

> I observed Helen's and Frank's lessons these days. And I taught the same lesson this week. In comparison with Helen, I did more speaking and Frank did more listening. All in all, however, the lessons we taught were deviant from innovative principles. (TJ: Mar. 9, 2012)

The same confidence was also observed as Marian and her fellow PTs disseminated effective innovative practices within the TRG, which was documented earlier in this sub-section.

Meanwhile, Marian was still strongly conscious of the comments on her teaching from her mentor teachers when she first came to HES. To deal with the problems concerned, she observed her mentor teachers' lessons two or three times every week, and raised the issue to teacher educators and other PTs to explore and seek for therapy to solve the problem.

> She told me I should pay attention to the transitional language I used in teaching, so I have always been concerned about this problem for these years. I found my teacher talk had improved because I observed a lot of my mentor teacher's lessons and she also gave me a lot of feedback on my teaching. (I13:28–29)

> In the speaking activity Marian conducted today, some students were quite reluctant to speak. She had no idea how to deal with their reticence. Yan told her if she had provided them with some useful word clues for reference, students might have something to scaffold their task performance. (FN: Mar. 7, 2012)

7.4.2.4 The Exam Stage

Despite a general tendency in the TRG to make pedagogical decisions highly influenced by and associated with exams, Marian was rather a maverick than a follower to the collectively designed lesson planning, in which the preemptive forms to focus on were closely linked to the so-called 'test points.' She expressed a slight resentment when telling about a conflict with her colleagues.

> They don't think I should include the phrase 'have a great influence on sth.' into the list of language points with 'have an effect on.' They think the phrase won't be included in the test, so there is no need to teach it at all. Moreover, they said presenting two phrases might be confusing to some students. But why, students do come across that phrase when doing reading. (I12: 23–26)

Not surprisingly, the peer relationship at this stage was infused with a spirit of competition. Though the difference of mean scores among classes was normally around 2 or 3 points, teachers who taught Level 9 students at HES were extremely sensitive about the ranking of their classes in the exam performance list issued by the Office of Teaching Affairs (*jiao wuchu*). Marian and Frank, because they taught project classes, suffered extra pressure, for their peers took it for granted that their classes would outperform those non-project classes on exams.

Another feature of peer interaction at this stage was found among those teachers who taught different subjects to the same class. Because the students were admitted based on the overall scores they got by summing up the scores of five subjects, those teachers tended to negotiate with each other, analyze an individual student' situation and find one or two subjects that were considered most possible to get improved. Once the decision was made, there was a tacit agreement that teachers who did not teach the "promising" subjects would leave time for the student to work on those hopeful subjects.

7.4.2.5   The Post-project Stage

On entering her new educational setting, Marian soon became the opinion leader who embraced, demonstrated, and propagated the ideas and practices of the DP. There were no the TRG or regular teaching research activities of any form at Yanling School. Despite the institutional constraints, Marian interacted quite frequently with the teacher who taught the same level of students as her on issues relating to teaching and students, to, as Marian saw it, "guide and help her." She thought working in the same office with other English teachers provided her with more flexibility to interact at their convenience (I14:15–16). Apart from daily informal contacts with her colleagues, Marian also taught public lessons and had meetings with them after class. Moreover, she voluntarily called on her colleagues to organize extracurricular activities relating to English learning, such as a school-wide phonetic symbol contest and an English speech contest (I14: 13).

Meanwhile, Marian kept in close contact with her colleagues at HES, especially Frank, who was teaching the same level of students Marian taught at YS. Her frequent contact with HES sprang out of three considerations. First, she thought it was necessary to keep observing her colleagues' lessons, otherwise she would fall behind. Second, she went back to help with subsequent research projects carried out by researchers. Third, she constantly exchanged opinions and information about teaching and students with Frank, and compared their students' performances at exams.

With respect to her mentor teachers at HES, Marian began to challenge them, and thought their ideas were sometimes "old-fashioned." She thought that, although her mentor teachers were experienced, they needed to learn more, as she had by participating in the DP.

> Most of the PhD students are younger than me. However, you are much more knowledgeable. I feel lucky to have the chance to learn from you. My mentor teachers, experienced as they are, still lack the knowledge and expertise that I learned in the project. Some of their ideas are rather old-fashioned doctrines. (I14: 99)

In a nutshell, peers were essential componential factors in the context in which Marian implemented the innovation project. Over the five stages of the project, Marian had not lived in a capsule isolated from her ordinary life; thus, the implementation of innovative principles was intertwined with the interactions and tension between Marian and her colleagues.

7.4.3   Leaders

7.4.3.1   The Pre-project Stage

As introduced in Chap. 1, Mr. Zhang, the principal of HES, was one of the initiators of the Danyang Project, and a deputy principal, Mr. Wang, was nominated to take charge of the project. Before the Danyang Project was initiated, the principals of HES were supportive of the prospective cooperation and enlisted logistical and political resources to make it possible. They made meticulous preparations for visits by Prof. Shu and the PhD students, and officials from the local education bureau were invited to attend meetings held for the preliminary negotiation on the project.

> The director general of the local Education Bureau met with the researchers in person. Two principals, Mr. Zhang and Mr. Wang, the director of the Office of Academic Affairs, the head teacher of English the TRG, and 6 English teachers attended the meeting today. They discussed with Prof. Shu and the PhD students in detail specific issues relating to the forthcoming project. Items included in the meeting agenda today are: project funding,... teacher training,...curriculum development,...selecting project classes,...project evaluation,... and the name of the project. (FN: May 25, 2009)

7.4.3.2 The Top-Down Stage

With the principals' support, the difficult times at the very beginning of the project became much easier. Apart from logistical support, the principles also communicated with researchers on the specifications for teaching and learning in project classes. The head of English attended almost all events concerning the project, and actively communicated with PhD students on relevant issues, encouraged the project teachers, and overtly expressed her opinions about the benefits and possible drawbacks of the project. Though both Mr. Zhang and Mr. Wang were math teachers, they seemed to have no difficulty understanding the principles of innovation.

> ...Beilei bought some books for PTs before she went to Danyang.... Mr. Wang said the school would reimburse PhD students for any expenses incurred. And he also said if the PhD students recommended a booklist for project teachers, the school would buy those books.... Getting to know that there would be learner portfolios for students in the project classes, Mr. Wang brought three folders of different sizes for PhD students to choose from....An office was allocated for the project, where researchers could work, store documents, and hold meetings.... Mr. Wang said a computer and a printer would be installed, and the walls would be decorated soon. (FN: Sep. 4, 2009)

> During the meeting,.... Mr. Zhang said he expected teachers would learn more about FLT theory and improve teaching skills through participating in this project. He cited some exemplar excerpts from two PTs' teaching journals to demonstrate how they benefited from the project.... (FN: Jan. 12, 2010)

7.4.3.3 The Bottom-Up Stage

At the bottom-up stage, with the unexpected failure of the first two project classes in a city-level exam, things became extremely difficult for people involved in the Danyang Project. As school leaders, the principals had to deal with criticism from parents and non-project teachers. Although it had been almost two years since the project was launched, people at HES valued exams greatly. Thus, the failure put significant pressure on Mr. Zhang and Mr. Wang, who had taken primary responsibility for the implementation of the project. Despite all the tacit and explicit doubts and criticism in the setting, the researchers were blamed by principals or the TRG head.

> The students did not perform well in the listening and speaking sub-test[5] of the senior high school entrance examination. At the news, Yan felt guilty and she went to talk to Mr. Zhang at his office…. However, Mr. Zhang said there was nothing wrong with the project and the researchers. Then there was a long silence. Yan got more guilt-ridden about the school. (FN: May 4, 2012)

7.4.3.4 The Exam Stage

About one year later, when Marian's and Frank's classes were at the last phase of the exam stage, the principals were much more relaxed than at the same time last year, partly due to the consistent good performance of the students in project classes in previous mock tests, and partly due to their changed expectations of the effect of the innovation project on students' scores. They became more liberal about students' academic achievements, in terms of their communicative competence, motivation, autonomy, etc. However, they were concerned about the sustainable, delayed effect of the innovation project on students.

> Mr. Wang told Yan he did a preliminary survey on students who had graduated from HES and was admitted by the key senior high school. Among 15 students who had recently won awards in an English competition, 13 were from HES. (FN: Nov. 28, 2012)

7.4.3.5 The Post-project Stage

At this stage, the researcher left HES for an overseas academic visit. While she was away, she communicated with the principals and the head of the TRG through Skype calls. During this period, Mr. Wang told the researcher about the updates at the school, and invited her to come back to HES when she had time. The head of the TRG also contacted her several times, consulting with her about issues relating to teaching and learning. When the researcher visited HES after coming back to China, she was received with the same hospitality and warmth as before the project was initiated.

> Mr. Wang said the school was developing rapidly and they had just got the permission from the local education bureau to enlarge the campus. In addition, they decided to build two

---

[5]In Danyang, the English senior high school entrance examination consists of two sub-tests: a computer-based sub-test of listening and speaking, which is in March, and a paper-and-pencil sub-test of grammar, reading and writing, which is in June.

e-learning labs for English learning. He said there was no problem with funding or technology, what they needed were innovative ideas, thus the input from PhD students would be great. (FN: Nov. 26, 2013)

To conclude, principals' support was an essential factor in guaranteeing the sustainable development of the Danyang Project.

7.4.4   School Timetable

Another theme relating to the institutional context was the hectic and inflexible academic schedule at HES and the rural school.

7.4.4.1   The Ordinary Timetable

Students were almost fully occupied with courses and routine activities from 7:50 to 20:30 at HES. With a prescriptive quota of lessons assigned to different subjects, there were constant conflicts among teachers as they competed to squeeze teaching into students' spare time, not to mention any free time left for students at their disposition.

Teachers at HES started working normally at 7:50 in the morning, or even earlier for those teachers who attended to students while they did morning reading. While most teachers finished working at 17:10, those who accompanied students when they did self-study in the evening would not leave school until 20:50. Besides their regular workload, teachers were called on to take on extra work when there was an emergency. In her teaching journal, Marian wrote,

> This morning, one of my colleagues got injured in an accident. The principal called on me to take over her class. (TJ: Oct. 19, 2010)

> Frank had to attend a training course outside school today, and I took over his class. I taught three classes in the morning. When I was in the third class, I was too tired to teach. (TJ: Oct. 23, 2010)

7.4.4.2   The Timetable for Exam-Preparation

Due to the approaching exam, students' daily routines got extremely busy, and they were rarely available for out-class self-directed learning, as teachers of various subjects were fighting to squeeze exam-oriented homework into their spare time. Marian regretted the situation, as she had to compromise to ensure that her students could succeed on the upcoming competitive exam.

> Let me tell you, there are three segments of time for student to learn autonomously every evening. The first one, from 17:40–18:55, is allocated to studying physics and chemistry. The second one, from 19:00–19:55, is for studying math. The third one, from 20:05–21:05, is for studying Chinese and English. I only have half an hour at my disposal. (I13: 32)

Table 7.1 Students' timetables at YS and HES

	YS	HES
Get up	5:50 a.m.	6:30 a.m.
Morning reading	6:30–7:10 a.m.	7:00–7:40 a.m.
Morning lessons	7:50–11:30 a.m.	7:50–11:30 a.m.
Afternoon lessons	13:00–17:10 p.m.	13:45–17:10 p.m.
Evening lessons	18:30–20:50 p.m.	18:30–20:10 p.m.

(I14: 24)

7.4.4.3 The Timetable at the Rural School

Students' academic schedule was no less busy at the rural school. When Marian taught there, she normally got up at 6:00 in the morning, and left school at 5:00 in the afternoon; when she accompanied her students to evening class, she would not come back home until 10:00 at night (Table 7.1).

> "It was frightening," Marian told Yan her experience on a winter night, "I left for home after I finished the evening class. When I was driving, the smog got so heavy that I could not even see the pavement markings. It was so dark, so frightening…." (FN: December 25, 2013)

To conclude, the school timetables vividly demonstrate how intensely busy students and teachers were at both HES and YS. It seemed as if there were a strong fortress in which teachers and students mechanically followed their routine, one so strong that the strength of a few external researchers was tenuous.

7.5 The Attributes of the Innovation Project

7.5.1 The Pre-project Stage

Most of the researchers involved in the Danyang Project had very limited knowledge of secondary education before they stepped into the field. Many had five to 12 years' teaching experience in colleges and universities, and some of them had three to eight years' research experience in the second language acquisition and foreign language teaching field. The PhD students were determined, diligent, tenacious, and cooperative with each other. None had ever been in Danyang before the project was initiated. At this stage, they visited HES to gather the preliminary information about the school, the teachers. and the students, and had frequent meetings to discuss about the project plan. Though there was consensus among researchers to involve PTs in the decision-making process, the project at this stage was still researcher-directed.

In an on-line meeting via QQ chat, Fei said we should invite the PTs to join us (discussing about the plan). She said it was the teachers that should be the center of this project. Prof. Shu agreed, saying this was a good idea....and the role of researchers was somewhat that of a guide or an advisor. (FN: Jul. 31, 2009)

7.5.2 The Top-Down Stage

Contrary to the university researchers' intentions to cultivate the initiative of PTs and enhance their engagement, the primary approach adopted to implement the Danyang Project at this stage was, as its name suggests, by imposing top-down model, with university researchers taking a directing and caring role in their interaction with the project teachers. The decision-making process for essential components of the project had quite limited input from the teachers, for it was virtually unrealistic to incorporate many teachers' ideas, when there was such a distance between those ideas and the innovative principles. Normally, the researchers taught PTs how to teach innovatively by presenting a prepared proposal with meticulous exemplification and clarification. Accordingly, PTs played a passive role as recipients of new knowledge in the learning process. In her field notes, an invited teacher educator, Pei Chen[6] wrote,

> I gave a teacher training session on the topic *Classroom Practices of Task-based Language Teaching* this afternoon. Around 30 teachers from the primary sector and the secondary sector came to my talk. There were three parts in my talk: theoretical underpinnings of TBLT, classroom practices of TBLT, and my comments on 4 lessons I observed this morning. For 2 and a half hours, those teachers listened to me very attentively and they also interacted with me sporadically.... However, I found almost none of them knew any theoretical basics of FLT, and terms such as communicative language teaching, PPP, etc., were completely new to those teachers.... Thus, I had to lower the level of difficulty of my lecture. (FN: Nov. 9, 2009)

Towards the end of the top-down stage, due to the incompatibility of the innovation project's principles and practices with local realities, there was a somewhat intense resistance among project teachers. The resistance grew even more intensive when the first group of project students did not perform as well as expected on the senior high school entrance exam. The resistance was evident when the researcher's comments on a project teacher, Alex's, lesson were politely rejected after a classroom observation.

> "Yes, probably you are right." Alex said, "But do you still remember how we were taught when we were at secondary school? What if I continue to teach in this [innovative] way, and my students get failed in the exam?" (FN: Sep. 29, 2011)

---

[6]Pei Chen, then a postdoctoral fellow at Shanghai International Studies University, participated in the Danyang Project during its early stage.

7.5.3 The Bottom-Up Stage

Realizing the negative effects a top-down approach might have on implementing the innovation project, and a recognition among university researchers that, with over one year's exposure to the teacher education program of the Danyang Project, teachers had gained substantial knowledge on the basics of FLT theory and practice, a decision was made to gradually convert the top-down approach to a bottom-up one. What teacher educators were supposed to do at this stage was to counsel, to facilitate, and to support. PTs' autonomy and initiative were considered of pivotal importance to implementing the project. PTs were encouraged to fine-tune the innovative principles to suit the realities of their classrooms, and to conduct classroom-based action research. In addition, a group leader, Frank, was selected to coordinate work and organize learning sessions for the project teachers.

In a meeting with the PTs and principals in Danyang, Prof. Shu said:

> …Actually, we know about [your resistance]. These days my PhD students and I have been reflecting on the implementation of this project so far. We also read some articles written by practitioners from other countries. We've begun to think, if the innovation is top-down in nature, there won't be a strong possibility of implementing it successfully. The changes are not likely to take place, if they are driven by external factors rather than internal motives. (FN: Feb. 16, 2012)

7.5.4 The Exam Stage

At the exam stage, the project was still bottom-up, and a compromise was made to keep a balance between teachers' practical needs and the objectives of the project— i.e., teachers' needs and voices were attended to, even though there was an obvious conflict with the innovative principles. Apart from the regular teacher education program, university researchers also offered Marian and Frank guidance and resources to help students cram for the exam.

> During her visit, Yan got to know that the students in Marian's class performed relatively worse than those in Frank's class. And Marian was a bit concerned about the scores of the blank-filling items. Yan suggested that Marian carefully analyze students' error types and focus on those types of errors that were more likely to appear. (FN: May 16, 2013)

7.5.5 The Post-project Stage

At the post-project stage, the university researchers withdrew from the project, seldom going to HES to hold seminars or workshops, or to observe classrooms. There was very limited external intervention in teaching and learning at either HES or YS. However, university researchers kept in contact with people in Danyang, mutually helping each other to do things relating to teaching and research.

> Yan conducted a classroom-based experimental study at HES. Marian and Frank actively helped her organize participants; video–and audio–record her teaching and mark some of the tests. …Yan promised to visit the rural school where Marian was teaching. She accepted the invitation to be the judge for an oral English competition organized by Marian. (FN: December 25, 2013)

To sum up, the implementation approaches of the Danyang Project changed from a drastic and purist top-down model at the pre-project stage, to a lenient and more eclectic bottom-up model, at the bottom-up stage and the exam stage, after which the intensity of innovation gradually faded as the project moved to the post-project stage.

7.6 Summary

In a nutshell, how Marian implemented the Danyang Project was influenced by manifold factors relating to her personal experience and the complexity of the interpersonal relationship where she lived, worked, and learned. As is shown in Fig. 7.1, these factors could be further categorized into two types—intrapersonal factors and interpersonal factors. Intrapersonal factors (indicated by the blue cells, below) impacted the cognitive and affective processed influencing Marian's response to the educational intervention. Interpersonal factors (indicated by the

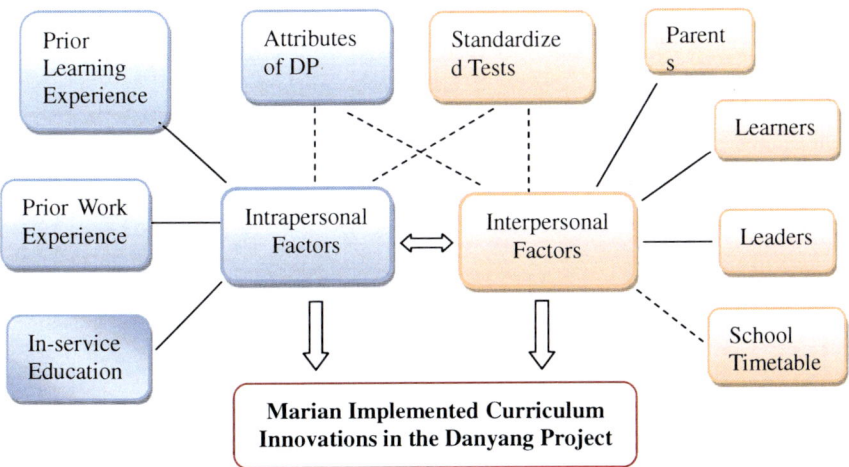

Fig. 7.1 Factors influencing the implementation of the danyang project

beige cells in the figure) refer to the external variables mediating teacher learning while she implemented the innovation project. There was no clear-cut boundary between these two types of influencing factors, as some factors pertained to both intrapersonal and interpersonal categories. These two types of factors were dynamically interactive and intertwined, exerting positive or negative impacts on the implementation of the innovation project.

Chapter 8
Conclusion

This chapter draws the whole study to an end by offering a synthesis of the answers found to the four research questions, discussing the research findings with reference to previous studies, and proposing a tentative exploratory model for foreign language teacher cognition and practices, followed by two sub-sections evaluating the effectiveness of the classroom teaching in the Danyang Project and the factors conducive to the uptake of innovation. The subsequent part dwells on the implications of this study, before its limitations are discussed, and suggestions provided for future studies.

8.1 Results

8.1.1 Research Question 1

8.1.1.1 What Changes Took Place in the Danyang Teacher's Cognition?

Depicting Marian's changes in cognition over the five stages, triangulated through comparisons between Marian and a non-project counterpart, it was found the project teacher's cognition changed in accordance with the goals of the innovative project, but the trajectory of that change was much more tangled and complicated than what was initially expected. Here is a summary of the changed aspects of Marian's cognition.

(1) Meaning versus form

At the outset of the DP, Marian held the belief that there was a dichotomy between language meaning and form, with the latter playing the dominant role in language learning and teaching. This ambivalence gradually changed to an attitude favoring meaning, at the top-down stage. When the innovation project proceeded to the bottom-up phase, Marian reverted to an apparent inclination to traditional teaching approach, thus subordinating communicative, meaning-oriented teaching. At the exam preparation phase, form-oriented teaching was of paramount importance to Marian; however, when Marian went to a new educational setting, she showed a belief in integrating meaning and form, and in maintaining the fundamental role that communicative activities or tasks play in enhancing learners' communicative capacity in the target language.

(2) *Learner participation and learner autonomy*

Before the DP was launched, Marian perceived learners as passive recipients of linguistic knowledge, in alignment with her belief in the predominance of linguistic form over meaning. Meanwhile, she was in favor of self-directed language learning, despite her obvious doubts about learners' capacity to learn autonomously. At the top-down stage of the DP, Marian was supportive of the rationale of fostering learner participation and learner autonomy in language teaching, and was confident of her expertise in facilitating, and learners' capacity to conduct self-directed learning. However, she was dubious about the effectiveness of the teaching method she adopted regarding the foreseeable evaluation with standardized tests. When the DP moved to the bottom-up stage, Marian was even more convinced of her expertise to enhance learner participation and conduct self-directed learning. However, she was still haunted by the conflict between innovative ways of teaching and standardized tests. At the exam preparation stage, Marian's enthusiasm for autonomous learning was almost completely abandoned in favor of exam-oriented, spoon-fed teaching. Nevertheless, when Marian began to teach a new group of students at YS, she explicitly espoused learner participation and self-directed learning.

(3) *Providing corrective feedback*

At the very beginning of the DP, Marian was quite concerned about the accuracy of both learners' written and oral language production, and held a rather firm belief that all errors should be corrected. Through the teacher training program at the top-down stage of the DP, Marian came to realize that learners' errors were inevitable and informative, and ought to be treated with different strategies; she came to favor correcting learners in an implicit way at this stage. When the DP moved to the bottom-up stage, Marian was once again uncertain about whether and how corrective feedback should be provided, and adopted some innovative strategies to correct learners' errors, particularly a preemptive way of preventing errors in learners' oral productions, and a learner-directed way to correct errors in learners' written production. At the exam preparation stage, Marian reverted to emphasizing accuracy, and asserted that all errors should be corrected. Then again, when Marian went to teach in a new educational setting, she gradually developed a sophisticated scheme for providing correct feedback by adopting strategies (implicit vs. explicit; teacher-correct vs. peer-correct, etc.) that were appropriate to individual learners' cognitive and affective differences, as well as the context-specific realities in her classroom.

(4) *Using textbooks*

At the preliminary stage of the DP, Marian was heavily reliant on the mandated textbook, and did not question its effectiveness for achieving educational goals, despite occasionally rearranging the positions of different sections therein. To a certain extent, Marian perceived 'teaching' as 'covering the textbook.' At the top-down stage of the DP, there was a tension in Marian's mental world between the quality of experimental textbooks, and their possible negative influence on learners' performance in standardized tests. This tension led to Marian's eclectic approach of incorporating the underlying principles of experimental textbooks into the mandated textbooks. At the bottom-up stage, although Marian almost exclusively resorted to the mandated textbooks in teaching, she was much more confident about adapting and developing instructional materials. Again, at the exam preparation phase, Marian adopted a safe strategy by relying on the mandated materials. The post-project stage also witnessed the revival of Marian's willingness to adapt the mandated textbooks and construct new materials to suit her teaching purposes.

(5) *Attitudes towards innovative project*

The DP was the first time Marian had joined a school-based innovation project by collaborating with university researchers. At the very beginning, Marian was optimistic about the project's prospects, anticipating that the university experts would provide a package of solutions to deeply-entrenched problems in secondary FLT classrooms. At the top-down stage, Marian viewed the university researchers as nice, knowledgeable teacher educators who caringly prepared theoretical and practical guides, as a set of dos and don'ts for the project teachers. Despite the beneficial development Marian thought she had gained from researchers, she also hinted that the 'guidance' she received from the teacher education program was not relevant to the realities of her classroom. At the bottom-up stage of the DP, Marian was still quite supportive of the DP, but became critical about the opinions and suggestions given by researchers. She took more initiative to raise questions and seek answers by referring to accessible resources. At the post-project stage, Marian saw the university researchers as her colleagues and collaborators, and believed the interaction between them was mutually beneficial.

8.1.2 Research Question 2

8.1.2.1 What Changes Took Place in His/Her Classroom Practices?

This question is of decisive importance to the whole project, for it is assumed only when changes are found in teachers' classroom practice could we claim the innovation project was beneficial to its participants—the learners, in this case. Chapter 5 addressed this question through inductively analyzing data concerning seven aspects of classroom instruction over our stages (exam-preparation lesson was excluded for its obvious incomparability) of the project. The findings were triangulated by comparing typical lessons taught by Marian and Jane (see Chap. 6). The following is a synthesis of the changes in Marian's classroom teaching behavior.

(1) *Time allotment to different activities of a lesson*

Before she participated in the DP, the activities in Marian's classroom followed the typical PPP (presentation, practice, and production) model, with linguistic forms being much emphasized. What is more, Marian was not familiar with using tasks in classroom instruction. At the top-down stage, the organization of classroom activities dramatically changed as Marian was trained to teach the LAP course, which was task-based. When it came to the bottom-up stage, Marian reverted to a combination of traditional PPP teaching and tasks designed to consolidate pedagogical content— i.e., task-supported teaching. At the exam preparation stage, the activities were exclusively based on covering items in moot test papers; however, at the post-project stage, the activities in Marian's lesson were much more communicative, incorporating aspects of more communicative teaching from the early stage.

In comparison with Jane, it was found Marian's lesson were more communicative, and more congruent with the stated teaching objectives and time allotted for different activities. Nevertheless, traditional teacher-centered activities still constituted a large part of Marian's classroom teaching.

(2) *Choice of instructional materials*

At the outset of the DP, Marian was highly reliant on the mandated textbooks, and exclusively based her teaching plan on covering their contents. By contrast, at the top-down stage, the mandated textbooks were abandoned and learners were involved in developing instructional materials. At the bottom-up stage, however, Marian returned to the mandated textbooks, which she adapted and supplemented when necessary. The exam stage was filled with mandated materials—specifically, exam preparation materials. At the post-project stage, Marian largely drew on materials designed by herself, combining student-provided materials and adapting the mandated materials.

Also, compared with Jane's lesson, Marian showed more knowledge and expertise to adapt and develop instructional materials, and was more confident in involving students in material development. However, the changes she made to the mandated textbook were additional, rather than substitutional; in other words, the mandated textbook was still seen as authoritative, regardless of its identified defects.

(3) *Teacher talk*

At the very beginning of the DP, teacher talk accounted for over half of the discourse in Marian's classroom, in terms of its overall length and time. A dramatic change took place at the top-down stage, as teacher talk decreased greatly. At the bottom-up stage, however, teacher talk went back to levels only slightly lower than those at the first stage, before increasing continuously and reaching almost the same levels as in the pre-project stage. Compared with NPTs, both the time and length of teacher talk were higher in Marian's classroom.

The complexity of teacher talk, measured by average length per move, varies in alignment with the learners' proficiency level. As her students moved from Level 7 to Level 9, Marian's teacher talk tended to become increasingly complex, and greatly decreased when she began to teach a new group of Level 7 students at YS. Her speaking speed, however, varied with the communicativeness of the lesson she taught. She tended to speak faster when the lesson was more communicative-oriented and at a lower speed when teaching in a traditional teacher-fronted manner. The same trend was found regarding the percentage of referential questions in Marian's classrooms—i.e., the more communicative the lesson tended to be, the more referential questions were asked.

By comparison, the average length per move was higher in Marian's classroom than in her NPT counterpart's, she spoke slightly faster, and the proportion of referential questions in her lesson was much higher.

(4) *Student talk*

Accordingly, the time and length of learner talk in Marian's classrooms varied according to the stages of the innovation project. Nevertheless, the complexity of learner talk tended to correlate jointly with the task design and the learner's proficiency level. In learner talk, the average length per move was influenced by task implementation and learners' proficiency level. Moreover, there was a general increase in the percentage of unrestricted moves in learner talk, with a slight dip from the top-down to the bottom-up stage. It seems neither the communicativeness of a lesson nor the intensity of the innovation project had a direct and sustained impact on this aspect of classroom teaching; rather, it was likely correlated with the teacher's increased awareness and capacity to enhance beneficial learner engagement in classroom discourse.

(5) *Participatory organization*

Student-student interaction comprised a very small part of classroom interaction at the pre-project stage. The percentage largely increased at the top-down stage, and dropped to almost the same level as in the pre-project stage, towards the end of the bottom-up stage. At the post-project stage, the percentage of student-student interactions moderately increased.

Compared with NPTs, the project teacher was more skillful in organizing classroom interaction, using a variety of participatory structures.

(6) *Focus on meaning versus form*

At the outset of the DP, form-focused exchanges accounted for nearly half of all exchanges. This percentage decreased greatly at the top-down stage, then rose to almost the same level as the pre-project stage at the bottom-up stage. At the post-project stage, the percentage of form-focused exchanges decreased to about half of the level seen in the pre-project stage.

Compared with NPTs, the percentage of form-focused exchanges in Marian's classroom discourse was much lower.

(7) *Discourse structure*

Throughout the four stages of the DP, the percentage of IRF patterns reached a peak at the top-down stage, and then slightly dropped at the bottom-up stage. Approaching the post-project stage, the figure decreased to much lower than the pre-project stage.

The percentage of student-initiated exchanges reached its highest point at the top-down stage, and then dropped to its lowest level before rebounding to a level higher than that at the pre-project stage.

To summarize, changes in the project teacher's teaching practices roughly took on an 'N' shape, as illustrated in Fig. 8.1; i.e., the newness of the teacher and her students' teaching behaviors reached a dramatically high level when the innovation project was at its height; then, when the innovation project faded out, the classroom instruction went back to being traditional. However, the new teaching behaviors revived in the project classrooms at the post-project stage.

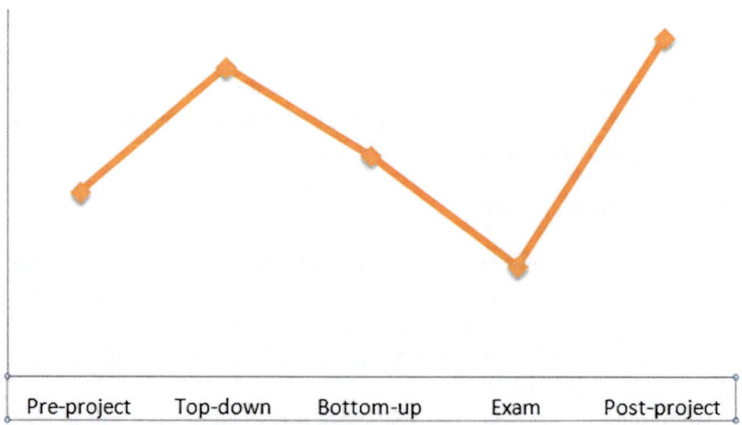

Pre-project   Top-down   Bottom-up   Exam   Post-project

Fig. 8.1 The trajectory of change in teaching practices

8.1.3 Research Question 3

8.1.3.1 What Relationship Is There between? the Changes in the Teacher's Cognition and Changes in His/Her Classroom Practices?

In this study, consistency between teacher cognition and classroom practices was found at the pre-project, bottom-up, and post-project stages. At the top-down and exam stages of the DP, changes in the teacher's cognition did not conform to the changes in her classroom practice; thus, it is hypothesized that the stresses that caused tensions between teacher's mental world and outside realities were likely to be salient factors in explaining the consistency and inconsistency at different stages. To be more specific, at the top-down stage, the tension sprang from the gap between the pressure on PTs to implement innovation project, and teachers' under-developed capacity to understand and accept the innovative principles. At the exam stage, however, the tension stemmed from an overwhelming pressure caused by all stake holders in the exam, stressing accuracy in learners' written production, and recognition of the effectiveness of communicative teaching in improving fluency, accuracy, and complexity in learners' oral production.

8.1.4 Research Question 4

8.1.4.1 What Factors Influenced the Teacher's Implementation of the Danyang Project?

The present study shows that teachers' implementation of curriculum innovation is influenced by intra- and inter-personal factors. Intra-personal factors refer to the cognitive and affective process that influence teachers' responses to educational intervention when learning, trying out, and reflecting on its impact on learning. Inter-personal factors refer to the external variables mediating teacher learning. In the Danyang project, intra-personal factors contained teachers' prior experience and knowledge, attitude and motivation, teaching style and personality, etc.—in short, the intrinsic and idiosyncratic attributes of an individual teacher. Inter-personal factors included the on-going in-service teacher learning program, the community of learning and practice, education management mechanism, and other socio-political issues.

8.2   Discussion

8.2.1   An Exploratory Model of Foreign Language Teacher Cognition and Practices

Based on an overview of the whole process, it can be argued that the changes in the project teacher's cognition and practices were gradual, non-linear, fluctuating, and sometimes regressive. Borg (2011) reminded researchers to properly operationalize 'impact' before concluding whether a teacher education program influences on teacher cognition. To that end, the author adopted a broad interpretation of 'impact' that "encompasses a range of developmental processes" (Borg, 2011, p. 178). In this study, it was found that the teacher's cognitions were considerably influenced by her educational background and prior work experience. Teacher cognition was also significantly impacted by the institutional context in which she interacted with learners, colleagues, and leaders. In addition, the mechanism under which the innovation project was enacted had an obvious effect on PTs' attitudes towards the project, and the principles it attempted to implement. Moreover, socio-political factors containing the washback effect of standardized tests (Hughes, 1989; Taylor, 2005), the parents, the community, etc., impacted on the change of teacher cognition.

Argyris and Schön (1974) termed different types of teacher beliefs as espoused theories and theory-in-use. Basturkmen (2012) defined explicit beliefs as "those which a person can readily articulate" (p. 283), and implicit beliefs as "those which are held unconsciously and can only be inferred from actions" (*ibid*). Compared with inexperienced teachers, Mitchell (2005) and Feryok (2004) reported, experienced teachers' beliefs more consistently corresponded with their teaching behaviors. Notwithstanding the ample evidence supporting the existence of two types of teacher cognitions in language teachers' mental lives, there was, however, a limited amount of studies on the interactive relationships between curriculum innovation, teacher learning, teacher practices, and the two types of cognition. The present study proposes a tentative exploratory model (Fig. 8.1) showing these two dimensions of language teacher cognitions and the mechanism through which internal and external factors play mediating roles. This model might be viewed as speculative, due to the small sample size of this study, yet it is still informative and enlightening to practitioners, teacher educators, and researchers.

This study found two types of teacher cognition: explicit cognition and implicit cognition. As shown in Fig. 8.2, explicit cognition can be built through teacher training, and is related to conscious pedagogical decision making, but is likely to be transient and vulnerable, due to external intervention. In contrast, implicit cognition is what the teacher holds as internalized beliefs and acquired knowledge through reflective practice. It pertains to the teacher's unconscious and automatic pedagogical decision making. Implicit cognition tends to be stable, deeply-entrenched, and resistant to external intervention.

(Community of Professional Learning and Practices)

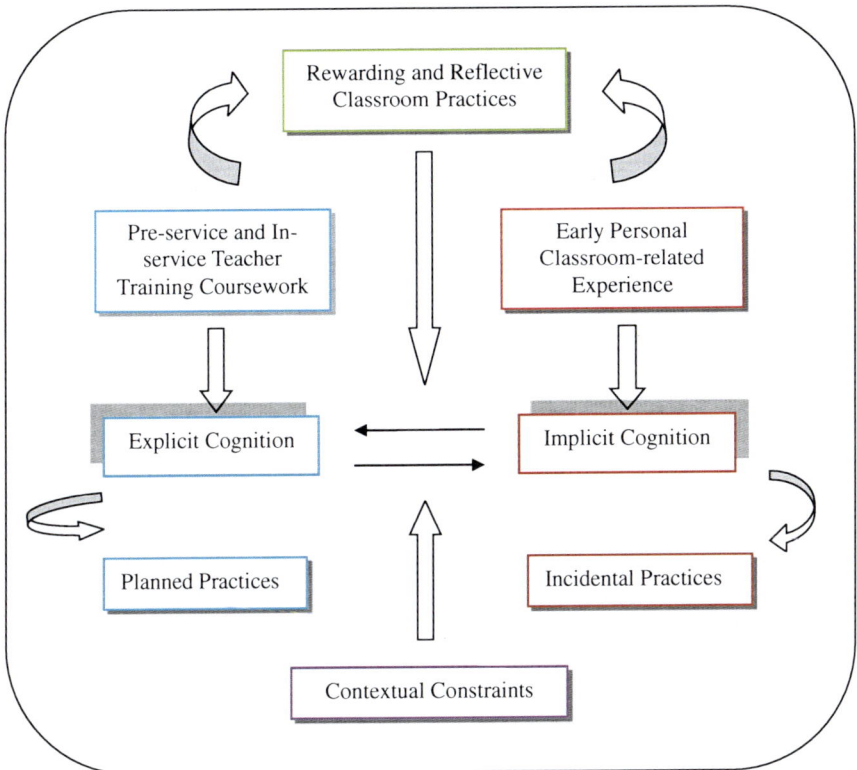

Fig. 8.2 An exploratory model of foreign language teacher cognition and practices

Drawing on the findings of this study, it is hypothesized that there is an interface between teacher's implicit and explicit cognition—that is, teacher's explicit cognition can be converted into implicit cognition through reflective practices, particularly the practice experienced by individual teachers working collaboratively in a community of learning and practice. In the present study, the interaction between implicit and explicit cognition was found to be bi-directional, such that there can be a conversion from explicit to implicit cognition, and vice versa. It is also hypothesized that explicit cognition and implicit cognition exist in juxtaposition in teachers' minds, and are accessed in accordance with the contextual realities that impact teachers' pedagogical decisions. For example, at the exam preparation stage, Marian primarily drew on her explicit cognition (favoring accuracy of linguistic forms) in regular teaching, whereas she used much more implicit cognition (communicative-oriented) when critiquing her colleagues' lessons, which were not taught for exam preparation.

8.2.2 Effectiveness of the Classroom Teaching in the Danyang Project

Given the theory-laden approach this study has adopted to evaluate the effectiveness of classroom teaching, the framework formulated in Sect. 2.1.2.3 is referred to here, to construct an evaluative review of the classroom teaching in the DP. As this study shows, the trajectory of teaching practices in project classrooms is a fluctuating upward process; thus, only established teaching behaviors are drawn on as evidence in support of the effectiveness of classroom teaching in the innovation project.

Generally, towards the end of the DP, while she still found it hard to break the routines she had been living with for so long, the focal project teacher began to deviate from traditional teaching with regarding to these salient aspects:

(1) There was a much clearer recognition of teaching objectives, and activities were designed and arranged to achieve the teaching purpose;

(2) Instructional materials were rather the means to facilitate teaching, rather than its ends—i.e., teaching no longer consisted of simply covering textbooks;

(3) It was the quality rather than the quantity of teacher talk that counted, and a major function of teacher talk was to provide learning opportunities;

(4) Student talk contributed to the effectiveness of teaching, as a manifestation of both the process (interaction) and product (output) of learning;

(5) The participatory organization was a reasonable mixture of teacher-student and student-student interaction, with the latter constituting proper proportion;

(6) Classroom interaction was predominantly meaning-oriented, although attention was still directed at linguistic forms;

(7) As to the IRF pattern in classroom discourse, it was in their follow-up moves that students' responses was evaluated, and suitable feedback given to facilitate learning by requesting expansion, clarification, justification, and exemplification.

8.2.3 Factors Conducive to the Uptake of Innovation

Based on the research findings, intrapersonal and interpersonal factors are conducive to teachers' uptake of an innovation project. The following principles are of vital importance to the implementation of educational change, and are proposed for planning, conducting, and managing an innovation project:

(1) There should be an on-going, in-service teacher education program that caters to the specific needs of project teachers. The program ought to be supportive, sustainable, and adaptive to contingencies in the target context.

(2) There should be a community of learning and practice in which teachers and researchers interact through identifying and investigating unexplored areas in learning and teaching, and by connecting theory with practice.

(3) There should be a pressure-free education management mechanism that respects, supports, and fosters teacher autonomy. External and prescriptive teacher training courses are by no means the only way; school-based in-service teacher learning has the potential to become an effective and legitimate alternative approach to promoting language teachers' professional development. Thus, sufficient financial and intellectual support should be allocated to promote self-directed teacher learning.

(4) There should be a socio-political climate that favors whole-person learner development, and that mitigates the negative impact of standardized language tests on learning.

(5) There should be local opinion leaders who are personally influential in the setting, and who have the capacity to allocate resources at the school level. Support from opinion leaders is of vital importance to the implementation of an innovation project.

(6) There should be acceptance of and readiness for failure. Educational change is destined to be an arduous long journey, full of bumps and falls. Success could come much later than expected.

8.3 Implications

The present study attempts to fill the identified research gap by sketching the lines of changes of teacher cognition and teaching practice within an EFL innovation project running deeply and continually in Chinese secondary classrooms. As there is a paucity of accessible studies that cover such an extended time span, and that investigate the dynamics of classroom instruction despite all their complexities, this study contributes to the field with implications in the following aspects.

(1) Educational innovation is not always as successful as expected. It is an arduous and long journey that may not end at the planned destination. However, the amount of time, energy, and resources stake-holders invest in it is still likely to predict its success.

(2) An on-going, in-depth, school-tailored teacher education program is an essential prerequisite for the implementation of innovation project. The program ought to be teacher-centered—that is, it should be designed to cater to teachers' contingent needs in specific educational contexts. The role of teacher educator is not that of knowledge provider, but that of a guide, facilitator, and collaborator.

(3) Explicitly stating innovation principles and appropriate teacher training by presenting, exemplifying, and demonstrating teaching practice at the initial stage of an innovation project is necessary, as it contributes to developing PTs'

explicit cognition. Nevertheless, a mechanism that encourages and supports self-directed teacher learning is more important to facilitate sustainable teacher professional development. It is through reflection on personal and peers experience that explicit cognition is converted into implicit cognition, and then related to established teaching practices.

(4) The stagnant phase in curriculum innovation does not necessarily indicate failure; rather, it might be a critical period in which the teacher's psycho-cognitive and socio-affective processing is involved in absorbing and decoding teacher learning and, in turn, changes in teaching practices.

(5) University-school collaboration is by no means a realm in which knowledge, ideology, and practices are 'taught' by university researchers to school teachers. Rather, both parts are collaborators with equivalent resources to contribute, and their interaction is a process of exploration by jointly constructing new knowledge, ideologies, and practices.

(6) When evaluating whether an innovation project is successful, a valid method to adopt is to observe whether there are beneficial and verifiable changes in PTs' cognition and teaching practices. Moreover, one needs to be mindful, as external pressure might lead to inconsistencies between what a teacher states, and what he or she does.

(7) The adoption of an innovation takes much longer than has been speculated. Four years is regarded as a long period for a doctoral study; however, it is still a short period for the adoption of an educational change. As illustrated by the by Rogers' (1983) widely-quoted S-shape curve (see in Fig. 8.3), the shaded area marks "the heart of the diffusion process" (Rogers, 2003, p. 274)—that is,

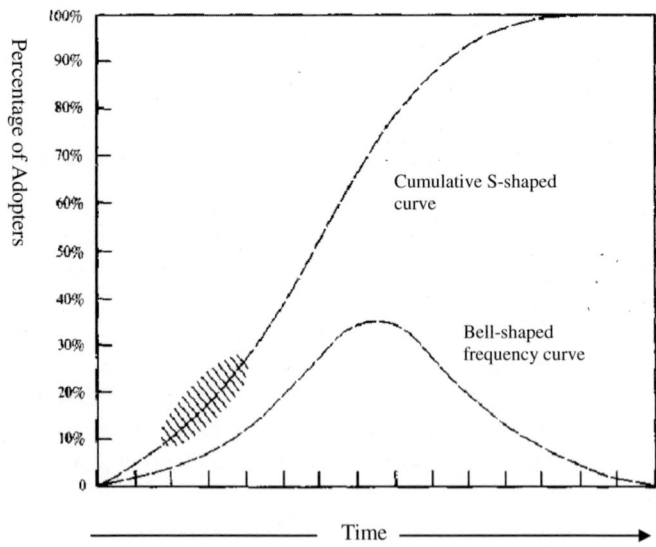

Fig. 8.3 The S-shape curve of adoption (based on Rogers, 1983, p. 243)

from about 10 to 20% adoption of the diffusion curve. According to Rogers, diffusion begins to accelerate after that point, and becomes impossible to stop. Regarding the Danyang Project, the number of PTs who completely accepted the innovative principles and who translated innovative cognition into teaching behavior is still very limited, as we were still at the initial stage of diffusion, even after over four years' implementation of the project.

8.4 Limitations

One major limitation in this study relates to the criticism of ethnographic studies in general—that is, it seems to be too grand and unmanageable to reach specific and convincing conclusions. Though ethnography has its intrinsic limitations, as do other research methods, it is a powerful tool for seeking answers to meaningful questions hidden behind the intricacies of human society (Dörnyei, 2007).

Another limitation, based on the scope of this study, concerns the number of focal participants. Among 10 teacher participants who had been the DP members for the past four years, only one teacher was selected to be reported on in this dissertation. Despite her typicality and representativeness, the author does not propose the changes that occurred to Marian must also happen to other teachers or in other educational settings. The route travelled by Marian is unique, integrating personal endeavors and external inputs to which she had been exposed. As with other qualitative studies rooted in the naturalistic paradigm, this study features an in-depth investigation of individual experience to illuminate and enlighten, rather than to inform readers with definite rules for generalization. Admittedly, more interesting findings would have been possible if more than one focal participant had been selected; however, this study can serve as a reliable reference informing ensuing research.

The third limitation of this thesis concerns the relationship between research and teaching. Research in SLA and language teaching to date still leaves numerous unexplored areas. While these unsolved questions continually give impetus to the development of this field, the researcher of this study, along with her fellow researchers involved in the Danyang Project, constantly find it difficult to give definite and satisfactory answers in response to PTs' enquiries. How corrective feedback should be provided, for example, is a question that has invoked a large body of research yielding somewhat controversial findings. As there is always a gap between research and classroom practices, the researcher regards unanswered questions as triggers informing future research.

8.5   Suggestions for Future Studies

Due to the limitations of the present study, it is suggested that future studies address questions concerning the constancy and inconsistency between teacher cognition and practices, using a more easily-manipulated method. It would be worthwhile to select one aspect of classroom instruction and involve teachers in immediate reflection thereon. In that case, more restricted methods, such as stimulated recall, could be employed to elicit teachers' belief, knowledge and attitudes about specific aspects of their teaching. The findings from a normative study would be a quite informative complement to both the present study and the field as a whole. As depicted in this study, despite all the ups and downs she experienced in the Danyang Project, Marian, when alone in a new educational setting, started a new professional journey full of fascinating uncertainties; similarly, studies relating to the field are always intriguing endeavors for more researchers to conduct.

Appendix A

The English classroom teaching evaluation form used for unfocussed classroom observation

English Classroom Teaching Evaluation Form

(Translated from Shu et al., 2012, pp. 412–414)

School		Teacher's name	Date			
Teaching contents				Grade		
Evaluation scheme				5	4	3
Teacher's teaching behaviors	Teaching principles	1. Develop learners' capacity to use target language and emphasize using language in contextualized situations;				
		2. Help learners form beneficial learning habits and train effective learning strategies;				
		3. Give respect, care and love to all students				
	Organizing classroom activities	1. The pedagogical objectives are clear				
		2. The teacher's presentation and instruction is explicit				
		3. There is a clear and reasonable division of teaching steps and natural transition in between				
		4. There is a variation of instructional activities that are in accordance with pedagogical objectives				

(continued)

(continued)

School		Teacher's name	Date			
		5. The teacher exhibits good questioning strategies that can promote learner engagement in classroom interaction				
		6. The teacher can accommodate the content and tempo of teaching to learners' performance				
	Using teaching resources	1. The teacher can select suitable instructional materials and appropriately make necessary adaptations				
		2. The teacher can use multi-media equipment to facilitate teaching				
	Achieving pedagogical objectives	1. The teacher can arrange teaching steps in a logical way and highlight the key points				
		2. The teacher can attain the pre-set pedagogical objectives				
	Teacher's presenting skills	1. teach with passion;				
		2. good pronunciation and clear articulation;				
		3. speak target language accurately and fluently;				
		4. communicate with learners and understand their needs;				
Students' learning behaviors	Students' performance	1. Students show interest in learning and actively participate in classroom activities				
		2. Students can understand and follow the teacher's instruction to do classroom activities as expected				
		3. Students can speak loudly in English and avoid using their L1				

Appendix B

A classroom observation scheme used for focused classroom observation

Classroom observation scheme for participatory structure								
Date:		Class:	Teacher:		Observer:		Teaching content:	
1	2	3	4	5	6	7	8	9
6 Zhu Y. M1		Yan X. M4				Wei Y. M3		Wu Y. M2
5 Zhang M. F3		Zhang C. M3		Liu Y. F2	Wu H. M2	Zhu S. F3	Leng F. M4	Li S. M3
4 Xu W. M3	Wu Q. F4	Zhou D. F2	Yu T. M4	Zhang Y. F3	Sun H. M3	Xu C. F3	Lu J. M3	Mao Y. F3
3 Tang J. M4	Zhang N. F4	Wu Y. F5	Xu Y. M3	Gong Y. F2	Li C. M2	He Jiao F4	Cao R. M2	Gong N. F4
2 Sun H. M3	Chen N. F4	Ma Y. F5	Zhu X. M5	Xu Y. F4	Jiang K. M3	He Jia F4	Cai S. M2	Zhuge Q. F5
1 Cheng Z. M4	Wang Y. F2	Fan W. F4	Jiang C. M4	Zhou Y. F4	Sun X. M5	Zhu J. F4	Tian X. M3	Zhu C. F3
			Teacher's Desk					

Note: This observation scheme was constructed in consultation with the teacher observee before he taught the class. The layout of this scheme was a miniature classroom map in which one cell stood for one learner. In each cell, there was a student's name, his or her gender (M/F) and proficiency level estimated by teacher (1-5 ranging from the lowest to the highest). When using this scheme, observers could draw lines with arrows to signal patterns of teacher-student and student-student interaction

© Springer Nature Singapore Pte Ltd. 2018
Y. Zhu, *Language Curriculum Innovation in a Chinese Secondary School*,
https://doi.org/10.1007/978-981-10-7239-0

Appendix C

Codebook for Coding Qualitative Data

1. **[Pre] teacher's pressure**

    (1) <EM> exam
    (2) <WL> workload
    (3) <SC> society and community
    (4) <Par> parents
    (5) <GSS> good students
    (6) <USS> under-developed students

2. **[EL] easy learning**

    (1) <EEL> expectation of easy learning
    (2) <TEL> teaching for purpose of easy learning

3. **[BLL] beliefs about language learning**

    (1) <L1&L2> L1 acquisition and L2 learning
    (2) <Mot> motivation
    (3) <LC> language communication
    (4) <LLB> learner's prior learning background
    (5) <RL> rote learning
    (6) <AI> audio recordings input
    (7) <LLA> learner's language aptitude
    (8) <GRM> grammar
    (9) <LS> learning strategy
    (10) <Voc> vocabulary
    (11) <PN> phonology
    (12) <LA> learner autonomy
    (13) <LAF> learner affective factors
    (14) <WLE> why learn English
    (15) <FS> Forms
    (16) <F&A> fluency & accuracy
    (17) <ER> extended reading

© Springer Nature Singapore Pte Ltd. 2018
Y. Zhu, *Language Curriculum Innovation in a Chinese Secondary School*,
https://doi.org/10.1007/978-981-10-7239-0

(18) <LJ> learning journal
(19) <OC> organized classroom
(20) <LO> learner output

4. [CCI] constraints on curriculum innovation

(1) <LLP> learner's language proficiency
(2) <TLP> teacher's language proficiency
(3) <LW> learner's workload
(4) <LBS> leaner's busy schedule
(5) <TAF> teacher's age factor
(6) <BH> bad health
(7) <TTK> teacher's theoretical knowledge

5. [TPB] teacher's professional background

(1) <BT> begin time
(2) <TT> teacher's teacher
(3) <Conf>confidence
(4) <TLS> teacher's learning strategy
(5) <TSL> teacher's success in learning
(6) <PTE> pre-service teacher education
(7) <TWE> teacher's work experience
(8) <TLE> teacher's learning experience

6. [TB] textbook

(1) <FT> follow textbook
(2) <AT> adapt textbook
(3) <STM> supplement teaching materials
(4) <DT> design task
(5) <DTB> difficult text book
(6) <ETB> experimental textbook
(7) <MTB> mandated textbook
(8) <MTM> mandated teaching materials
(9) <TM> teaching materials

7. [BLT] teacher's beliefs about language teaching

(1)   <GTT> grammar-translation teaching
(2)   <TFT> teacher-fronted teaching
(3)   <CLP> classroom presentation
(4)   <TL> teaching listening
(5)   <TR> teaching reading
(6)   <ST> story telling
(7)   <Comp> competition
(8)   <ES> emotional scaffolding and inspiration
(9)   <TS> teaching speaking
(10) <TW> teaching writing

(11) <NA> needs analysis
(12) <EA> extra-curricular activity
(13) <CA> classroom activity
(14) <TP> teaching pedagogy
(15) <TRL> teaching by rote learning
(16) <NC> national curriculum
(17) <TPI> teacher-parents interaction
(18) <TLR> teacher and learner's roles in classroom
(19) <SFB> student's feedback
(20) <CF> corrective feedback
(21) <KC> knowledge of culture
(22) <LP> lesson planning
(23) <CLI> contextualized language input
(24) <LES> Listening to English songs
(26) <IT> improve teaching
(27) <TDAL> teacher-directed autonomous learning
(28) <IA> innovative assessment
(29) <GS> goal setting
(30) <WM> watch movie
(31) <TBLT> task-based language teaching
(32) <M&F> meaning & form
(33) <DI> deductive instruction
(34) <II> inductive instruction
(35) <LLD> learner's long-term development

8. [CI] colleague interaction

(1) <CE> colleague encouragement
(2) <CP> colleague pressure
(3) <CL> colleague learning
(4) <CN> colleague negotiation

9. [CPL] community of practice and learning

(1) <HES> Huanan Experimental School
(2) <TRG> Teaching Research Group
(3) <PHD> PhD students
(3) <EXP> experts
(4) <COS> colleagues outside school
(5) <CIS> colleagues inside school
(6) <CIP> colleagues in innovation project
(7) <CAD> class advisor
(8) <WA> win awards
(9) <TTS> teacher's team spirit
(10) <RS> rural school
(11) <IR> institutional regulation

10. [CO] classroom observation

   (1) <CD> classroom discourse
   (2) <COF> classroom observation feedback
   (3) <PCO> peer classroom observation
   (4) <PGCO> project group classroom observation
   (5) <PL> public lesson
   (6) <POM> pre-observation meeting
   (7) <OS> classroom observation scheme
   (8) <NT> note taking
   (9) <GO> global observation
 (10) <FO> focused observation
 (11) <TA> time allotment

11. [TD] teacher development

   (1) <WI> awareness to improve
   (2) <TRT> teacher training
   (3) <GA> going abroad
   (4) <MD> master degree
   (5) <TRC> teacher-researcher collaboration
   (6) <TRP> teacher's research project
   (7) <TPL> teacher's professional level
   (8) <IP> innovation project
   (9) <ESC> explicit statement of change
 (10) <RB> read books for teacher development
 (11) <LTT> language teaching theory
 (12) <VBT> value of being a teacher
 (13) <TJ> teaching journal
 (14) <RP> reflective practice
 (15) <Ref> reflection
 (16) <TN> teacher's needs
 (17) <Pub> publication
 (18) <EP> exchange program
 (19) <LL> lifetime learning
 (20) <CT> charisma of teacher
 (21) <BC> being critical
 (22) <TTL> teacher training lectures
 (23) <DIP> difficulty confronted in innovation project
 (24) <SF> sense of fulfillmen

Appendix D

A coded classroom transcript[1]

---

[1]Due to the limit of space, columns containing the beginning time, the end time and the types of exchanges (Preparatory Ex./ Nuclear Ex./ Embedded Ex./Dependent Ex.) were omitted in this appendix.

© Springer Nature Singapore Pte Ltd. 2018
Y. Zhu, *Language Curriculum Innovation in a Chinese Secondary School*,
https://doi.org/10.1007/978-981-10-7239-0

Activity	Instructional Materials	Duration	Interlocutor	Utterance	Meaning- versus Form-focused	Participatory organization pattern	Student- versus teacher-initiated	IR/IRF	Types of teacher questions: Referential / Display	Types of learner talk: restricted/ unrestricted
A1: Greetings	N/A	0.85	TT	Hi class	m	T-AS	T	IRF		
		1.56	AST	Good morning, Miss Li						RL
		0.75	TT	Sit down, please						
		1.34	Silence	<Students sit down.>						
		5.73	TT	Today, so many students have come to our classroom, so let's welcome them	m	T-AS	T	IRF		
		2.65	AST	<Clap hands.>						
		2.64	TT	<Clap hands.>						
		1.46	TT	Thank you. Thank you						
A2: A student gave a presentation to introduce herself.	SPM	4.44	TT	And today, it is our demo time now	m	T-IS	T	IR		
		3.61	TT	Er…who is the next one?						
		0.82	TT	No. 7						
		0.65	Silence	(Wait time)						
		1.65	TT	S's name. Yes, please come here						
		5.01	Silence	<The presenter goes to the front.>						

(continued)

(continued)

Activity	Instructional Materials	Duration	Interlocutor	Utterance	Meaning- versus Form-focused	Participatory organization pattern	Student- versus teacher-initiated	IR/IRF	Types of teacher questions: Referential / Display	Types of learner talk: restricted/ unrestricted
		1.35	TT	Listen to her carefully	m	T-AS	T	IR		
		1.15	Silence	(silence)						
		4.85	IST	Hello, everyone. Now let's introduce my friend, S's name	m	IS-AS	S	IR		UL
		2.38	IST	She is 13 years old						UL
		1.37	IST	She is ***						UL
		3.72	IST	She is a new student in Yan Ling Middle School						UL
		2.25	IST	She is tall						UL
		1.29	IST	Her hair is long						UL
		1.41	IST	And she wear glasses						UL
		2.61	IST	She had many hobby						UL
		4.17	IST	reading, swimming, listening to music and playing chess						UL
		3.06	IST	She is good at playing chess and swimming						UL
		6.47	IST	She has a big family: her grandparents, her parents, her sister and she						UL
		4.68	IST	She is, she want to be an English teacher when she grow up						UL
		1.94	IST	This is her. Thank you						UL
		0.92	Silence	(silence)						
		0.93	TT	Ok, thank you	m	T-IS-AS	T	IR		
		1.08	TT	<Clap hands>						
		1.08	AST	<Clap hands.>						
		1.55	TT	Stop here. Stop here	m	T-IS	T	IRF		

(continued)

(continued)

Activity	Instructional Materials	Duration	Interlocutor	Utterance	Meaning- versus Form-focused	Participatory organization pattern	Student- versus teacher-initiated	IR/IRF	Types of teacher questions: Referential / Display	Types of learner talk: restricted/ unrestricted
		2.65	TT	Do you have any questions to ask them?					RQ	
		0.68	IST	Yes						RLL
		0.57	TT	Yes						
		3.49	IST	What my hobby? What are my hobby?	m	IS-T-IS	S	IR		ULL
		2.65	Silence	(wait time)						
		0.95	TT	Yes?						
		0.86	TT	Yes?						
		0.91	IST	S's name						
		3.19	IST	Your hobbies are swimming and reading						ULL
		3.27	IST	Em, no... ***						
		1.46	Silence	(pause)						
		1.13	TT	Some others	m	IS-T-IS	T	IRF		
		1.06	Silence	(wait time)						
		1.03	TT	S's name. Ok. Say						
		2.59	IST	Listen to music and the chess						ULL
		0.85	IST	Yes						
		1.12	Silence	(Silence)	m	T-IS	T	IR		
		2.47	TT	Yes, ok, so any questions?					RQ	ULL
		2.81	IST	Em. How many people are my family?						
		1.94	Silence	(wait time)						
		0.55	IST	S's name	m	IS-IS	S	IRF		RLL
		6.73	IST	Your grandparents, parents, sister and your						ULL
		1.86	TT	Yes, and your...						
		0.43	TT	And...	m	T-AS	T	IRF		
		1.06	AST	you						RLL

(continued)

(continued)

Activity	Instructional Materials	Duration	Interlocutor	Utterance	Meaning- versus Form-focused	Participatory organization pattern	Student- versus teacher-initiated	IR/IRF	Types of teacher questions: Referential / Display	Types of learner talk: restricted/ unrestricted
		2.88	TT	Yes, ok. Thank you. Very good						
		2.29	AST	<Clap hands.>						
		0.735	TT	Very good						
		3.85	TT	And now, we will give her some points	m	T-AS	T	IR		
		3.78	TT	Here, clearly? Is, does she speak clearly?					DQ	
		1.34	AST	Yes						RLL
		1.17	TT	And correctly?	m	T-AS	T	IR	DQ	
		1.27	AST	Yes						RLL
		1.05	TT	And loudly?	m	T-AS	T	IR	DQ	
		0.84	AST	Yes						RLL
		1.37	TT	And fluently?	m	T-AS	T	IR	DQ	
		1.15	AST	Yes						RLL
		2.66	TT	So how many point can she get?	m	T-AS	T	IRF	RQ	
		1.17	AST	Ten						
		1.77	TT	Yes, ten. Very good						RLL
		2.9	TT	Ok, so, let's give her claps again	m	T-AS	T	IR		
		2.41	AST	<Clap hands.>						
A3. Lead-in. The teacher showed some pictures of sport stars on PPT slides, asked the students some questions and teaches	TDM	8	TT	Ok, just now. S's name tells us she is good at swimming, right?	m	T-AS	T	IR	DQ	
		2.2	TT	She is good at swimming, right?						
		1.22	AST	Yes						RLL
		5.37	TT	And do you know what is Lin Dan good at?	m	T-SS	T	IRF	RQ	
		0.83	Silence	(wait time)						

(continued)

(continued)

Activity	Instructional Materials	Duration	Interlocutor	Utterance	Meaning- versus Form-focused	Participatory organization pattern	Student- versus teacher-initiated	IR/IRF	Types of teacher questions: Referential / Display	Types of learner talk: restricted/ unrestricted
several useful phrases		2.82	TT	What sport is Lin Dan good at?						
		1.16	TT	Do you know him?					DQ	
		0.71	Silence	(wait time)						
		1.26	TT	Do you know Lin Dan?						
		0.81	Silence	(wait time)						
		0.67	SST	Yes						RLL
		0.62	TT	Yes						
		3.49	TT	So he is good at…what?	m	T-IS	T	IRF	RQ	
		1.69	Silence	(wait time)						
		0.72	TT	Yes						
		2.09	TT	What? What is he good at?						
		2.24	Silence	(wait time)						
		0.84	TT	S's name. You						
		0.84	TT	Have a try						
		2.21	IST	He is good at tennis						ULL
		3.5	TT	He is good at tennis. Tennis, right?					DQ	
		2.37	TT	No, he is good at badminton						
		1.97	TT	Ok, sit down, please. Thank you						
		1.19	TT	Read after me. Badminton	f	T-AS	T	IR		RLL
		1.2	AST	Badminton						
		0.89	TT	Twice	f	T-AS	T	IR		
		2.37	AST	Badminton, badminton						RLL
		2.64	TT	Yes, so. Do you know, what's the meaning? The badminton	m	T-SS	T	IRF	DQ	
		0.89	Silence	(Silence)						
		1.28	SST	羽毛球。						RLL

(continued)

(continued)

Activity	Instructional Materials	Duration	Interlocutor	Utterance	Meaning- versus Form-focused	Participatory organization pattern	Student- versus teacher-initiated	IR/IRF	Types of teacher questions: Referential / Display	Types of learner talk: restricted/ unrestricted
		0.85	TT	Yes. Very good						
		3.18	TT	Next one, what sport is Li Na good at?					RQ	
		0.81	Silence	(wait time)	m	T-IS	T	IR		
		2.33	TT	Try to put up your hands						
		1.1	TT	Very good. You						
		1.69	IST	She is good at tennis						UL
		1.82	TT	Yes, do you think so?	m	T-AS	T	IR	DQ	
		1.07	AST	Yes						RL
		1.75	TT	Ok? Now read after me. Tennis	f	T-AS	T	IR		
		0.84	AST	Tennis						RL
		1.26	TT	Tennis, twice	f	T-AS	T	IR		
		1.33	AST	Tennis, tennis						RL
		0.97	TT	Here, tennis	f	T-AS	T	IR		
		1.55	AST	Tennis, tennis						RL
		0.52	TT	/e/	f	T-AS	T	IR		
		0.97	AST	/e/						RL
		0.6	TT	/e/	f	T-AS	T	IR		
		0.77	AST	/e/						RL
		0.76	TT	/e/	f	T-AS	T	IR		
		0.8	AST	/e/						RL
		0.39	TT	/e/	f	T-AS	T	IR		
		0.6	AST	/e/						RL
		1.27	TT	Yes, again. /e/	f	T-AS	T	IR		
		1.28	AST	/e/, /e/						RL
		0.74	TT	/i/	f	T-AS	T	IR		
		1.23	AST	/i/, /i/						RL
		0.57	TT	tennis	f	T-AS	T	IR		
		1.47	AST	tennis, tennis						RL

(continued)

(continued)

Activity	Instructional Materials	Duration	Interlocutor	Utterance	Meaning- versus Form-focused	Participatory organization pattern	Student- versus teacher-initiated	IR/IRF	Types of teacher questions: Referential / Display	Types of learner talk: restricted/ unrestricted
		1.48	TT	Again, tennis	f	T-AS	T	IR		RL
		1.57	AST	Tennis, tennis						
		0.49	TT	Good	m	T-IS	T	IRF		
		3.36	TT	Next one. What sport are they good at?					RQ	
		1.25	Silence	(wait time)						
		0.48	TT	You						
		1.25	IST	football						
		1.33	TT	Ok, football						RL
		2.02	TT	Ok, football or volleyball?	f	T-IS	T	IR	DQ	
		2.28	TT	Ok, the full sentence, you should say…						
		1.09	TT	Again						
		1.36	IST	at volleyball	f	T-IS	T	IR		RL
		1.89	TT	They are…again						
		1.5	IST	They are volleyball						UL
		1.29	TT	They are volleyball?	f	T-IS-AS	T	IRF	DQ	
		0.91	AST	<laughter>						
		0.5	TT	Ok						
		1.68	IST	They are playing volleyball						UL
		0.82	TT	Ok, thank you						
		1.645	TT	You, stand up. Again	f	T-IS	T	IR		UL
		2.31	IST	They are playing volleyball						
		1.13	TT	They are…	f	T-IS	T	IR		
		1.19	TT	They are…						
		1.37	IST	playing volleyball						RL
		2.72	TT	playing volleyball. They are good…at	f	T-IS	T	IRF		
		0.77	TT	Again						

(continued)

(continued)

Activity	Instructional Materials	Duration	Interlocutor	Utterance	Meaning- versus Form-focused	Participatory organization pattern	Student- versus teacher-initiated	IR/IRF	Types of teacher questions: Referential / Display	Types of learner talk: restricted/ unrestricted
		3.31	IST	They are good at playing volleyball						UL
		1.3	TT	Thank you. Very good						
		4.21	TT	Next one. Here, volleyball. Read after me	f	T-AS	T	IR		
		3.15	AST	Volleyball. Volleyball						RL
		0.92	TT	Volleyball	f	T-AS	T	IR		
		1.98	AST	Volleyball, volleyball	f	T-AS				RL
		0.62	TT	/o/						
		0.59	AST	/o/	f	T-AS	T	IR		RL
		0.59	TT	/o/						
		0.53	AST	/o/	f	T-AS	T	IR		RL
		0.48	TT	/i/						
		0.47	AST	/i/	f	T-AS	T	IR		RL
		0.46	TT	/i/						
		0.53	AST	/i/	f	T-AS	T	IR		RL
		0.64	TT	volleyball						
		1.16	AST	volleyball, volleyball	f	T-AS	T	IR		RL
		1.37	TT	Yeah, very good	m	T-IS	T	IR		
		4.64	TT	Next one. What sport is Yi Jianlian good at?					RQ	
		2.48	Silence	<Many students raise their hands.>						
		0.96	TT	Anybody? You						
		2.72	IST	He is good at playing basketball						UL
		1.21	TT	Do you think so?	m	T-IS-AS	T	IRF	DQ	
		1.13	AST	Yes						
		2.15	TT	Yes. Very clever answer						RL
		1.59	Silence	<prepare PPT>						
		1.18	TT	Ok. next one	m	T-IS	T	IR		

(continued)

(continued)

Activity	Instructional Materials	Duration	Interlocutor	Utterance	Meaning- versus Form-focused	Participatory organization pattern	Student- versus teacher-initiated	IR/IRF	Types of teacher questions: Referential / Display	Types of learner talk: restricted/ unrestricted
		3.54	TT	What sport is Li Xiaoxia good at?					RQ	
		0.9	Silence	<Many students raise hands.>						
		0.46	TT	S's name						
		3.5	IST	She is good at play, play table tennis						UL
		3.89	TT	She is good at playing table tennis	m	T-IS	T	IRF		
		1.31	Silence	(pause)						
		0.94	TT	Right?						
		1.87	TT	Think the ***						
		2.32	TT	She is good at play…						
		1.73	IST	Playing table tennis						UL
		1.99	TT	Yeah, thank you. You are right						
		1.14	Silence	(pause)						
		2.98	TT	She is good at playing table tennis	f	T-AS	T	IR		
		1.6	TT	Ok, together, table tennis						
		1.06	AST	Table tennis						RL
		1	TT	Again						
		2.31	AST	Table tennis. Table tennis	f	T-AS	T	IRF		
		1.05	TT	Good						RL
		3.23	TT	And what sport is Sun Yang good at?	m	T-IS	T	IR	RQ	
		1.22	Silence	(pause)						
		0.75	TT	Sun Yang						
		1.61	Silence	<Many students raise their hands.>						
		0.8	TT	S's name						

(continued)

(continued)

Activity	Instructional Materials	Duration	Interlocutor	Utterance	Meaning- versus Form-focused	Participatory organization pattern	Student- versus teacher-initiated	IR/IRF	Types of teacher questions: Referential / Display	Types of learner talk: restricted/ unrestricted
		3.48	IST	Sun Yang is good at swimming	m	T-SS	T	IR		UL
		1.74	Silence	(silence)						
		1.44	TT	Do you agree with him?					DQ	RL
		0.81	SST	Yes						
		0.86	TT	Yes or no?						
		0.77	AST	Yes						RL
		1.73	TT	Very good. Thank you	m	T-AS	T	IRF		
		1.07	TT	Very good answer						
		0.4	Silence	(pause)						
		3.29	TT	Ok, he is good at swimming						
A4: Students worked out an exercise in the textbook and then the teacher checked their answers	MMTA	5.07	TT	And what are the students good at?	m	T-AS	T	IR	RQ	
		4.07	TT	Now, you can open your books. Turn to page 19						
		6.04	TT	Page ***. Finish exercise 1, part A						
		31.16	Silence	<Students work on the exercise. The teacher walks among the students.>						
		1.4	TT	So, have you finished?	m	T-SS	T	IR		
		2.7	Silence	(wait time)						
		2	TT	Yes or no? Have you finished?						
		1.49	SST	Yes						RL
		2.57	TT	Ok, yes, the first one, you	m	T-IS	T	IR		
		2.9	Silence	<The student stands up.>						
		2.05	TT	The whole sentence. Read	m&f	T-IS	T	IR		
		1.55	Silence	(wait time)						
		1.05	IST	We are playing volleyball						UL

(continued)

(continued)

Activity	Instructional Materials	Duration	Interlocutor	Utterance	Meaning- versus Form-focused	Participatory organization pattern	Student- versus teacher-initiated	IR/IRF	Types of teacher questions: Referential / Display	Types of learner talk: restricted/ unrestricted
		1.26	TT	We are playing…						
		0.79	Silence	(wait time)	m&f	T-IS	T	IRF		
		2.17	TT	Look at the sentence carefully						
		2.05	TT	We like…						
		1.83	IST	playing foot, volleyball						UL
		1.97	TT	Yes, volleyball. Thank you						
		0.94	TT	Go on. Next one						
		1.54	Silence	(wait time)	m&f	T-IS	T	IR		
		2.59	IST	I'm good at playing table tennis						UL
		0.83	TT	Yes						
		1.92	TT	And next one, go on	m&f	T-IS	T	IR		
		1.7	IST	We are playing football						UL
		3.6	TT	Yes. That is Simon, right? Simon likes playing football						
		2.22	IST	I enjoy swimming	m&f	T-IS-SS	S	IRF		UL
		0.8	TT	Right?					DQ	
		0.5	SST	Yes						RL
		1.1	TT	Yes. Ok						
		4.02	TT	Anybody who get all the answer correctly, please put up your hands			T	IR		
		0.6	TT	Let's see	m	T-IS				
		1.36	Silence	<Many students raise their hands.>						
	TDM	2.53	TT	Yes, thank you, very good						
A5: The teacher asked		6.16	TT	And, now. S's name. S'a name						
		5.38	TT	What sport are you good at?					RQ	

(continued)

(continued)

Activity	Instructional Materials	Duration	Interlocutor	Utterance	Meaning- versus Form-focused	Participatory organization pattern	Student- versus teacher-initiated	IR/IRF	Types of teacher questions: Referential / Display	Types of learner talk: restricted/ unrestricted
some students about their favourite sports. Next students worked in pairs to practice the dialogue. Then students were asked to perform the dialogue in groups		1.89	IST	I'm good at…						UL
		3.6	Silence	(silence)						
		1.43	TT	What sport are you good at?	m	T-IS	T	IR		
		1.21	Silence	(wait time)						
		3.25	IST	I good at tabl..playing table tennis						UL
		0.89	TT	I good at	m	T-IS	T	IRF		
		1.17	TT	I good at						
		0.94	Silence	(wait time)						
		3.13	IST	I am good at playing table tennis						UL
		1.03	TT	Yeah, very good						
		2.24	TT	Next one, what's your favorite sport?	m	T-IS	T	IRF	RQ	UL
		3	IST	I'm good at playing basketball						
		1.16	TT	Ok, thank you						
		0.69	Silence	(pause)						
		4.72	TT	Next one, what sport do you like best?	m	T-IS	T	IR	RQ	UL
		3.52	IST	I like playing volleyball						
		3.13	TT	You like playing volleyball… best, right?	m	T-IS	T	IRF		
		1.59	TT	Ok, thank you, sit down, please						
		1.66	TT	And, you						
		1.09	Silence	<The student stands up.>						
		2.52	TT	What is your favorite sport?					RQ	
		3.63	IST	My favorite sport is…table tennis						UL
		1.43	TT	Yes, very good answer						

(continued)

(continued)

Activity	Instructional Materials	Duration	Interlocutor	Utterance	Meaning- versus Form-focused	Participatory organization pattern	Student- versus teacher-initiated	IR/IRF	Types of teacher questions: Referential / Display	Types of learner talk: restricted/ unrestricted
		5.16	TT	Please work in pairs. One ask, one answer						
		1.92	TT	What is your favorite sport						
		8.19	TT	Then answer I love, I enjoy, or I...I like. Or my favorite sport is….	m	T-AS	T	IR		
		1.24	TT	Ok. can you understand me?						
		2.38	TT	Yes, now, work in pairs. Be quick						
		25.25	PST	<Students work in pairs and practice the dialogue.>						
		1.69	TT	Ok, have you finished?						
		8.37	TT	Ok, now, I will ask you to do the dialogue in teams						
		3.6	TT	Clear? In teams. That is a team, team, team	m	T-AS	T	IR		
		4	TT	Ok. Now one ask, one answer. And then you ask, and you answer						
		2.26	TT	Ok, have you understood me?						
		1.4	TT	Now, let's have a try						
		3.12	TT	Oh, yes. This group. Stand up						
		1.63	Silence	<A column of students stand up>	m	T-SS	T	IR		
		2.63	TT	Please turn back, ask her						
		2.5	Silence	(Silence)						
		1.8	IST	What is your…	m	IS-T-IS	S	IR		UL
		1.56	Silence	<The student struggles.>						
		0.21	TT	favorite						
		2.15	IST	favorite sport?						UL

(continued)

(continued)

Activity	Instructional Materials	Duration	Interlocutor	Utterance	Meaning- versus Form-focused	Participatory organization pattern	Student- versus teacher-initiated	IR/IRF	Types of teacher questions: Referential / Display	Types of learner talk: restricted/ unrestricted
		6.77	Silence	(Silence)						
		1.99	IST	I like playing volleyball						UL
		2.74	IST	What is your favorite sport?	m	IS-IS	S	IR		UL
		1.98	IST	My favorite sport is running						UL
		1.62	IST	What is your favorite sport?	m	IS-IS	S	IR		UL
		2.74	IST	My favorite sport is running						UL
		1.74	IST	What is your favorite sport?						UL
		1.56	IST	I like ***	m	IS-T-IS	S	IR		UL
		2.64	TT	Ok, ok, now, thank you						
		1.47	Silence	(pause)						
		1.13	TT	Thank you, sit down, please	m	T-SS	T	IR		
		3.44	TT	Another group. This one. Stand up						
		2.16	IST	What is your favorite sport?	m	IS-IS	S	IR		UL
		3.3	IST	I like, I like playing table tennis best						
		2.72	IST	What is your favorite sport?	m	IS-IS	S	IR		UL
		2.9	IST	My favorite sport is ***						UL
		2.04	IST	What is your favorite sport?	m	IS-IS	S	IR		UL
		2.59	IST	My favorite sport is running						UL
		2.18	IST	What is your favorite sport?	m	IS-IS	S	IR		UL
		0.91	IST	My favorite is running						UL
		1.4	IST	What is your favorite sport?	m	IS-IS	S	IR		UL
		2.69	IST	My favorite sport is running						UL
		2.94	TT	Ok, thank you. Very good. Very good. Thank you	m	T-SS	T	IR		

(continued)

(continued)

Activity	Instructional Materials	Duration	Interlocutor	Utterance	Meaning- versus Form-focused	Participatory organization pattern	Student- versus teacher-initiated	IR/IRF	Types of teacher questions: Referential / Display	Types of learner talk: restricted/ unrestricted
		4.27	TT	Now, Simon and Amy are also talking about sports	m	T-AS	T	IR		
		7.55	TT	Now, please listen careful and finish the short passage						
		2.09	TT	Ok, so, are you ready?						
		0.69	Silence	(pause)						
		1.08	TT	Listen carefully						
A6: The teacher asked the students to listen to a conversation and completed an exercise in the textbook. Then the teacher checked students' answers, asked them to read the conversation and invited some students to present the conversation in pairs.		2.61	Silence	<prepare audio recording>						
		3.95	AI	I went to swim. What is your favorite sport, Simon?						
		4.72	AI	I want to play football. Do you often play football!?	m	AI-AS-T	T	IR		
		3.62	AI	Yes, I often play football after school						
		1.1	AI	What about you?						
	MMTA	2.83	AI	I go swimming every week						
		1.71	Silence	<Many students raise hands.>						
		2.48	TT	If you get the answer, put up your hands. Very good	m&f	T-IS	T	IRF		
		1.75	TT	The first one. You						
		2.46	Silence	<The student stands up.>						
		1.12	IST	Eddie like swimming						UL
		1.42	TT	Swimming, good						
		2.29	TT	Next one. You	m&f	T-IS	T	IRF		
		2.65	IST	Simon likes playing football						UL
		0.98	TT	Very good						
		2.56	TT	Next one. You. S's name	m&f	T-IS	T	IRF		
		2.79	IST	He often plays it after school						UL
		1.9	TT	Yes, very good. Thank you						

(continued)

(continued)

Activity	Instructional Materials	Duration	Interlocutor	Utterance	Meaning-versus Form-focused	Participatory organization pattern	Student-versus teacher-initiated	IR/IRF	Types of teacher questions: Referential / Display	Types of learner talk: restricted/ unrestricted
		3.96	TT	The last one. The last one. Ok. S's name						
		3.1	IST	Amy goes swimming every week	m&f	T-IS	T	IRF		UL
		1.44	TT	Every week. Do you think so?					DQ	
		1.68	Silence	(wait time)						
		1.68	TT	Every week. Yes or no?	m&f	T-IS-AS	T	IRF	DQ	
		1	AST	Yes						RL
		1.6	TT	Yes, ok. Thank you						
		1.47	TT	It's very good answer						
		1.26	TT	Let's read together	f	T-AS	T	IR		
		1.39	TT	Amy likes swimming. Begin						
		12.35	AST	Amy likes swimming. Simon likes playing football. He often plays it after school. Amy goes swimming every weekend						UL
		4.92	TT	Now, open your books. Turn to page 19, turn to page 19	m&f	T-AS	T	IR		
		11.69	TT	Please read the dialogue by yourself, try remember them. Then I will ask you act out the dialogue in front of… blackboard. Ok?						
		2.68	TT	One is Amy. One is Simon						
		1.92	TT	I'll give you two minutes. Be quick						
		58.37	PST	<Students work in pairs.>						
		2.8	TT	Ok. stop. Stop	m	T-AS	T	IR		
		0.91	Silence	(pause)						

(continued)

(continued)

Activity	Instructional Materials	Duration	Interlocutor	Utterance	Meaning- versus Form-focused	Participatory organization pattern	Student- versus teacher-initiated	IR/IRF	Types of teacher questions: Referential / Display	Types of learner talk: restricted/ unrestricted
		1.6	TT	Now, which pair?						
		1.51	TT	Any volunteers?						
		6.16	TT	Yes, em, S's name and your partner	m	T-SS	T	IR		
		1.17	TT	Please come here						
		3.6	Silence	<Two student walk to the front.>						
		0.56	PST	I'm Simon	m&f	IS-IS	S	IR		UL
		1.06	PST	I'm Amy						UL
		10.54	PST	What, what, what's your…I like swimming. What's your favorite sport?	m&f	IS-IS	S	IR		UL
		1.77	PST	I like playing football						UL
		2.12	PST	Do you often play football?	m&f	IS-IS	S	IR		UL
		3.8	PST	Yes, I often play football after school						UL
		1.79	PST	What about you?	m&f	IS-IS	S	IR		UL
		1.65	PST	I go swimming every weekend						UL
		2.35	TT	Every weekend? Or every week?	m&f	T-AS	T	IR		
		1.48	AST	Every week						UL
		3.88	TT	Ok, let's ***. Thank you. Go back to your seats	m	T-AS	T	IR		
		2.02	AST	<Clap hands.>						
		1.29	Silence	(pause)						
		5.33	TT	So do anybody has better, has better dialogues?	m	T-SS	T	IR		
		1.16	Silence	(wait time)						
		1.2	TT	Yes, you						
		1.19	TT	And your partner						

(continued)

(continued)

Activity	Instructional Materials	Duration	Interlocutor	Utterance	Meaning- versus Form-focused	Participatory organization pattern	Student- versus teacher-initiated	IR/IRF	Types of teacher questions: Referential / Display	Types of learner talk: restricted/ unrestricted
		6.2	Silence	<Two students walk to the front.>						
		1.13	PST	I'm Simon	m&f	IS-IS	S	IR		UL
		1.54	PST	I'm Amy						UL
		1.21	Silence	(pause)						
		3.43	PST	I like swimming. What's your favorite sport, Simon?	m&f	IS-IS	S	IR		UL
		1.9	PST	I like playing football						UL
		1.89	PST	Do you often play football?	m&f	IS-IS	S	IR		UL
		2.91	PST	I often play football after school. What about you?						UL
		2.25	PST	I go swimming every week						UL
		1.63	TT	Ok, thank you	m	T-AS	T	IR		
		2.03	AST	<Clap hands.>						
		2.55	TT	So do you think which pair is better?	m	T-SS	T	IR	DQ	
		1.56	SST	Yes, yes						RL
		2.39	TT	Do you think which group is better?	m	T-SS	T	IRF		
		0.91	Silence	(wait time)						
		1.39	TT	They or they?						
		1.58	SST	They, they						
		2.36	TT	Yes, they are better. Right?					DQ	RL
		2.08	TT	So, they are, they are better						
		5.81	TT	So pronunciation, and intonation, and their body language, right?					DQ	
		1.18	TT	Ok, very good						
A7: The teacher demonstrated a conversation	TDM	14.45	TT	And next one, I *** to look at another dialogue, just practice in pairs and talk about your favorite sports	m	T-AS	T	IR		

(continued)

(continued)

Activity	Instructional Materials	Duration	Interlocutor	Utterance	Meaning- versus Form-focused	Participatory organization pattern	Student- versus teacher-initiated	IR/IRF	Types of teacher questions: Referential / Display	Types of learner talk: restricted/ unrestricted
with one student, asked students to construct their own conversations in pairs and then called some pairs of students to present their conversations.		1.33	Silence	(pause)						
		3.35	TT	Now, please talk about your favourite sports						
		1.79	TT	I'll give you an example						
		2.71	TT	First one, you, boy	m	T-IS	T	IR		
		0.84	Silence	(pause)						
		1.59	TT	Hello. Stand up						
		3.61	TT	Hello, my name is Miss Li						
		1.82	TT	Do you love sports?					DQ	
		0.94	IST	Yes, I do						RL
		1.98	TT	Good. What is your favourite sport?	m	T-IS	T	IR	RQ	
		2.41	IST	I like ***, how about you						UL
		1.04	TT	I like swimming	m	T-IS	T	IR	RQ	
		5.87	TT	Do you often, do you often... Yeah, what do you like?						
		0.87	IST	I like...						RL
		1.48	TT	You like play football. Oh	m	T-IS	T	IR	RQ	
		1.71	TT	Do you often play football?						
		1.55	Silence	(pause)						
		5.08	IST	Yes, I often play football... er...after school. How about you?						UL
		4.52	TT	I often go swimming at weekend	m	T-IS	T	IR		
		0.93	Silence	(silence)						
		0.79	IST	Good						
		0.87	Silence	(Silence)						
		1.26	TT	Thank you, Bye	m	T-IS	T	IR		
		1.77	TT	Ok, thank you						

(continued)

(continued)

Activity	Instructional Materials	Duration	Interlocutor	Utterance	Meaning- versus Form-focused	Participatory organization pattern	Student- versus teacher-initiated	IR/IRF	Types of teacher questions: Referential / Display	Types of learner talk: restricted/ unrestricted
		3.9	TT	So please have your own dialogues like this. OK?	m	T-AS	T	IR		
		1.08	TT	Be quick						
		47.07	PST	<Students work in pairs.>						
		1.19	TT	<clap hands>	m	T-AS	T	IR		
		1.23	TT	Ok, stop here						
		3.55	TT	Stop here. Ok, any volunteers?						
		8.09	Silence	<Some students raise their hands.>						
		3.6	TT	Yeah, S's name. Yeah. And your partner. Please come here	m	T-SS	T	IR		
		4.97	Silence	<Two student come to the front.>						
		4.19	PST	Hello, my name is ***. Do you like sports?	m&f	IS-IS	S	IR		UL
		1.21	PST	Yes, I do						UL
		4.04	PST	Good. What is your favorite sport?	m&f	IS-IS	S	IR		UL
		2.14	PST	I like sport						UL
		2.19	PST	What about you?	m&f	IS-IS	S	IR		UL
		1.57	PST	I like sport too						UL
		2.34	Silence	(pause)						
		1.43	PST	Do you often play football?	m&f	IS-IS	S	IRF		UL
		3.06	PST	I often play football at ***						UL
		1.47	Silence	(pause)						
		0.76	PST	Good						UL
		2.43	Silence	(pause)						
		1.23	PST	Thank you. Bye						
		1.82	TT	Thank you. Bye	m&f	T-IS	T	IRF		UL

(continued)

(continued)

Activity	Instructional Materials	Duration	Interlocutor	Utterance	Meaning- versus Form-focused	Participatory organization pattern	Student- versus teacher-initiated	IR/IRF	Types of teacher questions: Referential / Display	Types of learner talk: restricted/ unrestricted
		2.23	Silence	(pause)						
		4.72	TT	Yes, he says goodbye to you, and what you should say?					RQ	
		1.92	Silence	(wait time)						
		0.99	TT	He says goodbye						
		0.58	PST	Bye						RL
		2.13	TT	Yeah, ok, thank you. Go back to your seats						
		1.12	TT	Ok	m	T-SS	T	IR		
		4.25	TT	And I think they did very well						
		1.55	TT	So anybody else?						
		1.51	TT	Any other group?						
		1.69	Silence	<Some students raise their hands.>						
		1.15	TT	And you, ok?						
		3.51	Silence	<Two students walk to the front.>						
		2.99	PST	Hello, my name is ***. Do you like sports?	m&f	IS-IS	S	IR		UL
		1.36	PST	I like ***						UL
		2.61	PST	Good. What, what is your favorite sport?	m&f	IS-IS	S	IR		UL
		4.55	PST	I like play football, playing football. What about you?						UL
		2.14	PST	I like playing basketball	m&f	IS-IS	S	IR		UL
		2.48	PST	Do you often play basketball?						UL
		1.57	Silence	(pause)						
		0.6	PST	football?	m&f	IS-IS	S	IR		UL

(continued)

(continued)

Activity	Instructional Materials	Duration	Interlocutor	Utterance	Meaning- versus Form-focused	Participatory organization pattern	Student- versus teacher-initiated	IR/IRF	Types of teacher questions: Referential / Display	Types of learner talk: restricted/ unrestricted
		6.04	PST	I often play football. How about you?						UL
		1.95	PST	I often play basketball						UL
		0.7	Silence	(pause)						
		0.65	PST	Good						UL
		1.37	PST	Thank you, goodbye	m&f	IS-IS	S	IR		UL
		0.56	PST	Goodbye	m	T-AS	T	IR		UL
		2.73	TT	Ok, thank you. Go back to your seats. Please give them claps						
		2.07	AST	<Clap hands.>						
		1.57	TT	They are great	m	T-AS	T	IR		
A8: The teacher played a guessing game with the students. She showed on PPT slides some pictures about playing sports, with parts of the pictures intentionally covered and asked the students to guess what sport was being played	TDM	5.33	TT	Now, I think we will play a game						
		2.1	TT	Would you like to play a game with me?					DQ	
		1.35	AST	Yes						
		2.29	TT	Yes, now, a guessing game	m	T-AS	T	IR		
		10.89	TT	Please look at the pictures carefully and try to think it over. What sport do they like?					RQ	
		1.06	Silence	(pause)						
		0.59	TT	Ok						
		3.51	TT	What sports do they like? Put up your hands						
		0.76	Silence	(wait time)						
		1.79	IST	Ok…girl	m	T-IS	T	IR		
		2.52	TT	They like playing volleyball						UL
		1.35	TT	Do you think so?	m	T-AS	T	IRF	DQ	
		1.04	AST	Yes						RL

(continued)

(continued)

Activity	Instructional Materials	Duration	Interlocutor	Utterance	Meaning- versus Form-focused	Participatory organization pattern	Student- versus teacher-initiated	IR/IRF	Types of teacher questions: Referential / Display	Types of learner talk: restricted/ unrestricted
		0.52	TT	Yes						
		0.53	TT	Ok						
		1	Silence	(pause)						
		4.04	TT	Let's see what are, what sport do they like?	m	T-AS	T	IR		
		1.98	Silence	<Show the word badminton on the PPT slide.>						
		1.52	TT	Do you think so?						
		1.37	Silence	(pause)						
		0.73	TT	Volleyball?	m	T-AS	T	IRF	DQ	
		3.28	TT	No, they like playing badminton						
		1.98	TT	Ok, now, read after me again						
		0.72	TT	Badminton						
		4.16	AST	Badminton, badminton, badminton						RL
		1.17	TT	Yes, very good						
		0.82	Silence	(pause)						
		1.07	TT	What is ***?	m	T-IS	T	IR	RQ	
		2.83	Silence	(wait time)						
		1.34	TT	S's name. Good						
		2.38	Silence	<The student stands up.>						
		2.43	TT	What sport do they like?					RQ	
		2.11	IST	They play table tennis						UL
		1.7	TT	Play table tennis?	m	T-IS	T	IR	DQ	
		0.47	Silence	(pause)						
		1.42	TT	Anybody else?						
		1.37	TT	Yeah, good						
		1.36	IST	They are running						UL
		1.14	TT	They are running?	m	T-IS	T	IR		

(continued)

(continued)

Activity	Instructional Materials	Duration	Interlocutor	Utterance	Meaning-versus Form-focused	Participatory organization pattern	Student-versus teacher-initiated	IR/IRF	Types of teacher questions: Referential / Display	Types of learner talk: restricted/ unrestricted
		1.21	TT	Anybody else?						
		1.42	Silence	(wait time)						
		1.11	TT	Yes, now, you						
		1.81	Silence	<The student stands up.>						
		1.33	IST	Play basketball						RL
		2.4	TT	Tell me the whole sentence	m	T-IS	T	IR		
		1.51	TT	They like…						
		2.13	IST	They like playing football						UL
		1.41	TT	Yes or no?	m	T-SS	T	IR	DQ	
		1.94	SST	No						RL
		0.75	TT	Sorry						
		2.75	TT	Who can give me the correct answer? S's name	m	T-IS	T	IR		
		2.49	IST	They want playing basketball						UL
		1.23	TT	Do you think so?	m	T-SS	T	IR	DQ	
		0.85	SST	Yes						RL
		3.75	TT	Yes. They like playing basketball	m	T-IS	T	IR		
		1.34	TT	And next one						
		1.47	Silence	(pause)						
		1.31	TT	It's easier						
		0.41	Silence	(pause)						
		2.04	TT	What do they like?					RQ	
		1.29	Silence	(wait time)						
		0.64	TT	S's name						
		1.08	IST	Playing football						RL
		1.82	TT	Playing football. Do you think so?	m	T-AS	T	IR	DQ	
		0.82	AST	Yes						RL

(continued)

(continued)

Activity	Instructional Materials	Duration	Interlocutor	Utterance	Meaning- versus Form- focused	Participatory organization pattern	Student- versus teacher- initiated	IR/IRF	Types of teacher questions: Referential / Display	Types of learner talk: restricted/ unrestricted
		2.18	TT	He…yeah, quite good	m	T-IS	T	IR		
		0.89	Silence	(pause)						
		0.91	TT	Next one						
		2.06	Silence	(silence)						
		2.42	TT	What sport do they like?					RQ	
		1.9	Silence	(wait time)						
		0.74	TT	S's name						
		2.23	IST	They like playing volleyball						UL
		2.12	TT	Volleyball. Do you think so?	m	T-SS	T	IR	DQ	RL
		0.92	SST	Yes						
		1.83	TT	Ok. S's name	m	T-IS	T	IR		
		1.74	IST	Playing tennis						RL
		2.15	TT	Playing tennis, right?	m	T-IS	T	IRF	DQ	
		5.47	TT	Now, let's see what's, what is their favorite sport?					RQ	
		1.05	Silence	<Show the answer on PPT.>						
		2.65	TT	Yeah, they are playing tennis						
		2.64	TT	Ok, they are playing tennis. Quite good						
		1.23	TT	Next one						
		2.09	Silence	(pause)						
		2.12	TT	Here, watch it carefully						
		4.13	Silence	(pause)						
		3.96	TT	Do you ***? If you can't, you can tell me in Chinese					RQ	
		2.24	Silence	(wait time)						
		1.31	TT	Good. S's name						

(continued)

(continued)

Activity	Instructional Materials	Duration	Interlocutor	Utterance	Meaning- versus Form-focused	Participatory organization pattern	Student- versus teacher-initiated	IR/IRF	Types of teacher questions: Referential / Display	Types of learner talk: restricted/ unrestricted
		3.85	IST	*** play baseball						RL
		4.86	TT	Baseball, baseball. No. I'm sorry. It is not base ball						
		1.07	Silence	(wait time)						
		0.59	TT	You	m	T-IS	T	IR		
		2.02	IST	They like go camping						UL
		2.53	TT	Go camping. Oh. I am sorry	m	T-SS	T	IR		
		1.53	TT	Anybody else?						
		1.93	IST	(wait time)						
		1.64	TT	Now, I will show you						
		2.43	Silence	<Show the answer on PPT.>						
		0.93	TT	What is that?					RQ	RL
		1	SST	Golf						
		3.84	TT	Yes, golf. Ok, they, they like playing golf	m	T-IS	T	IRF		
		1.29	TT	And next one						
		4.43	Silence	(pause)						
		3.15	TT	What do they like, do you, do they like?					RQ	
		1.56	TT	Ok, S's name						
		4.17	IST	They, they are like, they like playing volleyball						UL
		1.26	TT	Volleyball, yes						
		1.31	TT	Yes or no? Do you think so?	m	T-SS	T	IR	DQ	
		1.22	SST	No						
		1.98	TT	Any other answer? Any other answer?	m	T-IS	T	IR		RL
		1.44	Silence	(wait time)						

(continued)

(continued)

Activity	Instructional Materials	Duration	Interlocutor	Utterance	Meaning- versus Form-focused	Participatory organization pattern	Student- versus teacher-initiated	IR/IRF	Types of teacher questions: Referential / Display	Types of learner talk: restricted/ unrestricted
		0.51	TT	You						
		2.17	IST	They like ***						UL
		2.92	TT	Oh, yes. Er, pardon?	m	T-IS	T	IR		
		1.31	Silence	(pause)						
		1.03	TT	Pardon? Stand up						
		0.97	Silence	(pause)						
		1.17	TT	Please say it again						
		4.81	IST	They, they are playing beach volleyball						UL
		3.24	TT	Please tell us, beach volleyball, what does it mean?	f	T-IS	T	IRF	DQ	
		1.03	IST	沙滩排球。						RL
		2.33	TT	Ok, very good. Beach volleyball						
		3.32	TT	Yeah, and next one, what's your answer?	f	T-AS	T	IR	DQ	
		2.05	TT	Anybody else, any other answer?						
		1.86	Silence	(wait time)						
		3.06	TT	So, let's see, if they are right…						
		2.49	Silence	(pause)						
		2.37	TT	They are playing volleyball, right?						
		3.02	TT	So, S's name has the correct answer. Very good						
		0.53	Silence	(pause)						
		3.65	TT	And I, here, I should praise S's name						
		5.11	TT	She tells a new word that is beach volleyball. Very good						

(continued)

(continued)

Activity	Instructional Materials	Duration	Interlocutor	Utterance	Meaning-versus Form-focused	Participatory organization pattern	Student-versus teacher-initiated	IR/IRF	Types of teacher questions: Referential / Display	Types of learner talk: restricted/ unrestricted
		3.51	TT	Ok, and next one	m	T-AS	T	IR		
		5.44	TT	I'd like to play another game again						
		1.25	Silence	(pause)						
A9: The teacher organized a guessing game in which one student mimed to play a certain sport, another student who stood with his or her back towards the performer guessed the sport by asking some questions to the rest of the class		5.07	TT	This game, I'd ask some students to come to the blackboard						
		3	TT	And do some action						
		5.31	TT	And another student should turn back and guess						
	TDM	3.56	TT	and ask, "does he like playing…"						
		4.86	TT	and all the students, you should answer yes or no						
		0.95	TT	Clear?						
		1.35	TT	Ok						
		2.03	TT	Now, I think	m	T-SS	T	IR		
		0.7	Silence	(pause)						
		2.12	TT	This group, please stand up						
		0.78	TT	Come here						
		2.61	Silence	<A garoup of students stand up and come to the front.>						
		2.34	TT	And who would like to guess?	m	T-IS	T	IR		
		1.25	TT	would like to guess?						
		0.98	Silence	(wait time)						
		0.91	TT	Anything else?						

(continued)

(continued)

Activity	Instructional Materials	Duration	Interlocutor	Utterance	Meaning- versus Form-focused	Participatory organization pattern	Student- versus teacher-initiated	IR/IRF	Types of teacher questions: Referential / Display	Types of learner talk: restricted/ unrestricted
		1.93	Silence	(wait time)						
		2.49	TT	S's name. Can you have a try?						
		1.85	Silence	<One student comes to the teacher.>						
		0.86	TT	Yes, you turn back	m	T-IS	T	IR		
		2.34	TT	You, please come here						
		6.35	TT	Yes. One by one. One by one. Yes. Be quick						
		3.73	TT	And you should face the students, face the students						
		1.07	TT	Ok.						
		2.12	Silence	(pause)						
		1.87	TT	S's name. Are you ready?						
		0.52	IST	Yes						RL
		1.63	TT	Ok, let's go. One	m	T-IS	T	IR		
		2	IST	Does…						RL
		2.97	TT	Ai…you just do the action	m	T-IS-SS	T	IR		
		2.03	TT	Maybe for example						
		0.93	Silence	<show a gesture>						
		0.43	TT	Turn back						
		1.22	SST	<laughter>						
		2.2	TT	May be you can do it like this	m	T-IS	T	IR		
		2.17	Silence	<The teacher makes actions of playing badminton and swimming.>						
		0.88	TT	Or something like that						
		1.4	Silence	<The first student makes and action of swimming.>						
		0.9	TT	So, stop						
		1.07	Silence	(pause)						

(continued)

(continued)

Activity	Instructional Materials	Duration	Interlocutor	Utterance	Meaning- versus Form-focused	Participatory organization pattern	Student- versus teacher-initiated	IR/IRF	Types of teacher questions: Referential / Display	Types of learner talk: restricted/ unrestricted
		1.32	TT	You ask	m	T-IS	T	IR		
		1.02	Silence	\<The boy makes the action of playing badminton.\>						
		0.59	TT	You know?	m	T-SS	T	IR		
		1.3	SST	\<laughter\>						
		3.07	TT	You can ask, "does he like playing..."	m	IS-T-SS	T	IR		
		2.76	Silence	(pause)						
		3.46	IST	Does he, playing, playing running?						UL
		1.39	SST	No, no						RL
		2.96	TT	No, no, he doesn't	m	T-AS	T	IR		RL
		1.14	AST	Doesn't						
		1.85	TT	Yes, ok. Go on	m	T-IS	T	IR		UL
		4.3	IST	Does he playing football?						
		1.26	TT	Does he like...	m	IS-T-SS	T	IR		UL
		1.11	IST	Playing football						UL
		3.23	SST	No, he doesn't						
		4.37	Silence	(Silence)						
		2.26	TT	***, be quick	m	IS-T-AS	T	IR		
		2.14	Silence	(pause)						
		2.32	IST	Does he like playing basketball?						UL
		3.2	AST	No, he doesn't						
		4.01	Silence	(silence)						
		0.75	TT	***	m	IS-T-AS	T	IRF		UL
		4.29	IST	Does he like, like swimming?						UL
		1.59	AST	Yes						RL
		1.64	TT	Yes, he...						
		0.85	AST	Does						RL

(continued)

(continued)

Activity	Instructional Materials	Duration	Interlocutor	Utterance	Meaning- versus Form-focused	Participatory organization pattern	Student- versus teacher-initiated	IR/IRF	Types of teacher questions: Referential / Display	Types of learner talk: restricted/ unrestricted
		3.22	TT	Yes, you are great. Thank you. Go back to your seat	m	T-AS	T	IR		
		5.34	TT	Good. I think I can give you…I can give you a gift <point to a paper bag>						
		0.65	Silence							
		8.12	TT	They are all here. They are all here. Now, I won't let you know what is in it. After class, I will give you. Ok?						
		1.01	Silence	(pause)						
		2.06	TT	And anybody else? Who would like to come here?	m	T-AS	T	IR		
		1.01	Silence	(wait time)						
		1.09	TT	Ok. S's name. Thank you	m	T-IS	T	IR		
		8.84	Silence	<A student comes to the front.>						
		2.12	TT	Two, the girl	m	T-IS	T	IR		
		2.05	Silence	<The second student makes an movement.>						
		0.34	TT	Ok						
		1.85	Silence	(pause)						
		0.63	TT	Begin	m	T-IS	T	IR		
		0.74	Silence	(pause)						
		1.16	TT	S's name. Ask						
		3.55	IST	Does she like playing volleyball?	m	IS-AS	S	IR		UL
		3.09	AST	No, she doesn't.							RL
		2.59	IST	Does she like swimming	m	IS-AS	S	IR		UL
		2.87	AST	No, she doesn't							RL
		2.78	IST	Does she like running?	m	IS-AS	S	IR		UL
		3	AST	No, she doesn't							RL

(continued)

(continued)

Activity	Instructional Materials	Duration	Interlocutor	Utterance	Meaning- versus Form-focused	Participatory organization pattern	Student- versus teacher-initiated	IR/IRF	Types of teacher questions: Referential / Display	Types of learner talk: restricted/ unrestricted
		5.2	IST	Does she like… play…tennis, playing tennis?	m	IS-AS	S	IR		UL
		2.77	AST	No, she doesn't						RL
		3.32	IST	Does she like playing football?	m	IS-AS	S	IR		UL
		2.9	AST	Yes, she does						RL
		4.5	TT	Ok, very good. Thank you. Very clever. Ok/ Go back to your seat	m	T-SS	T	IR		
		3.72	TT	Ok, next one. Who will be here?	m	T-IS	T	IR		
		1.66	TT	S's name. Come here. Be quick						
		8.4	Silence	<A student comes to the front>						
		1.69	TT	Ok, begin, ask						
		2.04	Silence	(pause)						
		2.34	IST	Does he playing football?	m	IS-T-AS	S	IR		UL
		1.21	AST	No						RL
		1.69	TT	Like playing						
		1.09	TT	Ok, go on	m	IS-T-AS	T	IR		
		3.03	IST	Does he like volleyball?						UL
		3.26	AST	No, he doesn't						RL
		4.02	IST	Does he like playing football!?	m	IS-AS	S	IR		UL
		2.8	AST	No, he doesn't						RL
		5.29	IST	Does he like playing basketball?	m	IS-AS	S	IR		UL
		3.11	AST	Yes, he does						RL
		2.11	TT	You are great. Ok. thank you. Go back to your seats	m	T-SS	T	IR		

(continued)

(continued)

Activity	Instructional Materials	Duration	Interlocutor	Utterance	Meaning- versus Form-focused	Participatory organization pattern	Student- versus teacher-initiated	IR/IRF	Types of teacher questions: Referential / Display	Types of learner talk: restricted/ unrestricted
		1.29	Silence	(pause)						
		2.31	TT	Ok, ***. Next one, who?						
		1.59	Silence	(wait time)						
		0.89	TT	Ok, S's name. Go on	m	T-IS	T	IR		
		9.04	Silence	<The student comes to the front.>						
		1.6	TT	Ok, ask	m	T-IS	T	IR		
		3.15	IST	Does he playing football?						UL
		1.03	TT	Does he like…	m	IS-T-AS	T	IR		
		2.42	IST	Does he like playing football?						UL
		3.64	AST	No, he doesn't						RL
		2.29	IST	Does he like…swim?	m	IS-AS	S	IR		UL
		2.91	AST	No, he doesn't						RL
		3.49	IST	Does he like playing football?	m	IS-AS	S	IR		UL
		3.11	AST	No, he doesn't.						RL
		2.49	IST	Does he like playing volleyball?	m	IS-AS	S	IR		UL
		3.38	AST	No, he doesn't						RL
		1.82	Silence	(pause)						
		2.13	IST	Does he like playing *** games?	m	IS-AS	S	IR	DQ	
		2.25	AST	No, he doesn't						RL
		2.57	IST	Does he like ***?	m	IS-AS	S	IR		
		2.89	AST	Yes, he does						RL
		2.17	TT	Thank you. Go back to your seat. Very good	m	T-SS	T	IR		
		1.09	Silence	(pause)						
		3.14	TT	The last one. The last one. Who will come here?	m	T-SS	T	IR		

(continued)

(continued)

Activity	Instructional Materials	Duration	Interlocutor	Utterance	Meaning- versus Form-focused	Participatory organization pattern	Student- versus teacher-initiated	IR/IRF	Types of teacher questions: Referential / Display	Types of learner talk: restricted/ unrestricted
		4.79	TT	Yes. ***. This time you do the same action						
		1.63	TT	You can have a discussion						
		2.54	TT	Yeah, are you ready? Yes						
		3.02	TT	The same discussion. *** The same action						
		0.88	Silence	(pause)						
		2.95	TT	Ok, you do it together	m	T-SS	T	IR		
		5.93	Silence	<Two students do some actions.>						
		1.5	TT	Ok. Can you ask? You can ask.	m	IS-T-SS	T	IR		
		3.04	IST	Does he...does she...						UL
		1.34	SST	Do they?						RL
		2.07	TT	Do they...						
		2.61	IST	Do they like playing football?	m	IS-T-AS	S	IRF		UL
		3.43	AST	No, he doesn't						RL
		1	TT	Yeah, very good						
		5.46	IST	Do they like playing...em... basketball?	m	IS-AS	S	IR		UL
		3.37	AST	No, they don't						RL
		1.67	Silence	(pause)						
		3.2	IST	Do they like swimming?	m	IS-AS	S	IR		UL
		3.32	AST	No, they don't						RL
		5.44	IST	Do they like...Badminton?	m	T-IS	S	IRF		UL
		2.43	TT	Badminton. Not badminton. Badminton						
		0.87	IST	Badminton						RL
		1.37	TT	Yes or no? Yes or no?	m	T-AS	T	IRF		
		3.27	AST	No, they don't						RL

(continued)

(continued)

Activity	Instructional Materials	Duration	Interlocutor	Utterance	Meaning- versus Form-focused	Participatory organization pattern	Student- versus teacher-initiated	IR/IRF	Types of teacher questions: Referential / Display	Types of learner talk: restricted/ unrestricted
		2.29	TT	Yes or no. No						
		1.12	Silence	(pause)						
		6.7	IST	Do they like…tennis?	m	IS-T-AS	S	IRF		UL
		1.93	TT	Do they like tennis?					DQ	
		2.78	AST	No, they don't						RL
		1.08	Silence	(pause)						
		3.36	TT	Ah, it is a little difficult, yeah?	m	T-SS	T	IR		
		3.08	Silence	(pause)						
		5.21	TT	I think, maybe, turn back, you do the action for him						
		0.9	TT	Together						
		1.62	Silence	(pause)						
		2.1	TT	Do action again						
		3.06	Silence	<The students do the action again.>						
		0.8	TT	What's that?	m	T-AS	T	IR		
		1.66	Silence	(wait time)						
		5.48	IST	Do they like playing table tennis?	m	IS-AS	S	IR		UL
		2.84	AST	Yes, they do						RL
		3.39	TT	Ok, thank you. Go back to your seats. Thank you	m	T-AS	T	IRF		UL
		2.06	TT	Thank you for all. Ok						
		2.36	TT	Let's give ourselves claps.						
		1.65	AST	<Clap hands.>						
		0.61	TT	Good.						
		0.6	Silence	(pause)						
A10: The teacher presented two	MMTA	4.63	TT	And do you know, what does Eddie like doing?	m	T-AS	T	IR	RQ	
		0.7	Silence	(pause)						

(continued)

(continued)

Activity	Instructional Materials	Duration	Interlocutor	Utterance	Meaning- versus Form-focused	Participatory organization pattern	Student- versus teacher-initiated	IR/IRF	Types of teacher questions: Referential / Display	Types of learner talk: restricted/ unrestricted
questions on PPT slide. She asked the students to find the answers through listening to a dialogue. Then she taught some grammatical points in the dialogue, asked the student to read and acted it out in pairs before some students were called on to perform the dialogue.		4.87	TT	Now, let's listen to the tape. He is talking with Hobo						
		5.11	TT	Now listen to the tape and answer the question. What sport does Eddie like?						
		10.6	AI	Eddie, do you play sports? Yes, I like walking. Oh, really? Yes, I walk to my bowl many times a day	m	AI-AS	T	IR		
		0.99	Silence	(Silence)						
		0.81	TT	Ok	m	T-AS	T	IR		
		0.63	Silence	(pause)						
		1.62	TT	Do you get the answer?					DQ	
		0.95	Silence	(pause)						
		1.46	TT	Now, next one	m&f	T-IS	T	IR		
		2.24	Silence	(wait time)						
		1.95	TT	Guess. S's name						
		2.15	IST	Eddie likes the walking						RL
		1.41	TT	Walking. Right?	m&f	T-AS	T	IRF	DQ	
		1.25	AST	Yes.						RL
		0.97	TT	Yes, very good						
		1.49	TT	Now, read after me. Walking	f	T-AS	T	IR		RL
		0.79	AST	Walking						
		1.07	TT	Twice	f	T-AS	T	IR		
		1.83	AST	Walking, walking						RL
		0.72	TT	Walking		T-AS				
		1.61	AST	Walking, walking						
		4.45	TT	And…Does he really like walking?	m	T-SS	T	IR	DQ	

(continued)

(continued)

Activity	Instructional Materials	Duration	Interlocutor	Utterance	Meaning- versus Form-focused	Participatory organization pattern	Student- versus teacher-initiated	IR/IRF	Types of teacher questions: Referential / Display	Types of learner talk: restricted/ unrestricted
		2.31	TT	Does he really like walking?						
		1.21	TT	Yes or no?						RL
		1.67	SST	No						
		1.04	Silence	(pause)						
		0.61	TT	You	m	T-IS	T	IR		
		0.6	IST	No						RL
		1.12	TT	No, he...	m&f	T-IS	T	IRF		
		5.66	IST	No, he likes...walk to, walk to his bowl						UL
		1.85	IST	Many time a day						RL
		0.66	TT	Yes						
		1.53	TT	How do you know?	m	T-AS	T	IR	RQ	
		3.29	TT	Because he walks to his bowl many times a day						
		2.47	TT	Why does he go, walk to his bowl?						
		2.44	TT	Why does he walk to his bowl?					RQ	
		0.82	Silence	(wait time)						
		1.46	TT	Because he wants to…						
		1.53	AST	Eat						RL
		1.65	TT	Eat, read after me, eat	f	T-AS	T	IR		
		1.59	AST	Eat						RL
		0.88	TT	Eat	f	T-AS	T	IR		
		1.51	AST	Eat, eat						RL
		5	TT	He is lazy. He only want to sleep and… eat	f	T-AS	T	IR		
		4.29	TT	Yes, here, read after me, the word here. Bowl						RL
		2.01	AST	Bowl, bowl						

(continued)

(continued)

Activity	Instructional Materials	Duration	Interlocutor	Utterance	Meaning- versus Form-focused	Participatory organization pattern	Student- versus teacher-initiated	IR/IRF	Types of teacher questions: Referential / Display	Types of learner talk: restricted/unrestricted
		0.66	TT	/ou/	f	T-AS	T	IR		RL
		1.57	AST	/ou/, /ou/						
		0.51	TT	Bowl	f	T-AS	T	IR		
		1.31	AST	Bowl, bowl						RL
		0.81	TT	/ir/	f	T-AS	T	IR		
		1.51	AST	/ir/, /ir/						RL
		0.76	TT	Really	f	T-AS	T	IRF		
		1.43	AST	Really, really						RL
		1.36	TT	Ok, very good						
		7.05	TT	And here look at this sentence. He walks to his bowl to eat many times a day	f	T-AS	T	IR		
		3.21	TT	Here, walk, it is a verb						
		1.38	TT	It is a verb						
		4.18	TT	And here, eat, eat is another verb						
		7.43	TT	When we use two verbs, we should use, the second verb, we can use to do, to do						
		1.44	TT	Pay attention to 'to'						
		4.48	TT	当我们两个动词同时使用时，第二个东西前面应该加上什么啊?						
		0.78	AST	To						
		6.21	TT	表示一种目的。走到碗前的目的就是为了吃东西。Ok						RL
		1.21	TT	Now, so much for it						

(continued)

(continued)

Activity	Instructional Materials	Duration	Interlocutor	Utterance	Meaning- versus Form-focused	Participatory organization pattern	Student- versus teacher-initiated	IR/IRF	Types of teacher questions: Referential / Display	Types of learner talk: restricted/ unrestricted
		10.9	TT	Next one, please read, turn to Page 18, and read the dialogue by yourselves and act out the dialogue. I give you two minutes. Be quick	m	T-AS	T	IR		
		2.46	TT	You can use your body language						
		30.1	PST	<Students work in pairs.>						
		0.89	TT	Ok	m	T-SS	T	IR		
		2.87	Silence	<The teacher goes back to the front.>						
		1.02	TT	Now, stop here						
		2.16	Silence	(pause)						
		1.03	TT	Any volunteers?						
		1.87	Silence	(wait time)						
		3.17	TT	Yes, S's name and your partner						
		1.11	TT	Please come here						
		1.13	Silence	<Two students come to the front.>						
		0.6	TT	Let's welcome	m	T-AS	T	IR		
		2.72	AST	<Clap hands.>						
		7.36	Silence	<Two students come to the front.>						
		2.02	PST	Eddie, do you like sports?	m&f	IS-IS	S	IR		UL
		1.43	PST	Yes, I like walking						UL
		1.27	Silence	(pause)						
		0.99	PST	Oh, really?	m&f	IS-IS	S	IR		
		4.18	PST	Of course, I walk to my bowl many times a day						
		3.74	Silence	(Silence)						
		1.21	TT	Ok, thank you	m&f	T-AS	T	IR		

(continued)

(continued)

Activity	Instructional Materials	Duration	Interlocutor	Utterance	Meaning- versus Form-focused	Participatory organization pattern	Student- versus teacher-initiated	IR/IRF	Types of teacher questions: Referential / Display	Types of learner talk: restricted/ unrestricted
		3.98	TT	Do you, do they think they are, they acted very well?					DQ	
		0.79	AST	Yeah.						RL
		2.71	TT	Yes, very good. Thank you. Give them claps	m	T-AS	T	IR		
		2.34	AST	<Clap hands.>						
		0.81	TT	Another pair	m	T-SS	T	IR		
		0.79	Silence	(pause)						
		0.76	TT	Another pair?						
		0.62	TT	Boys?						
		1.51	Silence	(Pause)						
		0.76	TT	Boys?						
		0.91	Silence	(pause)						
		0.63	TT	You two?						
		1.1	Silence	(pause)						
		1.1	TT	Or you two						
		2.71	TT	I think you, ok, you two, come here						
		1.91	Silence	<Two students come the the front.>						
		1.07	PST	I'm Hobbo	m&f	IS-IS	S	IR		UL
		1	PST	I'm Eddie						UL
		2.4	Silence	(pause)						
		1.98	PST	Eddie, do you like sports?	m&f	IS-IS	S	IR		UL
		1.82	PST	Yes, I like walking						UL
		1.07	PST	Oh, really?	m&f	IS-IS-SS	S	IR		UL
		1.44	Silence	(pause)						UL
		5.08	PST	Yes, I want to walking to bowl many times a day						UL

(continued)

(continued)

Activity	Instructional Materials	Duration	Interlocutor	Utterance	Meaning- versus Form-focused	Participatory organization pattern	Student- versus teacher-initiated	IR/IRF	Types of teacher questions: Referential / Display	Types of learner talk: restricted/ unrestricted
		7.11	PST	Oh, you likes eat. You like eating very much. You are very fat						UL
		1.03	SST	<laughter>						
		0.8	TT	Yeah, Ok	m	T-SS	T	IRF		
		1.86	TT	Do you have anything to say?					RQ	
		0.59	PST	No						
		3.09	TT	No, ok. Thank you. Go back to your seat						
		0.72	TT	Thank you						
		2.47	AST	<Clap hands.>						
		4.87	TT	Yeah, he likes eating too much. He is so fat						
		2.03	TT	Very good dialogue. Thank you						
		0.39	Silence	(pause)						
		11.19	TT	Ok, now, I think, after class, you can make up your dialogues. Ok, And you can make the dialogue longer and more interesting	m	T-AS	T	IR		
		0.96	TT	Very good						
		0.62	Silence	(pause)						
A11: The teacher initiated a free discussion with the student on the issue "the meaning of playing	TDM	4.39	TT	Now, I think it's time for us to have a discussion						
		3.68	Silence	(pause)						
		2.47	TT	Can we just sleep and eat, why?					RQ	
		4.41	TT	What should we do and what sport can we do at school?					RQ	

(continued)

(continued)

Activity	Instructional Materials	Duration	Interlocutor	Utterance	Meaning- versus Form- focused	Participatory organization pattern	Student- versus teacher- initiated	IR/IRF	Types of teacher questions: Referential / Display	Types of learner talk: restricted/ unrestricted
sports" and then presented some proverbs about playing sports.		9.08	TT	And you can have a discussion in groups of four. Four students. And the last students. You can have a try.						
		51.18	GST	<Students work in groups. The teacher walks among them and works with one group.>						
		1.52	TT	Stop here	m	T-AS	T	IR		
		3.11	Silence	(pause)						
		6.13	TT	Ok. I like some student to tell us, what can, can we just sleep and eat?	m	T-IS	T	IR	RQ	
		4.85	TT	Who will ***. I think, S's name, have a try						
		1.58	Silence	(pause)						
		1.09	TT	Stand up						
		0.77	Silence	<The student stands up.>						
		3.95	TT	Can we just sleep and eat?	m	T-IS	T	IRF		
		2.86	IST	No, because we become fat.						UL
		3.78	TT	Good, we will get fat, we will be fat. Ok						
		1.27	Silence	(Pause.)						
		1.6	TT	And what should we do?	m	T-IS	T	IR	RQ	
		0.81	Silence	(wait time)						UL
		2.61	IST	We can... do exercise						
		2.71	TT	Ok, and what sport can we do at school?	m	T-IS	T	IR	RQ	
		5.18	IST	We can go running, we can running and playing						

(continued)

(continued)

Activity	Instructional Materials	Duration	Interlocutor	Utterance	Meaning- versus Form-focused	Participatory organization pattern	Student- versus teacher-initiated	IR/IRF	Types of teacher questions: Referential / Display	Types of learner talk: restricted/ unrestricted
		3.01	TT	We can running and playing?	m	T-AS	T	IRF	DQ	
		1.96	TT	We can play						
		2.92	TT	We can playing. We can running						
		1.39	Silence	(pause)						
		1.47	TT	We can…run						
		1.19	TT	We can…						
		0.81	AST	Play.						RL
		2.14	TT	Yes, ok. Thank you						
		1.97	Silence	(pause)						
		4.8	TT	I think sports is very important for us	m	T-AS	T	IR		
		0.91	TT	Do you think so?					DQ	
		2.92	TT	Here I have some proverbs for you	m&f	T-AS	T	IR		
		2.92	TT	See. Movement is life						
		1.24	Silence	(pause)						
		1.2	TT	Movement is life						
		1.5	TT	Say it together. Chinese						
		3.81	AST	生命在于运动。						
		4.12	TT	And happiness comes from sports	m&f	T-SS	T	IR		
		2.76	SST	***						
		3.06	AST	快乐来自运动。	m&f	T-AS	S	IR		
		5.37	TT	It means, 我运动,我快乐。						
		0.64	Silence	(pause)						
		0.54	TT	Ok.	m&f	T-SS	T	IR		
		1.09	TT	Another. ***						

(continued)

(continued)

Activity	Instructional Materials	Duration	Interlocutor	Utterance	Meaning- versus Form-focused	Participatory organization pattern	Student- versus teacher-initiated	IR/IRF	Types of teacher questions: Referential / Display	Types of learner talk: restricted/ unrestricted
		2.66	TT	Health comes from sports.						
		1.74	Silence	(pause)						
		1.49	TT	Health comes from sports. It means…						
		2.41	SST	我运动,我健康。						
		1.3	TT	Oh, yes. Say it together.	m	T-AS	T	IRF		
		4.58	AST	我运动,我健康。						
		2.73	TT	You are quite clever, quite clever						
		1.47	TT	Fantastic, ok						
		0.96	Silence	(pause)						
		6.66	TT	And, you should love sports, and love your life						
		8.28	TT	And try to do exercise if you have time, so that you can keep healthy						
		1.03	Silence	(pause)						
A12: The teacher gave a brief review of what's been learned in this class by asking the students to work out a blank-filling exercise, and then she assigned the homework	TDM	3.75	TT	Ok. Now. What have you learned today?	f	T-AS	T	IR	RQ	
		1.56	TT	What have you learned today?						
		4.89	TT	New word here, and some sentences here						
		3.11	TT	Now I think you can fill in blanks now						
		1.42	TT	What sports do they like?	f	T-AS	T	IR	RQ	
		0.85	TT	They like…						
		2.08	TT	They like, playing…						
		1.66	AST	playing volleyball						RL
		4.56	TT	They like playing. They like doing something	f	T-AS	T	IRF		

(continued)

(continued)

Activity	Instructional Materials	Duration	Interlocutor	Utterance	Meaning- versus Form-focused	Participatory organization pattern	Student- versus teacher-initiated	IR/IRF	Types of teacher questions: Referential / Display	Types of learner talk: restricted/ unrestricted
		3.17	Silence	<The teacher writes on the blackboard.>						
		4.49	TT	And does ehe like…yes, she or he…						
		1.06	AST	does						RL
		2.12	TT	Very good. Yes, he does						
		1.31	TT	No, he or she…	f	T-AS	T	IRF		
		1.11	AST	Doesn't						RL
		1.91	TT	Very good. Very good						
		1.58	TT	Do they like…	f	T-AS	T	IRF		
		1.68	TT	For example, do they like running?					DQ	
		0.81	TT	Yes, they…						
		0.98	AST	Do						RL
		1.37	TT	Do, good						
		1.31	TT	And no, they…	f	T-AS	T	IRF		
		0.81	AST	didn't.						RL
		2.59	TT	Good. Quite good						
		3.15	TT	Ok. Now. So much for today	m	T-AS	T	IR		
		8.14	TT	Today's homework is, one, tell your friend your favorite sport, two, write a short passage about your favorite sport						
		1.88	TT	Class is over. Stand up.						
		2.77	Silence	<Students stand up.>						
		0.78	TT	Goodbye, class						
		1.15	AST	Goodbye. Miss Li						RL

References

Abrami, P. C., D'apollonia, S. & Rosenfield S. The Dimensionality of Student Ratingsof Instruction: What We Know and What We Do Not [A]. Perry R. P. & Smart J. C. (eds.) *Effective Teaching in Higher Education* [C]. New York: Agathon Press, 1997. 321-367.

Adamson, B., & Morris, P. (1997). The English Curriculum in the People's Republic of China. *Comparative Education Review, 41,* 3–26.

Allen, L. Q. (2002). Teachers' pedagogical beliefs and the standards for foreign language learning. *Foreign Language Annals, 35,* 518–529.

Allwright, D. & Hanks, J. (2009). *The developing language learner: An introduction to exploratory practice.* Houndmills, Basingstoke, Hampshire; New York: Palgrave Macmillan.

Allwright, D., & Lenzuen, R. (1997). Exploratory practice: Work at the Cultura Inglesa, Rio de Janeiro, Brazil. *Language Teaching Research, 1,* 73–79.

Allwright, D. (2005). Developing principles for practitioner research: The case of exploratory practice. *The Modern Language Journal, 89,* 353–366.

Allwright, D. (2003). Exploratory practice: Rethinking practitioner research in language thinking. *Language Teaching Research, 7,* 113–141.

An, L. (2012). *The role of textbooks in modifying teacher beliefs and practices: A project-based study in middle schools in China.* Shanghai: Shanghai International Studies University.

Argyris, C., & Schön, D. A. (1974). *Theory in practice: Increasing professional effectiveness.* San Francisco: Jossey Bass.

Bailey, K. L. (1996). The best laid plans: Teachers 'in-class decisions to depart from their lesson plans. In K. M. Bailey & D. Nunan (Eds.), *Voices from the language classroom: qualitative research in second language education* (pp. 15–40). Cambridge: Cambridge University Press.

Bailey, K. M. (1990). The use of diary studies in teacher education programs. In J. C. Richards & D. Nunan (Eds.), *Second language teacher education* (pp. 215–226). New York: Cambridge University Press.

Bartlett, L. (1990). Teacher development through reflective teaching. In J. C. Richards & D. Nunan (Eds.), *Second language teacher education* (pp. 202–214). New York: Cambridge University Press.

Basturkmen, H. (2012). Review of research into the correspondence between language Teachers' stated beliefs and practices. *System, 40,* 282–295.

Beretta, A., & Davies, A. (1985). Evaluation of the Bangalore Project. *ELT Journal, 39,* 121–127.

Beretta, A. (1990). Implementation of the Bangalore Project. *Applied Linguistics, 11*(4), 321–337.

Borg, S. (2012). Current approaches to language teacher cognition research: A methodological analysis. In R. Barnard & A. Burns (Eds.), *Researching language teacher cognition and practice: International case studies* (pp. 11–29). Bristol; Buffalo: Multilingual Matters.

Borg, S. (2006). *Teacher cognition and language education: Research and practice.* London; New York : Continuum.

Borg, S. (2003). Teacher cognition in language teaching: A review of research on what teachers think, know, believe, and do. *Language Teaching, 36,* 81–109.

Borg, S. (2011). The impact of in-service education on language teachers' beliefs. *System, 39,* 370–380.

Borich, G. D. (2011). *Observation skills for effective teaching.* Boston: Pearson Education.

Boyd, J., & Boyd, S. (2005). Reflect and improve: Instructional development through a teaching journal. *College Teaching, 3,* 110–114.

Bradburd, D. (1998). *Being there: The necessity of fieldwork.* Washington, DC: Smithsonian Institution Press.

Breen, M. P., & Candlin, C. N. (1980). The essentials of a communicative curriculum in language teaching. *Applied Linguistics, 2,* 89–112.

Breen, M. P., Hird, B., Milton, M., & Thwaite, A. (2001). Making sense of language teaching: Teachers' principles and classroom practices. *Applied Linguistics, 4,* 470–501.

Brown, H. D. (2001). *Teaching by principles: An interactive approach.* Beijing: Foreign Language Teaching and Research Press.

Brown, H. D. (2007). *Teaching by principles: An interactive approach to language pedagogy (3rd edition).* White Plains, NY: Pearson Education.

Brown, J. D., & Rodgers, T. S. (2003). *Doing second language research.* Oxford: Oxford University Press.

Brumfit, C. J. (1984). The Bangalore procedural syllabus. *ELT Journal, 4,* 233–241.

Burden, P. R., & Byrd, D. M. (2003). *Methods for effective teaching.* Boston: Pearson Education.

Burns, A. (1996). Starting all over again: From teaching adults to teaching beginners. In D. Freeman & J. C. Richards (Eds.), *Teacher learning in language teaching* (154–177). Cambridge: Cambridge University Press.

Burns, A. (1992). Teacher belief and their influence on classroom practice. *Prospect, 3,* 56–66.

Carless, D. R. (2001). *Curriculum innovation in the primary EFL classroom: Case studies of three teachers implementing Hong Kong's Target-oriented Curriculum (TOC).* The University of Warwick.

Carless, D. R. (2003). Factors in the implementation of task-based teaching in primary schools. *System, 31,* 485–500.

Carless, D. R. (2004). Issues in Teachers' reinterpretation of a task-based innovation in primary school. *TESOL Quarterly, 4,* 639–662.

CCP Central Committee & State Council. (1993). *Zhongguo jiaoyu gaige he fazhan gangyao* [Program for China's educational reform and development.]. Beijing: CCP Central Committee & State Council.

CCP Central Committee & State Council. (1999). *Zhonggong zhongyang guowuyuan guanyu shenhua jiaoyu gaige quanmian tuijin sushi jiaoyu de jueding.* [Decision on deepening educational reform and promoting quality education.]. Beijing: CCP Central Committee & State Council.

CCP Central Committee. (1985). *Zhonggong zhong yang guangyu jiaoyu tizhi gaige de jueding.* [Decision on reforming China's educational system.]. Beijing, CCP Central Committee.

Clandinin, J. D., & Connelly, M. F. (1987). Teachers' personal knowledge: What counts as personal in studies of the personal. *Journal of Curriculum Studies, 6,* 487–500.

Cornelissen, F., Swet, J., Beijarrd, D., & Bergen, T. (2011). Aspects of school-university research networks that play a role in developing, sharing and using knowledge based on teacher research. *Teaching and Teacher Education, 27,* 147–156.

CPC. (1985). *Zhonghua renmin gongheguo yiwu jiaoyufa.* [Compulsory education law of the People's Republic of China]. Beijing: CPC.

Crookes, G., & Arakaki, L. (1999). teaching idea sources and work conditions in an ESL Program. *TESOL Journal, 1,* 15–19.

Cullen, R. (2002). Supportive Teacher Talk: the Importance of F-move [J]. *ELT Journal, 2,* 117–127.

Cullen, R. (1998). Teacher talk and the classroom context. *ELT Journal, 3,* 179–187.

Curdt-Christiansen, X.-L., & Silver, R. E. (2012). Educational reforms, cultural clashes and classroom practices. *Cambridge Journal of Education,* (2), 141–161.

Curdt-Christiansen, X.-L., & Silver, R. E. (2013). New Wine into Old Skins: The enactment of literacy policy in Singapore. *Language and Education*, (3), 246–260.

Cynthia, A. B. (1986). The effects of referential questions on ESL classroom discourse. *TESOL Quarterly, 1,* 47–59.

Dalton, S. S. (2008). *Five standards for effective teaching: How to succeed with all learners.* San Francisco: Jossey-Bass.

Debbie, G. E. H. (2005). Why do teachers ask the questions they ask? *RELC Journal, 3,* 297–310.

Denzin, N. K. (1978). *The research act: A theoretical introduction to sociological methods* (2nd ed.). New York: McGraw-Hill.

Dörnyei, Z. (2007). *Research methods in applied linguistics.* Oxford: Oxford University Press.

Duff, P. (2000). Repetition in foreign language classroom interaction. In J. Hall & L. Verplaetse (Eds.), *The development of second and foreign language learning through classroom interaction.* Mahwah, NJ: Lawrence Erlbaum.

Dunne, R., & Wragg, T. (2005). *Effective teaching.* New York: Routledge.

Eisenhart, M. A., J. L. Shrum, Harding, J. R., & Cuthbert, A. M. (1988). Teacher beliefs: Definitions, findings and directions. *Educational Policy*, (1), 51–70.

Ellis, R. (1990). *Instructed second language acquisition.* Oxford, UK; Cambridge, Mass., USA: B. Blackwell.

Ellis, R. (1990). Researching classroom language learning. In C. Brumfit & R. Mitchell (Eds.), *Research in the language classroom* (54–70). London: Modern English Publications.

Ellis, R. (1994). *The study of second language acquisition.* Shanghai: Shanghai Foreign Language Education Press.

Ellis, R. (1997). *SLA research and language teaching.* Oxford; New York: Oxford University Press.

Ellis, R. (2003). *Task-based Language Learning and Teaching [M].* Oxford: Oxford University Press.

Ellis, R., & Barkhuizen, G. (2005). *Analyzing learner language.* Oxford: Oxford University Press.

Ellis, R. (2005). Principles of instructed language learning. *System, 33,* 209–224.

Ellis, R. (2006). Current Issues in the teaching of grammar: An SLA perspective. *TESOL Quarterly, 1,* 83–107.

Ellis, R. (2009a). Corrective feedback and teacher development. *L2 Journal*, (1), 3–18.

Ellis, R. (2009). Task-based language teaching: Sorting out the misunderstandings. *International Journal of Applied Linguistics, 3,* 221–246.

Ellis, R. (2012). *Language teaching research and language pedagogy.* Malden, Mass: Wiley-Blackwell.

Fang, Z. (1996). A review of research on teacher beliefs and practices. *Educational Research, 1,* 47–65.

Feng, Z. (2002). Bilingual education and integrated english program. *Journal of Tianjin Normal University (Elementary Education Edition), 4,* 54–58.

Feng, Z. (2012). *Problems and solutions of EFL in China: An experimental study.* Speech given in Shanghai International Studies University.

Feryok, A. (2004). *Personal practice theories: Exploring the role of language teacher experiences and beliefs in the integration of theory and practice.* University of Auckland.

Foster, P., & Ohta, A. (2005). Negotiation for meaning and peer assistance in second language classrooms. *Applied Linguistics, 3,* 402–430.

Freeman, D. (1993). Renaming experience/reconstructing practice: developing new understandings of teaching. *Teaching and Teacher Education*, (5/6), 485–497.

Freeman, D. (2002). The hidden side of the work: Teacher knowledge and learning to teach. A perspective from North American educational research on teacher education in english language teaching. *Language Teaching, 1,* 1–13.

Fullan, M. (2001). *The new meaning of educational change* (3rd ed.). New York and London: Teachers College Press.

Gardner, D. C. (2011). Characteristic collaborative processes in school-university partnerships. *Planning and Changing*, (1/2), 63–86.

Geng, F. (2012a). *Developing learner autonomy and language speaking proficiency through LAP Class: A project-based research at a secondary school in China*. Shanghai International Studies University.

Glaser, B. G., & Strauss, A. (2008). *The discovery of grounded theory*. New Brunswick, N. J.: Aldine Transaction.

Gourlay, L. (2005). Ok, Who's got number one? Permeable triadic dialogue, covert participation and the co-construction of checking episodes. *Language Teaching Research, 4*, 403–422.

Graden, E. C. (1996). How language teachers' beliefs about reading instruction are mediated by their beliefs about students. *Foreign Language Annals, 3*, 387–395.

Hamilton, J. (1996). *Inspiring innovations in language teaching*. Clevedon England; Philadelphia: Multilingual Matters.

Hammersley, M., & Atkinson, P. (1983). *Ethnography: Principles in practice*. London: Tavistock Publications.

Harmer, J. (2007). *How to teach English (new edition)*. Harlow: Pearson Longman.

Harmer, J. (2001). *The practice of English language teaching (3rd ed.)*. Harlow: Longman.

He, K. (2005). Transcendence basic education experiment (I). *IT Education in Primary and Secondary Education, 11*, 58–60.

He, K. (2005). Transcendence basic education experiment (II). *IT Education in Primary and Secondary Education, 12*, 45–48.

Hedge, T. (2000). *Teaching and learning in the language classrooms*. Oxford: Oxford University Press.

Ho, B., & Richards, J. C. (1993). Reflective thinking through teacher journal writing: myths and realities. *Prospect: A Journal of Australian TESOL*, (8), 7–24.

Holt Reynolds, D. (1992). Personal history-based beliefs as relevant prior knowledge in course work. *American Educational Research Journal*, (2), 325–349.

Hu, G. (2005). English language education in China: Policies, progress, and problems. *Language Policy, 4*, 5–24.

Hu, G. (2005). Professional development of secondary EFL teachers: Lessons from China. *Teacher College Record, 4*, 654–705.

Hu, G. (2002). Recent important developments in secondary English-language teaching in the People's Republic of China. *Language, Culture and Curriculum, 1*, 30–49.

Hughes, A. (1989). *Testing for language teachers*. Cambridge: Cambridge University Press.

Johnson, K. E. (1994). The emerging beliefs and instructional practices of preservice english as a second language teachers. *Teaching and Teacher Education, 1994*(4), 439–452.

Johnson, K. E. (1992). Learning to teach: instructional actions and decisions of preservice ESL teachers. *TESOL Quarterly, 3*, 507–535.

Johnson, K. (1992). The relationship between teachers' beliefs and practices during literacy instruction for non-native speakers of English. *Journal of Reading Behaviour, 1*, 83–108.

Johnson, K. (1995). *Understanding communication in second language classrooms*. Cambridge: Cambridge University Press.

Kagan, D. (1992). Professional Growth among Preservice and Beginning Teachers [J]. *Review of Educational Research, 62*, 129–169.

Kam-yin, W. (1993). Classroom interaction and teacher questions revisited. *RELC Journal, 2*, 49–68.

Kasper, G. (2001). Four perspectives on L2 pragmatic development. *Applied Linguistics*, (22), 502–530.

Kern, R. (1995). Students and teachers' beliefs about language learning. *Foreign Language Annals, 1*, 71–92.

Kırkgöz, Y. (2008). A case study of teachers' implementation of curriculum innovation in English Language teaching in Turkish primary education. *Teaching and Teacher Education, 24*, 1859–1875.

Kumar, K. (1992). Does class size really make a difference?—Exploring classroom interaction in large and small classes. *RELC Journal, 1,* 29–47.

Kumaravadivelu, B. (2003). *Beyond methods: Macrostrategies for language teaching.* New Haven: Yale University Press.

Kumaravadivelu, B. (1993). Maximizing learning potential in the communicative classroom. *English Language Teaching Journal, 1,* 12–21.

Kumaravadivelu, B. (1994). The postmethod condition: (E)merging strategies for second/foreign language teaching. *TESOL Quarterly, 1,* 27–48.

Kumaravadivelu, B. (2001). Toward a postmethod pedagogy. *TESOL Quarterly., 4,* 537–560.

Kumaravadivelu, B. (2006). *Understanding language teaching: From method to postmethod.* Mahwah, N.J.: Lawrence Erlbaum Associates.

Kyriacou, C. (1997). *Effective Teaching in Schools: Theory and Practice (2nd edition) [M].* United Kingdom: Nelson Thornes Ltd.

Labov, William Sociolingustic. (1972). *Patterns.* Philidelphia: University of Pennsylvania.

Larsen-Freeman, D., & Long., M. H. (1991). *An introduction to second language acquisition research.* London: Longman.

Lau, K. L. (2013). Chinese language teachers' perception and implementation of self-regulated learning-based instruction. *Teaching and Teacher Education, 31,* 56–66.

LeCompte, M., & Goetz, J. (1982). Problems of reliability and validity in ethnographic research. *Review of Educational Research, 1,* 31–60.

LeCompte, M., & Schensul, J. J. (1999). *Analyzing and interpreting ethnographic data.* Walnut Greek, CA: Altamira Press.

LeCompte, M., & Schensul, J. J. (1999). *Designing and conducting ethnographic research.* Walnut Greek, CA: Altamira Press.

Lenneberg, E. (1967). *Biological foundations of a language.* New York: Willey.

Lerner, G. H. (1995). Turn design and the organization of participation in instructional activities. *Discourse Processes, 19,* 111–131.

Li, D. (1998). "It is Always More Difficult Than You Plan and Imagine": Teachers' perceived difficulties in introducing communicative approach in South Korea. *TESOL Quarterly, 4,* 677–703.

Li, S. (2010). The Effectiveness of Corrective Feedback in SLA: A Meta-analysis [J]. *Language Learning, 2,* 309–365.

Littleton, D. M. (1998). Preparing professionals as teachers for the urban classroom: A university/school collaborative model. *Action in Teacher Education, 4,* 149–158.

Littlewood, W. (1981). *Communicative language teaching: An introduction.* Cambridge England; New York: Cambridge University Press.

Long, M., & Sato, C. (1983). *Classroom foreigner talk discourse: Forms and functions of teacher's questions.* Rowley, Mass: Newbury House.

Long, M. (1991). Focus on form: A design feature in language teaching methodology. In K. de Bot, R. Ginsberg, & C. Kramsch (Eds.), *Foreign language research in cross-cultural perspective.* John Benjamin, Amsterdam (pp. 39–52).

Long, M. H. (1985). Input and second language acquisition theory. In S. M. Gass & C. G. Madden (Eds.), *Input in second language acquisition* (pp. 377–393). Rowley, MA: Newbury House, 1985.

Long, M. H. (1996). The role of the linguistic environment in second language acquisition. In W. C. Ritchie & T. K. Bhatia (Eds.), *Handbook of second language acquisition* (pp. 413–468). New York: Academic Press, 1996.

Lortie, D. (1975). *School teacher: A sociological study.* Chicago: University of Chicago Press.

Mackey, A. & Goo, J. (2007). Interaction research in SLA: A Meta-analysis and research synthesis. In A. Mackey (Ed.), *Conversational interaction in second language acquisition: A series of empirical studies* (pp. 407–452). Oxford: Oxford University Press.

Mackey, W. F. (1965). *Language teaching analysis.* Bloomington: Indiana University Press.

Markee, N. (1997). *Managing curricular innovation.* Cambridge: Cambridge University Press.

Marsh, C. J. (2009). *Key concepts for understanding curriculum* (4th ed.). London and New York: Routledge.

Marta, A. (1999). The discourse of a learner-centered classroom: sociocultural perspectives on teacher-learner interaction in the second-language classroom. *The Modern Language Journal, 3,* 303–318.

Marzano, R. J. (1998). *Snowflake Bentley [M]*. Boston: Houghton Mifflin.

McIntyre, E., et al. (2009). *6 Principles for teaching English language learners in all classrooms.* Thousand Oaks, CA.: Corwin Press.

Merrill, S., Lindsay, B., & Agustina, T. (2002). Peer-peer dialogue as a means of second language learning. *Annual Review of Applied Linguistics., 22,* 171–185.

Miles, M. B., & Huberman, A. M. (1994). *Qualitative data analysis* (2nd ed.). Thousand Oaks, CA: Sage Publications.

Ministry of Education. (2010). *Jiaoyubu caizhengbu guanyu shishi zhongxiaox jiaoshi guojiaji peixun jihua de tongzhi* [Announcement for implementing national training programs for primary and secondary teachers by Ministry of Education and Ministry of Finance]. [EB/OL]. Retrieved from http://www.moe.gov.cn/publicfiles/business/htmlfiles/moe/s4667/201212/xxgk_146071.html2010.

Ministry of Education. (2001). *Jichu jiaoyu kecheng gaige gangyao (shixing)* [The outline of basic education curriculum reform (trial)]. [EB/OL]. Retrieved from http://www.moe.gov.cn/publicfiles/business/htmlfiles/moe/moe_309/200412/4672.html2001a.

Ministry of Education. (2000). *Jiunian yiwu jiaoyu quanrizhi chuji zhongxue yingyu jiaoxue dadang (shiyong xiudingban) [English syllabus for nine-year compulsory education full-time junior secondary schools] [Z]*. Beijing: People's Education Press.

Ministry of Education. (2000). *Quanrizhi gaoji zhongxue yingyu jiaoxue dagang (shiyan xiudingban) [English syllabus for full-time senior secondary schools] [Z]*. Beijing: People's Education Press.

Ministry of Education. (1982). *Quanrizhi liunianzhi zhongdian zhongxue yingyu jiaoxue dagang (zhengqiu yijiangao) [English syllabus for six-year full-time key secondary schools] [Z]*. Beijing: People's Education Press.

Ministry of Education. (1978). *Quanrizhi shinianzhi zhongxiaoxue yingyu jiaoxue dadang (shingxing caoan) [English syllabus for ten-year full-time primary and secondary schools]*. Beijing: People's Education Press.

Ministry of Education. (2001b). *Quanrizhi yiwu jiaoyu putong gaoji zhongxue yingyu kecheng biaozhun (shiyangao)* [English curriculum for full-time general senior secondary schools of compulsory education (experimental)] [Z] Beijing: Beijing Normal University Press, 2001b.

Ministry of Education. Yiwu jiaoyu yingyu kecheng biaozhun. (2011). *English curriculum for compulsory education.* Beijing: Beijing Normal University Press.

Mitchell, E. W. (2005). *The influence of beliefs on the teaching practices of high school foreign language teachers.* University of Massachusetts, Amherst.

Murchison, J. M. (2010). *Ethnography essentials: Designing, conducting and presenting your research.* San Francisco: Jossey-Bass.

Nassaji, H., & Wells, G. (2000). What is the use of 'Triadic Dialogue'?: An investigation of teacher-student interaction. *Applied Linguistics, 3,* 376–406.

Nespor, J. (1987). The role of beliefs in the practice of teaching. *Journal of Curriculum Studies, 4,* 317–328.

Newby, P. (2010). *Research methods for education.* Harlow: Pearson Education.

Numrich, C. (1996). On becoming a language teacher: insights from diary studies. *TESOL Quarterly, 1,* 131–153.

Nunan, D., & Bailey, K. M. (2010). *Exploring second language classroom research: A comprehensive guide.* Beijing: Foreign Language Teaching and Research Press.

Nunan, D. (2003). The impact of English as a global language on educational policies and practices in the Asia-Pacific region. *TESOL Quarterly, 37,* 589–613.

Nunan, D. (1992). The teacher as decision-maker. In J. Flowerdew, M. Brock & S. Hsia (Eds.), *Perspectives on second language teacher education* (pp. 135–165). Hong Kong: City Polytechnic.

Orafi, S. M. S., & Borg, S. (2009). Intentions and realities in implementing communicative curriculum reform. *System, 37,* 243–253.

Patton, M. Q. (2002). *Qualitative Research and Evaluation Methods.* Thousand Oaks, CA: Sage Publications.

Peacock, M. (2001). Pre-service ESL Teachers' beliefs about second language learning: A longitudinal study. *System, 29,* 177–195.

Peters, J. (2002). University-school collaboration: Identifying faulty assumptions. *Asia-Pacific Journal of Teacher Education, 3,* 229–242.

Phipps, S., & Borg, S. (2009). Exploring tensions between Teachers' grammar teaching beliefs and practices. *System, 3,* 380–390.

Pike, K. L. (1964). *Language in relation to a unified theory of structures of human behavior.* The Hague: Mouton.

Pratt, D. D., & Associates. (1998). *Five perspectives on teaching in adult and higher education.* Malabar: Krieger.

Prithvi, N. S. (2013). English language classroom practices: Bangladeshi Primary School Children's perceptions. *RELC Journal, 2,* 147–162.

Richards J. C., & Rodgers T. S. (1986). *Approaches and methods in language teaching: A description and analysis.*Cambridge, New York: Cambridge University Press.

Richards, J. C., & Rodgers, T. S. (2001). *Approaches and methods in language teaching (2nd ed.).* New York: Cambridge University Press.

Richards, K. (2003). *Qualitative inquiry in TESOL.* New York: Palgrave, Macmillan.

Richards, J. C., & Bohlke, D. (2011). *Creating effective language lessons.* Cambridge: Cambridge University Press.

Richards, J. C., & Lockhart, C. (1996). *Reflective teaching in second language classrooms.* Cambridge: Cambridge University Press.

Richards, J. C., Ho, B., & Giblin, K. (1996). Learning how to teach in the RSA Cert. In D.A. Freeman & J.C. Richards (Eds.), *Teacher learning in language teaching* (pp. 242–259). Cambridge: Cambridge University Press.

Richards, J., Platt, J., & Platt, H. (1992). *Longman dictionary of language teaching and applied linguistics.* London: Longman.

Richards, J. C., & Pennington, M. (1998). The first year of teaching. In J. C. Richards (Ed.), *Beyond training* (pp. 173–190). Cambridge: Cambridge University Press.

Richardson, V., Anders, P., Tidwell, D., & Llody, C. (1991). The relationship between teachers' beliefs and practices in reading comprehension instruction. *American Educational Research Journal, 3,* 559–586.

Roebuck, R. F., & Wagner, L. C. (2004). Teaching repetition as a communicative and cognitive tool: Evidence from a Spanish conversation class international. *Journal of Applied Linguistics, 1,* 70–89.

Roehler, L., &Duffy, G. (1991). Teachers' instructional action. In R. Barr, et al. (Eds.), *Handbook of reading research* (pp. 861–884) New York: Longman.

Rogers, E. M. (1983). *The diffusion of innovations* (3rd ed.). London: Macmillan.

Rogers, E. M. (2003). *The diffusion of innovations* (5th ed.). London: Macmillan.

Russell, J., & Spada, N. (2006). The effectiveness of corrective feedback for acquisition of L2 Grammar: Ameta-analysis of the research. In J. Norris & L. Ortega (Eds.), *Synthesizing research on language learning and teaching* (pp. 133–164). Amsterdam: John Benjamins.

Schmidt, R. W. (1993). Awareness and second language acquisition. *Annual Review of Applied Linguistics, 13,* 206–226.

Schmidt, R. W. (1990). The role of consciousness in second language learning. *Applied Linguistics, 2,* 129–158.

Seedhouse, P. (1996). Classroom interaction: Possibilities and impossibilities. *ELT Journal, 1,* 16–24.

Serrano, R. M., et al. (2012). University-school collaborative networks: A strategy to improve the professional skills of future teachers. *Education Research International, 1,* 1–12.

Skehan, P. (1998). *A cognitive approach to language learning.* Oxford: Oxford University Press.

Skehan, P. (1998). *A cognitive approach to language learning.* Oxford University Press.

Skinner, B. F. (1957). *Verbal behavior.* Harvard University Press.

Spada, N., & Fröhlich, M. (1995). *The communicative orientation of language teaching observation scheme (COLT).* Australia: The National Centre for English Language Teaching.

Spada, N., & Massey, M. (1992). The role of prior pedagogical knowledge in determining the practice of novice ESL teachers. In J. Flowerdew, M. Brock & S. Hsia (Eds.), *Perspectives on second language teacher education* (pp. 23–37). Hong Kong: City Polytechnic.

Spada, N. (1987). Relationships between Instructional Differences and Learning Outcomes: A process-product study of communicative language teaching. *Applied Linguistics, 8,* 137–161.

Spradley, J. P. (1979). *The ethnographic interview.* New York: Holt, Rinehart and Winston.

Sprenger, M. (1999). *Learning and memory: The brain in action.* Alexandria, VA: Association for Supervision and Curriculum Development.

State Council. (2001). *Guowuyuan guanyu jichujiaoyu gaige yu fazhang de jueding* [Decision on reform and development of basic education].

State Education Commission. (1986). *Quanrizhi zhonguxe yingyu jiaoxu dagang [English syllabus for full-time secondary schools].* Beijing: People's Education Press.

State Education Commission. (1990). *Quanrizhi zhonguxe yingyu jiaoxue dagang (xiudingben) [English syllabus for full-time secondary schools].* Beijing: People's Education Press.

State Education Commission. (1988). *Quanrizhi zhongxue yingyu jiaoxue dagang (xiudingben) full-time junior secondary schools].* Beijing: People's Education Press.

Stern, H. H. (1983). *Fundamental concepts of language teaching.* Oxford: Oxford University Press.

Sternhouse, L. (1975). *An introduction to curriculum research and development.* London: Heinemann.

Swain, M. (1995). Three functions of output in second language learning. In G. Cook & B. Seidhofer (Eds.), *For H.G. Widdowson: Principles and practice in the study of language.* Oxford: Oxford University Press.

Taylor, L. (2005). Washback and impact. *ELT Journal, 2005*(2), 154–155.

Thornbury, S. (1996). Teachers research teacher talk. *ELT Journal, 4,* 279–289.

Ten Tileston, D. W. (2000). *Best teaching practices: How brain research, learning styles, and standards define teaching competencies.* Thousand Oaks, CA: Corwin Press.

Tileston, D. W. (2004). *What every teacher should know about effective teaching strategies.* Thousand Oaks, CA: Corwin Press.

Tomlinson, B. (1990). Managing change in indonesian high schools. *ELT Journal, 1990*(1), 25–37.

Underwood, P. R. (2012). Teacher beliefs and intensions regarding the instruction of English grammar under national curriculum reforms: A theory of planned behavior perspective. *Teaching and Teacher Education, 28,* 911–925.

Ur, P. (2012). *A course in language teaching: Practice and theory (2nd ed.).* Cambridge England; New York: Cambridge University Press.

Ur, P. (1996). *A course in language teaching: Practice and theory.* Cambridge England; New York: Cambridge University Press.

van Lier, L. (1996). *Interaction in the language curriculum: awareness, autonomy and authenticity.* London: Longman.

van Lier, L. (2000). Constraints and resources in classroom talk: Issues in equality and symmetry. In C. Candlin & N. Mercer (Eds.), *English language teaching in its social context: A reader* (pp. 90–107). New York: Routledge.

van Lier, L. (2000). Constraints and resources in classroom talk: Issues in equality and symmetry. In C. Candlin & N. Mercer (Eds.), *English language teaching in its social context: A reader* (pp. 90–107). New York: Routledge.

van Lier, L. (1994). Language awareness, contingency, and interaction. *AHA Review, 11,* 69–82.

van Lier, L. (1988). *The classroom and the language learner: ethnography and second language classroom research*. London: Longman.

Vargas, J. S. (2013). *Behavior analysis for effective teaching*. New York: Routledge.

Wang, B. (2012a). Fostering learner autonomy via ELP-based assessment in the Chinese Context. Shanghai International Studies University.

Wang, Q., & Mu, H. (2013). The roles of university researchers in a University-school collaborative action research project- A Chinese experience. *Multidisciplinary Journal of Educational Research, 2,* 101–129.

Waring, H. Z. (2009). Moving out of IRF (Initiation-Response-Feedback): A single case analysis. *Language Learning, 4,* 796–824.

Watson, C. W. (1999). *Being there: Fieldwork in anthropology*. Sterling, VA: Pluto Press.

Watson-Gegeo, K. A. (1988). Ethnography in ESL: Defining the essentials. *TESOL Quarterly, 4,* 575–591.

Wells, G. (1993). Reevaluating the IRF sequence: A proposal for the articulation of theories of activity and discourse for the analysis of teaching and learning in the classroom. *Linguistics and Education, 5,* 1–37.

Widdowson, H. G. (1990). *Aspects of language teaching*. Oxford: Oxford University Press.

Wilen, W., Bosse, M. I., Hutchison, J., & Kindsvatter, R. (2004). *Dynamics of effective secondary teaching (5th ed.)*. Boston: Pearson Education.

Woods, D. (1996). *Teacher cognition in language teaching*. Cambridge England; New York: Cambridge University Press.

Woods, D. (2011). Two dimensions of teacher knowledge: The case of communicative language teaching. *System, 39,* 381–390.

Yalden, J. (1981). *Communicative language teaching: Principles and practice*. Toronto, ONT: Ontario Institute for Studies in Education.

Yo-An, L. E. (2006). respecifying display questions: interactional resources for language teaching. *TESOL Quarterly, 4,* 691–713.

Yoshida, R. (2008). Teachers' choice and learners' preference of corrective feedback types. *Language Awareness, 17*(1), 78–93.

Yu, L. (2001). Communicative language teaching in China: Progress and resistance. *TESOL Quarterly, 35,* 194–198.

Yuan, G. R. (2001). *Dali tuijin zhongxioaxue jiaoshi jixu jiaoyu gongcheng, buduan kaichuang jixu jiaoyu gongzuo xinjumian* [Invigorate the continuing education project for primary and secondary teachers; open up new prospects for continuing education].

Zheng, X., & Davison, C. (2008). *Changing pedagogy: Analyzing ELT teachers in China*. London, New York: Continuum International Publishing Group.

Zheng, X. M. (2005). *Pedagogy and pragmatism: Secondary English language teaching in the People's Republic of China*. The University of Hong Kong.

An, L. (2012). Developing in-house ELT materials for an English teaching reform project in a middle school. *Foreign Languages and Their Teaching, 5,* 10–14.

An, L. (2012). *The role of textbooks in modifying teacher beliefs and practices: A project-based study in middle schools in China. Unpublished doctoral thesis.* Shanghai: Shanghai International Studies University.

Chen, X., & Keith, S. (2005). Research on effective teaching in modern western countries: Systematical review and some inspirations. *Comparative Education Review,* (8), 56–60, 71.

Cui, Y. (2001). Effective teaching: Principles and strategies (I). *People's Education, 6,* 46–47.

Cui, Y. (2001). Effective teaching: Principles and strategies (II). *People's Education, 7,* 42–43.

Duan, W. (2013). Current situation and solutions to problems in primary and secondary EFL teacher education. *Education and Management, 6,* 59–61.

Geng, F. (2012). Fostering learner autonomy in secondary EFL classrooms. *Foreign Languages and Their Teaching, 5,* 6–9.

Geng, F. (2012b). *Developing learner autonomy and language speaking proficiency through LAP Class—A project-based research at a secondary school in China.* Unpublished Doctoral Thesis. Shanghai: Shanghai International Studies University.

Hu, D. (1999). A review of 97 years' history of English education in China. *Shandong Foreign Languages Journal, 4,* 55–57.

Hu, W. (2009). The strengths and weaknesses of China's foreign language education in the past 60 years. *Foreign Language Teaching and Research, 3,* 163–169.

Curriculum and Textbook Research Institute. (1999). *A collection of EFL curricular and syllabi in China's basic education in 20th Century.* Beijing: People's Education Press.

Liu, D. (2008). *Development of Foreign Language teaching and learning in China's basic education (1978–2008).* Shanghai: Shanghai Foreign Language Education Press.

Pan, M. (2011). *Reconceptualising and exploring oral communicative competence: A multimodal perspective. Unpublished doctoral thesis.* Shanghai: Shanghai International Studies University.

Ren, Q., & Liang, W. (2010). Investigating the effects of SLA studies on the professional development of foreign language teachers. *Foreign Language World, 4,* 76–83.

Shen, Y., & Cui, Y. (2008). *Classroom observation: Moving towards professional observation and evaluation.* Shanghai: East China Normal University Press.

Shen, Y., Lin, R., Wu, J., & Cui, Y. (2007). Frameworks and instruments for classroom instruction. *Contemporary Educational Science., 24,* 17–21.

Shu, D. (2013). Developing an EFL PhD program through "learning in using and social service". *Language Education, 1,* 9–12.

Shu, D. (2005). China needs FLT theories with Chinese characteristics. *Foreign Language World,* (6), 2–7,60.

Shu, D. (2013). An evaluative review of the Third SFLEP National Foreign Language Teaching Contest. *Foreign Language World, 2,* 43–49.

Shu, D. (2012). Exploring an EFL teaching approach with Chinese characteristics: Exploratory practices in a secondary school. *Foreign Languages and Their Teaching, 5,* 1–5.

Shu, D. (2012). The SFLEP National Foreign Language teaching contest and teacher development. *Foreign Language World, 3,* 34–41.

Shu, D. (2010). Classroom instruction for college English teaching and learning: What to teach, and how to teach? *Foreign Language World, 6,* 26–32.

Shu, D. (2011). The functions and objectives of EFL classroom instruction. *Foreign Language World, 1,* 5–8.

Shu, D., An, L., Geng, F., Wang, B., & Yuan, Y. (2012). *English curriculum innovation towards and EFL teaching approach with Chinese characteristics.* Shanghai: Shanghai Foreign Language Education Press.

Song, Q. (2007). The implication and features of effective teaching. *Exploring Education Development., 6,* 39–42.

Sun, Y. (2004). *Research on the Effectiveness of the Framework for Classroom Teaching Standards. Unpublished doctoral thesis.* Shanghai: East China Normal University.

Wang, B., & An, L. (2012). Exploring an evaluative framework for College English classroom instruction. *Foreign Language World, 3,* 42–50.

Wang, B. (2012). Portfolio-based assessment in EFL secondary classrooms. *Foreign Languages and Their Teaching, 5,* 15–19.

Wang, B. (2012). *Fostering learner autonomy via ELP-based Assessment in the Chinese context. Unpublished doctoral thesis.* Shanghai: Shanghai International Studies University.

Wang, D. (2004). *College EFL teachers' cognition: A qualitative study and its implications for teacher development. Unpublished doctoral thesis.* Shanghai: Shanghai International Studies University.

Wang, Q., Zhang, W., & Lin, Z. (2010). The practical exploration into the collaborative action research between universities and basic education teachers. *Curriculum, Teaching Material and Method., 12,* 87–93.

Wang, Q. (2013). Deepening the curriculum reform, improving the quality of teaching: Interpreting the major changes of the Nine-Year Compulsory Education English Curriculum Standards. *Curriculum, Teaching Material and Method., 1,* 34–40.

Wen, Q., & Han, S. (2011). *Research methods for english teachers: Case analysis.* Shanghai: Shanghai Foreign Language Education Press.

Wu, Y. (2008). Researching foreign language teachers: Results and implications. *Foreign Language Learning Theory and Practice, 3,* 32–39.

Wu, Y. (2005). Towards a professional profile for effective university EFL teachers. *Foreign Language Teaching and Research, 3,* 199–205.

Yang, H. (2011). Effective teaching: Reflective comments on The SFLEP National Foreign Language Teaching Contest. *Foreign Language World, 2,* 14–18.

Yao, L. (2005). A review of studies on effective teaching. *Primary & Secondary Schooling Abroad, 8,* 23–27.

Yi, B. (2010). *A study on English Curriculum Change of China's basic education during the thirty years of reform and opening up. Unpublished Doctoral Thesis.* Changsha: Hunan Normal University.

Yu, X. (2010). On the seven links in effective teachers' training: Taking the "National Training Plan—Trainers' research and studies program" as an example. *Educational Research, 2,* 77–83.

Yuan, Y. (2012). University-school collaboration targeting appropriate educational goals: Exploring an effective approach for foreign language teacher education. *Foreign Languages and Their Teaching, 5,* 20–23.

Yuan, Y. (2013). *Multi-interative model of School-based English Teacher Education: Theory and practice. Unpublished doctoral thesis.* Shanghai: Shanghai International Studies University.

Zhang, F. (2012). *A Sociocognitive Study of English Teacher Cognition and Its Influencing Factors in Chinese Secondary Schools.* Unpublished doctoral thesis. Changchun: Northeast Normal University.

Zhang, X., & Huang, L. (2014). Combining vertical and horizontal view of teaching expertise: Three threads of discussions on teacher learning and professional development of teachers. *Global Education, 4,* 59–67.

Zhang, Y., & Zhou, J. (2012). Foreign language teacher cognition and needs: A case study on teacher participants of a summer school. *Foreign Languages and Their Teaching, 1,* 6–10.

Zheng, X. (2006). Exploration on teachers' cognition in college English teaching innovation and change: A case study. *Computer-Assisted Foreign Language Education, 2,* 32–39.

Zhou, W., & Cui, Y. (2008). How to conduct classroom observation? *Management in Primary and Secondary Schools, 4,* 18–20.

Zhu, X. (2010). On the value of the National Training Plan. *Teacher Education Research, (11),* 3–8, 25.

Zhu, Y. (2013). Key factors to ensure the effectiveness of EFL classroom instruction. *Foreign Language World, (2),* 50–58, 68.

Zhu, Y. (2014). *An ethnographic study on foreign language teacher cognition and classroom practice within curriculum innovation in a Chinese Secondary School. Unpublished doctoral thesis.* Shanghai: Shanghai International Studies University.

Printed by Books on Demand, Germany